The Scholar and the Tiger

The Scholar and the Tiger

A Memoir of Famine and War in Revolutionary China

DAVID WEN-WEI CHANG AND ALDEN R. CARTER

ROWMAN & LITTLEFIELD PUBLISHERS, INC.

Lanham • Boulder • New York • Toronto • Plymouth, UK

ROWMAN & LITTLEFIELD PUBLISHERS, INC.

Published in the United States of America
by Rowman & Littlefield Publishers, Inc.
A wholly owned subsidiary of The Rowman & Littlefield Publishing Group, Inc.
4501 Forbes Boulevard, Suite 200, Lanham, Maryland 20706
www.rowmanlittlefield.com

Estover Road, Plymouth PL6 7PY, United Kingdom

British Library Cataloguing in Publication Information Available

Library of Congress Cataloging-in-Publication Data

Chang, David W., 1929–
    The scholar and the tiger : a memoir of famine and war in revolutionary China /
David Wen-wei Chang and Alden R. Carter.
        p. cm.
    ISBN-13: 978-0-7425-5761-1 (cloth : alk. paper)
    ISBN-10: 0-7425-5761-8 (cloth : alk. paper)
    ISBN-13: 978-0-7425-5763-5 (electronic)
    ISBN-10: 0-7425-5763-4 (electronic)
    1. Chang, David W., 1929– 2. Sinologists—United States—Biography. 3. Chang
family. 4. China—Genealogy. I. Carter, Alden R. II. Title. III. Title: Memoir of
famine and war in revolutionary China.
DS734.9.C3A3 2009
951.04'2092—dc22
    [B]
                                                                    2008043714

Printed in the United States of America

⊚™ The paper used in this publication meets the minimum requirements of
American National Standard for Information Sciences—Permanence of Paper for
Printed Library Materials, ANSI/NISO Z39.48-1992.

For my beloved wife, Alice,
and our wonderful sons, Christopher and Victor

—D. W. C.

For my sister,
Cynthia Carter LeBlanc,
and Wayne, Kelley, Julie, and Kyle

—A. R. C.

Contents

Preface

I WAS BORN IN 1929, not long after the beginning of a quarter century of famine, invasion, and war in my homeland. The story of my upbringing in revolutionary China revolves around two people: my mother, Chang Wei-sze (who started life as Wei Jing-shuang), and my eldest brother, Wen-po. My father died when I was still an infant, forcing my mother to raise her family under the most extreme conditions. Once the wife of a well-to-do and educated man, she was reduced almost to beggary in our village near the old imperial capital of Xi'an.

Eighteen years my senior, Wen-po joined the army to help support the family. He was a born soldier and rose quickly. His ferocity and tactical acumen earned him the rank of general and the feared nickname Tiger Chang. He became my idol and surrogate father, though his duties often kept him away for years at a time. My father had seen to it that his eldest son had a good education, and Wen-po insisted on the same for me. I had an aptitude for learning and soon led my class in our small, drafty schoolhouse. By my teens, I seemed destined for the life of a scholar and civil servant, one of that class of "mandarin" bureaucrats who had governed China in the name of emperors, conquerors, and strongmen for two thousand years.

War would shatter those plans well before I earned my university degree. Wen-po was forced to flee the mainland with the Communist victory in 1949. By then, Mother was ill and a patient in the Shanghai Radium Hospital. Though I believed in Dr. Sun Yat-sen's vision of a democratic and socialist China, I was not particularly political. I expected to remain in China, caring for my mother and doing my best to be of use in the People's Republic declared by Mao. But I was naive. The Communist authorities forced me to undertake a doomed mission to Wen-po, who commanded one of the offshore islands. He forbade me to return to live under Communist rule.

I would not learn for more than two decades what had become of my mother and the rest of my family on the mainland. By then I had emigrated to America, earned a doctorate in political science, and built a modest reputation as a teacher, scholar, and writer. My wife, Alice, had given me two wonderful sons: Christopher and Victor, both of whom would grow up to become illustrious members of their chosen fields.

Through all those personally eventful years, a day never passed without my feeling a deep sadness and remorse for leaving my mother's side. Though I had long supposed that she had passed out of this life, not until 1972 did I receive news of her death in 1955. Beginning with my first trip in 1979, I have returned to my homeland on numerous occasions. I recovered relationships long lost to me and made friends with many nieces, nephews, and cousins who had been born since my departure from China in 1950. I have met influential figures in the government and universities of the People's Republic and carried their private expressions of friendship to people in similarly prominent positions in the United States and the Republic of China on Taiwan.

I have also had the pleasure of guiding small groups of Americans on their first visits to China. One of these trips led to my friendship with the writer Alden R. Carter and his wife, the photographer Carol Shadis Carter. I was happy to review Alden's manuscripts for three introductions to China for various ages. Following my retirement from teaching, I wrote a memoir of my childhood and youth in China. Though generous in his praise of my initial effort, Alden challenged me to revise my story to include the personal details that I had been loath to reveal. I asked him to help me do so.

I did not appreciate then the time it would take nor the painful memories the process would involve. Like all traditional Chinese, it is unnatural for me to discuss highly personal matters. But Alden insisted that I bare my emotions, no matter how wrenching. For many months, we passed chapter drafts back and forth. He rewrote my work extensively, reconstructing scenes and restructuring my discursive narrative until it flowed like the story I had always dreamed of telling. For his skill, diligence, and particularly his uncanny sense of what it means to be Chinese, he has my deepest gratitude.

I now find myself in the autumn of my years, a time when I should like to reflect on and perhaps learn some wisdom from my past. With the encouragement of my beloved wife and my wonderful sons, I choose now to recall the life of my mother, my brother Wen-po, and all the dear ones who peopled my life in China. I hope that this testament honors both the living among them and those whose spirits have passed beyond this world.

My gratitude to my parents, brothers and sisters, my missionary teacher, Miss Lillian Wells, and all the rest of my family and friends will become obvious in the pages that follow.

David Wen-wei Chang
Silver Spring, Maryland

Coauthor's Note

DAVID CHANG ONCE SAID TO ME: "The world is such a cruel place. You Americans don't understand that." I don't think most of us do, and that is a pity. I would not, of course, like to see great suffering visited on my country. But in not understanding the suffering experienced by so many of the world's people, I think we miss appreciating the great courage and fundamental decency of our less fortunate brothers and sisters. David Chang experienced more hardship before the age of twenty than most Americans know in a lifetime. Yet suffering did not embitter him, and he is today a smiling, ebullient, compassionate, and profoundly wise man. It has been my great privilege to travel and write in partnership with him and, through his memories, to know his remarkable family.

Alden R. Carter
Marshfield, Wisconsin

The Spelling and Pronunciation of Chinese Words

THE CHINESE LANGUAGE IS WRITTEN in ideograms representing ideas. By combining various ideograms, different ideas can be expressed. For example: combining the character for "speak" and the character for "bright" produces "explanation."

Chinese has at least fifty thousand ideograms, and probably no one knows them all. About six thousand characters are commonly used, and the government has simplified about three thousand to ease the task of learning written Chinese. Literacy is particularly valuable in China because the pronunciation of Chinese varies widely from region to region while the written language is universal. All schools in China now teach Mandarin, the most widely spoken dialect, as part of an effort to standardize pronunciation across China.

A number of systems have been devised to spell Chinese words in the Latin alphabet used in most of the West. Chinese words in this book are spelled according to the pinyin system adopted by the State Council of the People's Republic of China in 1979 to replace the Wade-Giles system developed in Great Britain in the nineteenth century. Since Chinese is a tonal language, no system can exactly duplicate the actual spoken sounds of Chinese words. Nevertheless, a fair approximation can be made by using the equivalent English sounds for pinyin consonants, with these exceptions:

c is **ts** when it is the initial sound in a word
q is **ch**
x is a soft **sh**, nearly **sy**
z is **dz**
zh is **j**

Chinese vowels are most commonly pronounced:

a as in the **ah** in far
e as in the **eh** in bet

i as in the **ee** in free, except when it is a final vowel following *c, s,* or *z* when it is
 pronounced **uh**, or following *ch, sh,* or *zh* when it is pronounced **ur**
o as in the **aw** in law
u as in the **oo** in pool

When two vowels are written together, each retains an individual sound.
Hence, *Mao* is pronounced like the **mou** in **mou**th.

About Traditional Chinese Names

THE CHINESE NAMING TRADITION CAN seem all but impenetrable to Westerners. Among Han Chinese, the surname comes first and is the name of the bearer's clan (or family in a broad sense). It is followed by a given name of one or two characters. If two characters, the first element is usually capitalized in English followed by a hyphen and a second lowercased element. (Chinese has no capital letters, and they are added for convenience in the romanization process.)

Although there are hundreds of Chinese family names, the vast majority of Han Chinese share one of the fifty or so most common names. These names have their origins in antiquity and are borne with great pride. The descendents of Confucius (Kong Fuzi) have carried the family name Kong or Kung for 2,500 years. The surname Chang may be of even greater antiquity; one explanation of its origin dates it to the reign of the legendary Yellow Emperor (Huang Di) some 4,500 years ago.

If a Chinese name has two characters, the first is the family (or clan) name, the second the personal name. For example, David Chang's father was Chang Ying. Since the Communist revolution, two character names have become commonplace.

If the family name is followed by a two-character given name, the first character is the generational name, the second the personal name. Traditionally, the generational name was selected by clan elders. All male cousins within the patrilineal kinship group would bear this name. In some cases, the word might come from a poem about the clan. David Chang (Chang Wen-wei) and his brothers Chang Wen-po, Chang Wen-hui, and Chang Wen-shuan all shared the generational name *Wen*.

The second character of the given name is the personal name, selected by the parents to express a hoped-for quality in the child's character. For example, the four Chang brothers received the personal names -*po* (*generous*), -*hui* (*adaptable*), -*shuan* (*selective*), and -*wei* (*prosperous*). Neither the generational name nor the personal name was ever used alone but always in combination with the other.

Outside the family circle, the given name of a male might drop from use and a male would be addressed or referred to by his clan name and his birth-order number within the patrilineal kinship group. For example: David Chang's maternal uncles were referred to as *Wei San* (*San* meaning *third born*), *Wei Sze* (*fourth*), and *Wei Ba* (*eighth*).

Female names were traditionally constructed with the clan name again coming first, followed by a hyphenated given name. The generational name was not insisted on for females, and the first element of the given name was usually the distinctly personal name and the second element usually the same for all the daughters of the immediate family. For example, David Chang's sisters Bei-yeh, Chu-yeh, Koo-yeh, Reou-yeh, and Ling-yeh were all given names of flowers followed by the second element *-yeh* meaning *petals*.

In the traditional system, when a woman married she adopted the clan name of her husband. Her original clan name then became the first element in her given name. The second element was always *-sze*, meaning *wife of.* For example: David Chang's mother, Wei Jing-shuang (*she of the Wei clan who is like morning dew reflecting sunlight*) became Chang Wei-sze (*Chang's wife from the Wei clan*) on her marriage to Chang Ying. Members of her birth family would, however, continue to use her original given name of *Jing-shuang* among themselves.

On emigrating, many overseas Chinese localized their names to reflect the traditions of their country of residence. Those who took up new homes in the Occident began following the Western practice of placing the personal name first, the family name last. Because of the difficulty many Westerners had in pronouncing Chinese names, immigrants frequently adopted or were given Western first names. This was also common practice in schools in China and Taiwan run by Western missionaries. At Tamkang English College in Taiwan, Chang Wen-wei was given the name David by his teacher, Miss Lillian Wells.

Beginning in the 1930s it became popular for many educated Chinese young people to adopt the example of the Nationalist finance minister, T. V. Soong, the Harvard-educated brother of Madame Chiang Kai-shek, in both the order of their names and the use of initials for the elements of the given name.

Since the Communist revolution, many of the naming traditions have broken down, reflecting the changing status of women, revolutionary fervor, and the assault on Confucian tradition during the Cultural Revolution. However, many aspects of the naming tradition continue in practice today.

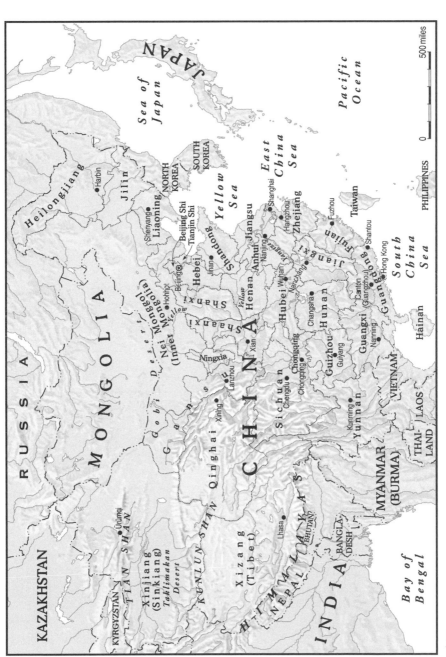

China

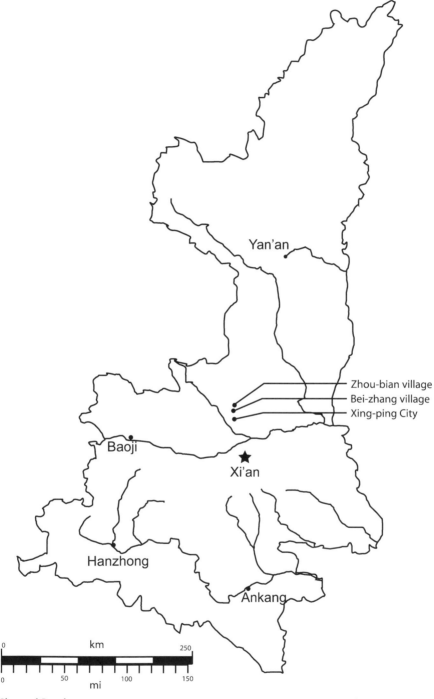

Yan'an

Zhou-bian village
Bei-zhang village
Xing-ping City

Baoji

★

Xi'an

Hanzhong

Ankang

| 0 | | | | | | km | | | | 250 |
| 0 | | 50 | | | 100 | mi | | | 150 | |

Shaanxi Province

Map by Brian P. Carter

CHAPTER 1

The Lucky Daughter

MY MOTHER ENJOYED A PROPITIOUS start in life. She was born on September 5, 1883, in the Chinese year of the Monkey. The year was not an easy one for the peasant families of rural China. Bedeviled by Western intervention and internal unrest, the Manchu dynasty had entered its final decades of decline, depriving the peasants of the political stability they had known in better days under the imperial system. This uncertainty came atop the traditional threats to rural families: flood, drought, famine, pestilence, and banditry. Yet my mother was the first girl-child born into the extended family in years, and she was welcomed, dandled, doted on, and greatly loved. For all the uncertainties of her future and the future of China, Wei Jing-shuang was considered a lucky child.

My mother grew up in the farming village of Bei-zhang in the province of Shaanxi in northwestern China, an area chilled by the wind out of Mongolia in winter and baked by the same wind in summer. Bei-zhang village was part of Xing-ping county, whose seat was the small city of Xing-ping, five miles to the southeast. The capital of Shaanxi province lay eighty miles farther east-southeast at the famous city of Xi'an. There, on the south bank of the Wei River, the great Ch'in Shih Huang Ti, unifier of China, had built his fabulous palace and mausoleum guarded by its great army of terra-cotta warriors.

Mother's parents, grandparents, uncles, aunts, and cousins were peasant farmers: poor, illiterate, and locked into a system that offered only the rare child an opportunity for advancement. Yet the peasants of rural China loved the land, loved the crops that thrived by their sweat, and honored the traditions of one of the world's oldest and richest civilizations. The Confucian philosophy that had guided Chinese society for over two thousand years accorded the place of highest respect not to royalty, generals, bureaucrats, doctors, craftsmen, or tradesmen, but to the peasant farmers. They might be poor, they might have little concept of the wider world, but they had been granted honor by the greatest sage of all.

But traditions could be cruel. In my mother's childhood, foot binding was both custom and law. For hundreds of years, this heinous practice was imposed on little girls by Chinese standards of beauty. The origin of the practice is clouded, but the popular legend is that the clubfooted eleventh-century empress Taki decreed that all aristocratic ladies should imitate her disability. The practice spread to the other classes, much to the agony of generations of little girls.

At about the age of five, girls had their feet bound with ten-foot strips of cloth so that the toes bent under the sole and the heel was forced forward. Every day or two, the strips were unwound, soaked, and the feet more tightly bound. This practice continued from four to six years until the feet were horribly misshapen. Ideally, a mature woman's feet measured no more than four inches long and two inches wide. To walk at all, women with "lotus feet" wore shoes with high wooden heels to balance the body's weight between bent-under toes and deformed (suspended) heels. The result was a shuffling, stiff-legged "willow walk."

My mother did not object to the foot binding. She wanted to please her mother and her family by having the smallest, most "beautiful" feet in the village. The charm of her tiny feet and "walking beauty" would attract well-born and well-off suitors for her parents to choose from. A good match would bring honor to the family and perhaps a higher standard of living. So she summoned her courage and asked each time for a tighter binding. Many years later she told me how she and her mother would weep together each time the strips were soaked and tightened. But they never considered violating tradition, and my mother's stoicism made the experience less painful for all those who loved her so dearly.

Though the family's love and my mother's courage were devoted in this case to a sad and brutal custom, she did emerge from the ordeal with pride, ambition, and confidence. She returned love with love, earning both the respect and affection of her family and her fellow villagers. She would need a large store of courage, kindness, and willpower in the years ahead as great trouble came to China and her own life.

The Qing dynasty that ruled China in my mother's girlhood came to power in 1644 when Manchu armies from northeast of the Great Wall overthrew the last Ming emperor. Co-opting the ancient mandarin civil service, the Manchus ruled effectively until the early decades of the nineteenth century, when corruption and foreign intrigue began eroding the dynasty's authority. At the heart of many of China's problems lay opium. The British East India Company made fabulous profits importing opium from India through the port of Guangzhou (Canton). Distributed throughout China, opium created a social catastrophe. When Chinese authorities attempted to shut off the trade at

Guangzhou in 1839, the British retaliated with modern warships and infantry. The medieval weapons of the Chinese were no match. The dynasty capitulated, ceding control of Hong Kong to the British and opening five new ports to Western trade. The dismemberment of China had begun. British victory in the Arrow War of 1856–1858 (often called the Second Opium War) resulted in the opening of eleven more treaty ports. The immense Taiping Rebellion (1850–1864) cost twenty million lives and destroyed much of the dynasty's remaining authority. The conservative Dowager Empress Cixi indulged in astounding extravagance while her corrupt favorites drained the empire.

Under the pressure of overpopulation and economic want, hundreds of thousands of coastal Chinese emigrated. They sent home money and news of the prosperity and power of the industrialized nations. Some of China's brightest students went abroad to study medicine, engineering, and democracy. They were both appalled and enthralled by what they saw. Among them was Dr. Sun Yat-sen, the future founder of the Republic of China. At home, forward-looking ministers instituted a number of "self-strengthening" programs in the 1870s and 1880s. By the time of my mother's birth in 1883, the Chinese were constructing modern factories, railroads, and warships. But a minor territorial clash on the border of Indochina in 1884 led to the destruction of almost the entire "self-strengthening" fleet in a single hour by a powerful French squadron at Fuzhou. Worse humiliation was to come. In 1894 recently modernized Japan challenged China's traditional suzerainty over Korea. The Sino-Japanese War of 1894–1895 cost China control of Korea and Taiwan, a huge indemnity, and virtually any claim to existence as a cohesive state. The Western powers and Japan carved China into "spheres of influence" where they ruled in all but name.

In Bei-zhang village, my mother grew to womanhood largely ignorant of these events. In vast areas of rural China, the farmers worked on, little heeding the signs of the deluge that would engulf China in the years to come. I have no photograph of my mother as a girl or a young woman, and I doubt if she had one taken until later in life. Cameras were almost unknown in rural China, and many Chinese held these Western inventions in superstitious awe, fearful that they might steal part of their spirit. Family tradition has it that Jing-shuang was an energetic girl. She was highly intelligent and dedicated to mastering all the skills demanded of the Chinese housewife. She learned to sew, spin, weave, and cook, to sing and tell stories, and to care for children, the sick, and the elderly. She sought out villagers particularly esteemed for virtue: good housewives, neighbors with a strong sense of justice, elders respected for their wisdom, skillful speakers and debaters, clever craftsmen, and upright citizens whatever their age, gender, or social position. Although she never learned to read or write, she managed a considerable education by observation and careful listening. She was an intuitive psychologist, equipped with great empathy and a knack for judging character.

Within the strictures placed on her by tradition, Jing-shuang grew into a strong-willed and ambitious young woman. She hoped to marry a young, kind, intelligent, handsome, and energetic man from a good, perhaps even a wealthy, family. Unfortunately, a happy marriage was not to be her fate. My mother's parents were simple people, an uneducated farming couple of meager means and mild manners, who were easily swayed by more assertive people. My mother had great respect for her honest, hardworking oldest brother, Wei San, who was a cotton-oil salesman employed by a land-rich family in another village. She was very fond of her younger brother, Wei Ba, who was generous and good-natured. But she did not get along at all with Wei Sze, her middle brother, who viewed his pretty, small-footed, and accomplished younger sister as a commodity to advance the family fortunes. He convinced his parents that my mother should be married to one of his friends as quickly as possible.

Chang Ying, the friend Wei Sze selected and the man who was to become my father, was a widower twice my mother's age. To overcome my grandparents' hesitation, Wei Sze emphasized that Chang Ying came from a prosperous family and had the rudiments of a scholarly education. No one consulted my mother about the match. Despite her parents' great love for her, they were traditional Chinese villagers who would never have thought to give their daughter a voice in the most important decision in her life. They listened to Wei Sze and let themselves be swayed. For the rest of her life, my mother would resent Wei Sze for determining so much of her future and causing so much of her unhappiness.

In 1900, at the age of seventeen, having never met her betrothed until their wedding day, the girl known as Wei Jing-shuang became Chang Wei-sze (Chang's wife from the Wei clan). As tradition demanded, she moved into his widowed mother's home in the nearby village of Zhou-bian.

The villagers of Zhou-bian received little news from the outside world in ordinary times, but my guess is that Mother and her neighbors heard of the flight of the imperial family from Beijing to Xi'an in the first year of her marriage. The imperial family existed so far removed from the daily lives of ordinary Chinese that it enjoyed an almost mythical status, more the stuff of fairy tale than reality. The news that the empress dowager, the young emperor, and their retinue had arrived in Xi'an in a state of undignified haste and startling tangibility must have spread across the province as fast as tongues could repeat it.

The cause of the imperial family's relocation was the rebellion of the Society of Righteous and Harmonious Fists, or the Boxers as they were known in the West. Drawing mainly from the peasant and poor working classes, the Boxers were reactionaries who sought to revive China's glory by driving out the foreigners and restoring the ancient customs under attack by modernization. In 1900, the year predicted for a great religious and cultural revival by Boxer leaders, they began a campaign against the "foreign devils" and their influence. They executed some two hundred Western traders, engineers, and missionaries, and hundreds of Christian converts. Under pressure from the Western powers, the dynasty at first opposed the Boxers. But as the Boxers flooded into Beijing in early June, the dynasty changed sides. Army troops joined the Boxers in laying siege to the foreign legation quarter. The legation's small band of defenders held out for eight weeks while a multinational army of twenty thousand landed on the coast and marched inland to raise the siege. Horrified at the impending catastrophe, the imperial family fled to Xi'an.

The Western troops entered Beijing on August 14, scattering the Boxers. In the months that followed, the Western troops looted Beijing and rounded up and executed thousands of Boxers and their sympathizers. The foreign powers forced the dynasty to accept a treaty that expanded the Western and Japanese spheres of influence and imposed a $333 million indemnity that bankrupted the imperial treasury. The Boxer Rebellion did not extend into the vicinity of Xi'an, and I doubt that Mother knew much about it beyond the news that a fight with the foreign devils had forced the imperial family to seek shelter in the city. Chang Ying, her scholarly husband, probably understood and cared a good deal more. But she was far too busy.

With her marriage, Mother entered a state of near servitude in my father's house. As in all traditional Chinese homes, the eldest female member of the family ruled the daily domestic affairs of the household. My father's mother, Chang Nan-sze, was not an unkind woman, but she was unsophisticated and very traditional, expecting Mother to play the role of the dutiful daughter-in-law without complaint or even a momentary laxity in attention to her many duties. Should my mother err, Grandmother felt it her duty to correct her sternly.

To make Mother's integration into the new family even harder, she had inherited an adolescent stepdaughter, Bei-yeh, by my father's first marriage. Bei-yeh resisted my mother's efforts to be friendly. She pouted, criticized, and complained to her father and her grandmother. My father's mediation might have done much to establish a harmonious relationship among the women of his household, but Chang Ying was a brooding, angry man who had known much disappointment in his life. He could not be concerned with women's petty bickering. He ignored it until his patience was pushed beyond endurance and then intervened in a harsh and arbitrary manner. My mother almost always took the blame.

A large part of Chang Ying's unhappiness came from the frustration of his personal ambitions. As a youth he had hoped to equal or surpass the accomplishments of his paternal grandfather, Chang Jing-shue, who had achieved great success within traditional Chinese society. Chang Jing-shue had been born about 1820. As a young man he became a peddler of small, useful articles. Daily, he pushed his wheelbarrow from village to village, selling his goods. He worked fifteen hours a day, saving every penny he could. Though greasing the axle would have made his wheelbarrow easier to push, he rarely spent the money. For this he acquired the nickname, "the screeching-wheel man." The irritating sound of his approach soon became good advertising. In a trade that knew many unscrupulous hawkers, he was an honest man who sold his goods for a fair profit and no more. People were soon greeting the "screeching-wheel man" with smiles and pennies for their small purchases. Slowly and painfully, he built up his savings until he could buy a little land and then a little more. After fifteen years of incessant labor and careful investing, he had become a respected landowner. After twenty-five years, he owned 150 acres of farmland and was the second richest man in Zhou-bian village—an astonishing achievement for a man who had started off in the world as a simple peddler.

Though he was personally thrifty to a fault, Jing-shue was a generous and community-spirited man. He helped the less fortunate and always contributed when money was raised for a good cause. He was a man of high moral standards and good judgment whom other people sought out for advice. He was the village spokesman and a leader in village affairs. He funded the building of the village school entirely out of his own wealth. In my childhood in the 1930s, I could still read his name high on a remaining wall of the old school.

When Chang Jing-shue died, his eldest son, my grandfather Chang You-tao, took charge of managing the family holdings. Grandfather was not personally ambitious, but he had great hopes for his eldest son, my father, Chang Ying. He wanted my father to have a thorough Confucian education so that he could become a scholar and enter the mandarin class of government civil servants.

Until recent historical times, China was unique in the world for its government by meritocracy. In ancient China, scholars were revered. Emperors listened to their advice during the long centuries China was developing into a single, cohesive state. The Western Han dynasty (202 B.C.E.–24 C.E.) institutionalized government by the scholar class through a rigorous examination program. Bright young men of good character were recruited for the government civil service from across China. Those admitted to the nine highest levels of the civil service became mandarins, holding positions from humble county magistrates to counselors to the emperor himself. The mandarins became indispensable to the administration of the vast empire. Although dynasties rose and fell, the mandarins maintained their power for more than two thousand years.

Becoming a mandarin was the ultimate achievement in Chinese society, bringing great honor on the family and the entire village. Even a boy of small means could pass the government examinations if he had the intelligence, energy, preparation, and judgment. Candidates studied the Confucian texts for years to learn the principles of good government and harmonious society. Usually in their late twenties or early thirties, they sat for the grueling government examinations. Locked in tiny cubicles for days on end, some candidates went mad or committed suicide. Others did so poorly that they were given only minor positions as clerks and tax collectors at the local level. But those who emerged with high scores could look forward to careers of responsibility, wealth, and power.

This was the future my paternal grandfather hoped for my father. But, sadly, Grandfather Chang You-tao died at thirty-nine in the prime of life. His widow, my grandmother Chang Nan-sze, did not trust Grandfather's younger brother, a lazy, foolish man, to manage the family's affairs. She insisted that Chang Ying give up his studies and his scholarly ambitions. Out of honor and filial affection, he complied. Father might have taken the imperial examinations and entered the civil service, perhaps even traveled abroad to complete his education, but those possibilities were suddenly as remote as the face of the moon. He stayed in the village and became the head of the family, a role that required him to spend most of his days working in the fields alongside the hired men and his evenings balancing the family accounts.

Chang Ying was only nineteen when his father died and his own ambitions crumbled. The disappointment never left him, and he remained all his life an unhappy and frustrated man. Many years later, my eldest brother, Wen-po, wrote in his autobiography that our father was "by nature an introvert, stone silent most of his life." As an educated person, Father had no one in the village to share his interests. He was uncertain when confronted by aggressive, younger men, who often got the better of him in a bargain. He would return home, frustrated and humiliated, to take out his anger on my mother. Try as he might, Father could not simply retreat to his books. Though head of the household, tradition required that he show great respect to his foolish uncle and particularly to his grieving and frequently complaining mother, Chang Nan-sze.

Fortunately, his uncle soon moved out of the family home with his family to set up a separate household. But my father and grandmother Chang Nan-sze continued to quarrel. She demanded of him warmth that he could not by temperament provide. Disappointed, she turned to her younger son, my uncle Chang Weng, who was a smiling, outgoing man, very much the opposite of my father. When my father made a decision, Chang Nan-sze would often contradict him, though it was often an excellent, well-reasoned decision.

My mother was frequently caught in the middle of arguments between her husband and her mother-in-law. She was far too young and inexperienced to be an effective peacemaker. In her daily life she saw more of her mother-in-law, but if she appeared to listen too closely to the older woman, her husband became angry. Likewise, if she seemed to be siding with her husband, this only antagonized her mother-in-law, who would become particularly bossy and demanding the next time my father left the house.

Poor Mother. Both her husband and mother-in-law were often unhappy with her. Her stepdaughter, Bei-yeh, challenged her authority and complained behind her back. My uncle Chang Weng, though good-hearted, was prevented by temperament and Confucian laws of filial respect to play the conciliator. His wife, whose name I no longer remember, was an unintelligent and spiteful woman who tried to win favor with Grandmother Chang Nan-sze by being particularly mean to my mother.

Mother worked from dawn until long after dark. She assumed a heavy burden of cooking and cleaning, her every step complicated by her tiny, painful feet. Pressure mounted on her to produce a male heir for the family. Since my father was the elder son of two, my grandmother was eager to have a grandson from my parents as soon as possible. My father, too, longed for a son. Chang Weng and his wife already had a son, Pao-wa, and this threatened my father. If something should happen to him before the birth of a son, his daughter and new wife would be at the mercy of his younger brother's generosity. Moreover, there would be a sort of celestial loss of face since my father's patrilineal line would end with his death.

Chinese tradition placed a huge emphasis on the birth of male descendants. In economic terms, a son was of more value as a working member of a rural family than a daughter, particularly since girls spent years crippled by painful foot binding. At a marriageable age, a son would bring a wife into the family while a daughter, after all the expense of raising her to womanhood, departed to increase the labor force of her husband's family. The eldest son of the eldest son would eventually assume leadership of the family, carrying on the family name into another generation. One of his principal obligations would be to maintain the customs venerating his deceased parents and all the family's ancestors.

Given all the hopes and anxieties of Chang Ying and Chang Nan-sze, one can only imagine the pressure on my mother. Her status and recognition depended upon the arrival of a healthy son. But fate did not work in her favor. She became pregnant after about two years of marriage. The delivery of a boy was anticipated with the greatest hope by all in the family, but despite my mother's fervent prayers, her first child was a daughter, my sister Chu-yeh, in 1903. The girl-child was welcomed to the family with the usual clucking that at least she might be a good playmate for her little brother once he was born.

The birth of Chu-yeh added to Mother's heavy workload. Grandmother Chang Nan-sze often spent the afternoon with other elderly women in gossip and mah-jongg. Bei-yeh married in 1904 and moved away. Mother endured, all the while hoping her next pregnancy would bring a boy-child and a better reputation in the family. But again fate wasn't kind and the next child was a girl, my sister Koo-yeh, in 1905. This time Mother was bitingly criticized.

Today our basic knowledge of modern science is so much a part of our outlook that it is difficult to imagine the attitude of these rural folk in the interior of China a century ago. They did not see gender as the result of an arbitrary biological process. Rather, they saw the birth of a daughter as punishment for my mother's failure as a wife. If she adopted the proper spiritual balance, she would have a son. That she'd now had two daughters could only be the result of a curse, spiritual ineptness, carelessness, or downright disobedience to the wishes of her husband.

After the birth of Koo-yeh, my mother's life became nearly intolerable. Her husband and mother-in-law criticized her constantly. Other family members were ashamed. The neighbors whispered about what an unfit, unfortunate wife she was. Many years later, she told me that she did not feel life worth living in this period. She was still a young woman. She adored her beautiful daughters. But her days were filled with sorrow and self-criticism for having failed to present her husband with a son. Her suffering also brought a great deal of pain to her parents, who were treated rudely and sarcastically by her husband and her mother-in-law whenever they came to visit. Her mother went many times to the Buddhist temple to pray and to offer donations for the birth of a son to my parents. So it was a terrible disappointment when my mother gave birth to her third daughter, my sister Reou-yeh, in 1907. This time my mother couldn't hide her sorrow. Her mother-in-law berated her as an unworthy daughter-in-law. My father was furious, alternately chastising and shunning her. My mother's parents did not dare visit for fear of the jeers and embarrassment. They turned to superstition and prayers, insisting that my mother swallow a silver coin to ensure her giving birth to a son next time. My mother swallowed a coin the size of an American quarter. For days she was sick and unable to hold down food.

All the superstition concerning procreation may seem quaint, but the ignorance of these rural folk put my mother under terrible stress. Her parents became more ashamed, her mother-in-law more shrill, the neighbors more snide, and my father more abusive. And all the while, Mother was loaded down with household chores and the care of three young daughters. How she managed I will never understand, but she did and emerged a stronger person than ever. Finally, in the early summer of 1909, she gave birth to a fat, healthy son, my brother Wen-po.

Wen-po's birth redeemed my mother in the eyes of her family and village. My mother's parents rushed to the Buddhist temple to promise a big worship donation. Following Buddhist custom, a blessed necklace was placed around Wen-po's neck to protect him from evil spirits. The necklace could not be taken off until his twelfth birthday, when he would be brought to the temple to thank Buddha for his life. The tradition applied only to first sons, and my brothers and I would not be similarly honored or protected. But we never thought to question this: Wen-po was the eldest son and forever deserving of his favored position in the family.

Mother's relationship with her mother-in-law greatly improved after Wen-po's birth. Grandmother Chang Nan-sze was not a cruel woman. She had no formal education and no particular intelligence. She acted the role of dictatorial mother-in-law, as she believed tradition demanded. Behind this facade, she was capable of affection and good humor. Quite probably, she felt that her severity had helped Mother achieve the proper conduct and spiritual attitude that made her at last worthy of becoming the mother of a son. She now judged her to be a good wife and mother, and they had many good conversations and happy hours as they worked together to care for Wen-po and his sisters. Uncle Chang Weng's wife granted a grudging respect to Mother after they both had sons. Eventually, she came to depend on Mother's judgment and intelligence, which were much superior to hers.

Unfortunately, the new respect Mother had won in Father's opinion soon faded. Pursued by his demons, lost dreams, and his own dark nature, he became increasingly abusive to her. Mother was innately a strong-willed person and that will had been strengthened by the years of disappointment, abuse, and criticism before the birth of Wen-po. Since her marriage, she'd done her best to weather my father's anger without fighting back, but now she increasingly used her sharp tongue whenever he criticized her unfairly. That, of course, only enraged him further, and he beat her many times.

Mother stood between her angry husband and an extension of his abuse to her children. She protected them, often taking the blows that he might have rained on them. To her great relief, she was able to stop binding her daughters' feet, sparing them the torture and lifelong disability suffered by generations of Chinese women.

Great changes were coming to China, and some of the wicked old traditions were cast into the dustbin of history where they belonged. In 1903, Emperor Kwang-shu issued a decree banning many ancient practices, including foot binding. By this time the Manchu dynasty was so weak that it no longer had the power to enforce or even promulgate its decrees. It took years for word to spread into the interior, but eventually people began putting aside the practice. I have the sense that Mother was one of the first women in the village to adopt the new outlook. She was a traditional Chinese woman, had herself submitted to rigorous foot binding, but she was also a loving mother and a humane person. Foot binding had been an aesthetic, sexual, and cultural aberration. She couldn't change her own victimization by tradition, but she could spare her daughters. The mothers of many young girls who would now have "big" feet worried whether their daughters would ever find suitable mates. But Mother's attitude was, let the men change or remain single.

I can only imagine her joy as she watched her daughters run and skip. She loosened her own bindings, began to adopt slippers in place of the traditional high shoes that promoted the "willow walk." There was no undoing the damage to her feet, but at least she would enjoy modestly better mobility in the years to come as her children grew up around her.

CHAPTER 2

The Enduring Cycle

MY MOTHER LIVED NEARLY HER entire life within a village society that had not changed greatly in more than two thousand years. Village life was regulated by customs and traditions whose origin few understood: people had simply always lived this way. Not all Chinese villages were the same, of course. China is a huge and diverse country. Climate, geography, and population density all had an effect on village life and traditions. Inter-rural transportation and communication were miserably inadequate in my mother's childhood. Villagers near the coast experienced more contact with Westerners and were more likely to have relatives living overseas, but many villagers in rural China had never seen a "foreign devil." In the remoter parts of the interior, half a hundred ethnic minorities practiced their own traditions. Some Chinese had converted to Islam or Christianity. Despite all these factors, the similarities between villages from one end of China to the other far outweighed the differences since the vast majority of Chinese were ethnically Han and culturally Confucian.

Confucianism is misunderstood by many in the West, where it is often dismissed as mere ancestor worship. Confucianism has always been primarily an ethical system for the achievement of social harmony. Confucius (c.551–479 B.C.E.) and his followers taught that human beings were primarily social creatures endowed with *jen*, a natural sympathy for other people. *Jen* is expressed in five relationships: friend and friend, husband and wife, older and younger brother, parent and child, ruler and subject. To repress less admirable human traits, the Confucian philosophers outlined a system of etiquette and ritual called *li*, whose basic tenet is identical in all but wording to the Christian golden rule. Strict adherence to *li* made the *jen* relationships function smoothly. Thus, social harmony was preserved in family, clan, village, and empire.

Since respect for elders was a major element of *li*, pre-Confucian practices honoring ancestors grafted easily onto Confucianism. In the first century C.E., Han rulers perceived the advantages of a state religion and began venerating Confucius with rituals and sacrifices performed in special shrines. Yet the basic nature of Confucianism as an ethical system remained unaltered, functioning with efficiency and durability well into the twentieth century.

The ethnic and cultural uniformity of the great majority of China's people provided a foundation for traditional village self-government. It is a misunderstanding of Chinese history to see imperial organization as a looming, highly centralized presence overseeing the daily lives of the people. Most villagers worked their fields and lived their lives with practically no contact with the central government. They expected neither help nor protection from it and rarely received any. Banding together, they kept their own peace; fought floods, pests, and fires; protected themselves from bandits; and celebrated the harvest and ritual days of the year. Occasionally, the government might exact a levy for a public works project or impress young men into the army. But even these incidents might come only once in a generation. For the vast majority of rural folk, a visit from the imperial tax collector was their only regular contact with the central government.

The absence of outside government aid or interference bred a strong sense of mutual reliance and cooperation among the villagers. Village women assisted each other in giving birth, looking after the young, caring for the sick, and preparing the dead for burial. The entire village turned out for birthdays, marriages, and funerals. If flood or fire threatened the village, the ringing of a bronze gong brought all able-bodied men running. In years of famine and unrest, the men mounted guard at the village gate and formed patrols to drive off bandits, thieves, and vagrants. At planting and harvest time, the men joined to accomplish the arduous work.

Rich families—and the standards of rural wealth usually represented only a modest step above the norm—had special obligations. They were expected to lend money or food to neighbors who fell on hard times and to donate generously to public works for the community's good. When a rich family celebrated an occasion of good fortune, it would formally invite a few people as a sign of special honor, kinship, or mutual interest. But a formal invitation was not necessary to attend the celebration, and the whole village turned out, expecting entertainment and a memorable feast.

As in any society, an individual would occasionally try to avoid the social obligations demanded by tradition. The offender paid a heavy price. Neighbors would criticize and shun him, making his family miserable. In time of trouble, he might receive grudging assistance once, but if he wasn't fulsome in his thanks and continued in his antisocial ways, he would find himself entirely alone the next time disaster or hardship came knocking. Few could or wanted to live long in the village without the respect and aid of neighbors. In China, rugged individualism was not considered a virtue but evidence of a selfish and disharmonious character at odds with the cooperative and conformist nature of village life. For all the harshness of village condemnation, redemption was readily granted for all but the most grievous antisocial behaviors. If the contrite offender made an honest self-criticism, neighbors were delighted to forgive him. Such a restoration of social compliance and harmony was considered a triumph for the whole village.

Learning moral character was the key to obtaining a prosperous life and, even more important, a good reputation in the village. Mothers were fiercely determined to educate their children according to the village standards of good conduct. Elders, both men and women, felt it a duty to observe the young and to judge their worthiness. A bad impression in the eyes of an elder could take a young person months, perhaps years, to overcome. It was not only a duty but greatly in the self-interest of every young person to build a reputation for hard work, fair dealing, and respect for elders.

Zhou-bian village had some 150 families divided among the surnames of Chang, Lu, Chen, and Liu. The Changs were the largest clan, constituting about half of the total village population of around eight hundred. The people were hardworking farmers who owned horses, cows, and mules to help cultivate the sticky yellow clay of the region. Wheat was the principal crop, followed by millet, buckwheat, barley, corn, cotton for both oil and fiber, and an assortment of fruits, including pears and melons. Garlic and hot peppers were raised for home consumption and export. Rice was imported from the south for those who could afford it, but noodles and wheat bread made up the staple foods in our area. Eggs were a frequent item in the diet. Farmers raised poultry and hogs for eating on special occasions, but few families could afford meat on a regular basis.

Zhou-bian village consisted of the mud-brick homes of the farmers, the schoolhouse, and little more. The houses shared common walls with adjoining houses. The village wall constituted the rear wall of each home. Our house was fairly typical for an independent farmer of some means. Facing the street was a stable for the family ox, a sleeping area for the hired man, and a room for farming implements. Beyond the stable was the enclosed courtyard where many of the family activities took place in good weather. Beyond this lay a living area with two bedrooms opening off one side and another bedroom and a storage room off the other. The next room was the kitchen and dining area taking up the full width of the house. Outside the rear door was the family's private outhouse, used almost exclusively by the women.

Shopkeepers, tradesmen, and artisans congregated in the bigger towns, and the villagers had to walk the nine miles to Xing-ping City or wait until the appropriate traveling craftsmen or peddlers came through the village. A compensation for this inconvenience was the absence in the village of gamblers, thieves, prostitutes, opium sellers, professional beggars, and society's other unsavory characters. In Chinese culture, the village life was considered the most beneficial to mind, body, and spirit. Many of the brightest and most ambitious young men left the village to seek advancement in government service or the commercial life of the city. But in old age they would return to the village of their birth to enjoy a retirement of quiet honor.

Ownership of land provided the standard of wealth and poverty. Landless families had no hope of becoming self-sufficient unless they, like my great-grandfather Chang Jing-shue, the "screeching-wheel" peddler, managed to save enough to buy land. Even with good luck, it usually took several decades, even generations, for a family to achieve wealth. Few families had both the determination and the good fortune to greatly improve their status when a single drought, opium-smoking son, or untimely death could wipe out years of hard work almost overnight.

Most of the villages of northwest China did not have the rural aristocracy of very rich landlords who exploited the landless farmers with heavy rents. Farms in our area were small and the standard of living low, even for those considered comparatively wealthy, like my family. Families that had more land than they could farm themselves were considered rich. In our region, excess holdings rarely amounted to more than a few extra acres. Even families considered rich by local standards could rarely afford ease or luxury. Like their poorer neighbors, they were up at dawn to work long hours in the fields. Farming implements were primitive, the larger items and beasts of burden often shared by several families. Farmers combined their labor in the harvest and planting seasons. By rural tradition, farmers helped widows without mature male children to put in and harvest crops. Families that had gained a bit more wealth than the average were obligated to be especially generous in support of the less fortunate.

All but the few truly wealthy families lived year to year on a perilous edge. Harvests were entirely dependent on good weather. No general irrigation system existed, and only the lucky farmers with land beside the river could irrigate. Two or three bad years of too much or too little rain would force many farmers into selling their land and joining the unfortunate class of laborers who worked for other people.

The summers in Shaanxi were usually very hot for a few weeks but otherwise mild. Springs and autumns lasted for many pleasant weeks. The winters saw stretches of subfreezing temperatures and bitter winds, but the frequent mild days melted the occasional snows. For many centuries scholars had observed the changing of the seasons, and their advice on when to plant was available in the Chinese equivalent of the *Farmer's Almanac*. The farmers' country wisdom usually validated the scholars' predictions and vice versa so that planting times took on the force of custom. Barley and winter wheat were planted in September for harvest in May, after which the other cereal crops were planted for harvest in the fall. May was the busiest month of the year with school dismissed so that sons could join fathers and older brothers in the fields. Farmers from farther north came to the area to earn extra money before returning to harvest their own winter wheat.

As in all rural societies, the village life changed with the cycle of the seasons. Farmers rose very early in the busy months, arriving in the fields before dawn. After an hour or two, they would return home for a light breakfast, typically wheat bread, tea, and barley soup or millet porridge. They would rest from their work again at noon to eat the largest meal of the day, typically wheat bread, tea, and large quantities of noodles with peppers and whatever vegetables were available. After an hour's nap, the workers would return to the fields. In the busy times of the year, when work went on until dark, children and women would bring an additional meal to the fields in midafternoon. A light supper, again bread, tea, and noodles, rounded out the day's diet. Many older people did not eat supper in the belief that digestion interfered with a good night's sleep.

Work continued at a deliberate pace through the summer. A good fall harvest brought celebrations and happy talk of what the family might afford in the next year. A poor harvest brought gloom. Farmers calculated and recalculated how much they would have to borrow to get through to the spring harvest. Two or three poor harvests in a row could bring disaster: starvation, the loss of family lands, the sale of young daughters into prostitution, and the suicide of fathers unable to pay their debts. Debt was both a necessity and a great curse for the rural families, and few could avoid it entirely. Tradition counted those able to pay off their debts at year's end as most fortunate.

After the planting of winter wheat and barley in September, the work in the fields eased. Young people usually married in these months. Late autumn brought cool days and preparations for the winter. Housewives hung out the families' heavy blankets and clothes to air. The men did repairs on their homes and equipment. In November they covered the windows with heavy paper that would keep out the wind but let in light during the daylight hours. At dark, every family would close its shutters against the cold and the howl of prowling wolves.

December and January were cold, dry months with occasional light snow. Families stayed close to home. By tradition, Chinese families had three, four, or even five generations living under the same roof. Luxuries like electricity, telephones, gas stoves, running water, and indoor plumbing were unknown. Animals lived in an attached stable. Well-to-do families could afford homes large enough for married couples and the elderly to enjoy some privacy. Poorer families had to endure long weeks of tight crowding. The hours together made for some squabbling, but even in the poorer homes the anticipation of the coming New Year's celebration fostered a happy atmosphere.

The people's health suffered because of crowding, the lack of modern medicines and vaccinations, dietary insufficiencies in poor homes, and the absence of refrigeration for food preservation. Yet in times of adequate food supply, villages were generally healthy. Custom promoted household cleanliness and personal hygiene. Every family had its favorite herbal cure for maladies, and these were willingly exchanged with other families. In every village a few elders enjoyed special reputations as herbal and acupuncture healers. They were summoned in cases of serious illness, treating the sick person without thought of compensation beyond gratitude and perhaps an invitation to a family meal or a small gift of food or money. Some healers practiced exorcism and other dubious superstitions, but most of the traditional healing arts were directed toward promoting recovery though balancing the *yin* and *yang* components of the Taoist life force *Qi*. Few ailing people dreamed of going to the city for treatment. As in most traditional societies, the rural folk of China lived and died in acceptance of the dictates of nature and fate.

Like all rural girls of her generation, my mother had no opportunity to go to school. Few families could afford to send more than a single child to school, and the honor was restricted to boys. The selection was a matter of great significance. A boy who studied hard and achieved good marks brought honor to the family. He was excused for the hours of the school day and from family chores when he had homework to do. However, family expectations could exert great pressure, and youngsters laboring over their lessons sometimes envied brothers who worked in the fields. But usually Chinese schoolchildren felt greatly honored and pursued their studies with diligence. There was no formal taxation to support village schools. Families with children in school paid for the upkeep of the building and the services of the schoolmaster. Sometimes a well-to-do elder, like my great-grandfather Chang Jing-shue, would fund the building of a school or sponsor the schooling of some village children out of a spirit of generosity.

According to Confucian tradition, all family decisions of importance were made by the oldest adult male unless, as in my great uncle's case, he was considered foolish or of poor moral character. Issues might involve who should get married, which boys should go to school and who should stay home to help with the farmwork, and whether the family could afford to rent land or employ a laborer. The wise family head consulted with other respected members of the household, both male and female, before making a decision. Critical household decisions often required long thought and discussion. Once made, decisions were rarely questioned.

The eldest married female exercised great authority over the day-to-day life of the household. With several married couples living under the same roof, disputes often arose, particularly among rival sisters-in-law. They would, of course, try to recruit their husbands to their side. Such "pillow talk" could lead to arguments among brothers who had grown up in harmony. But a skillful mother-in-law could defuse the conflict by bringing the women to a sisterly understanding.

Beyond the nuclear and extended family, surname clans were the significant units of self-government. Clan leaders gave advice, dispensed inherited wisdom, led clan ceremonies, and arbitrated disputes between families. The system was informal, carrying the force of tradition but not of law. The elders did not need a regular schedule of meetings since they met one another in the course of daily routines. They would exchange news and discuss village problems. If a problem were particularly vexing, they might meet over tea or a meal to discuss it or to interview participants. In times of great crisis they would call an assembly of the clan for a public discussion and a vote on the proper course of action.

Every child knew the identity of the clan leader. At Lunar New Year and on an elder's birthday, young people made a formal visit to do him honor. They would kowtow, touching forehead to floor. The elder responded with a blessing and perhaps a small gift of candy or money. Adults who had gone off to work in the city or to join the army always stopped to pay respect to their clan leaders on visits home.

The leadership provided by the clans worked so well that the village required little formal government. From among the clan leaders, the men of the village selected a village magistrate by voice vote in assembly. The members of the school board were the only elected officials in the village besides the magistrate. Tradition dictated curriculum, and the board's main duties were hiring the schoolmaster, collecting money to pay his salary, and maintaining the schoolhouse. Though and perhaps because the vast majority of the rural folk were illiterate, learning was greatly respected, and the school board could expect willing support from the villagers.

The magistrate served as a sort of village executive, seeing that streets and public privies were maintained. He might occasionally have to punish a petty criminal, but his main responsibility was dealing with the representatives of the central government: the tax collector, the commander of troops marching through the village, and the county executive, who was the next direct link in the long chain upward to the emperor himself.

Roughly ten villages made up a township with an executive appointed by the county executive in consultation with the village heads. About ten townships made up a county, its executive appointed by the provincial governor. The provincial governor was an immensely powerful figure with his own army and the responsibility for governing a population of millions. Though he submitted his reports through the interior ministry of the imperial court, he was to a large extent a law unto himself. In times when the central authority was weak, the provincial governors maneuvered to assume greater power through secret alliances or outright rebellion. So it had always been, and so it would continue until almost the end of my mother's life.

Evenings and slack periods in the farming year provided time for recreation. Boys and fathers flew kites. Children played the games common in most cultures: hide-and-seek, tag, keep-away, and the like. Young adults practiced rigorous martial arts while their elders preferred *taijiquan*, the ancient discipline of slow movement and breathing. Adults played mah-jongg, sang, told stories, and gossiped. Many people from an early age to very late in life enjoyed the ancient art of folding paper into birds, boats, fish, and animals. Sometimes neighborhoods held competitions to see who could fold fastest and with the greatest skill.

Any sort of theater production drew large audiences. If the harvest had been very good, the village might sponsor a performance by a traveling troupe of actors. More often, an enthusiastic amateur company from the village itself would present a production. Each province had its own traditional opera in the local dialect. The stories were well known and easy to follow even for the young. All were didactic, teaching respect for the past, elders, and custom, although some would also caution against too rigid an adherence to tradition. There was, for example, the story of the rich man during the Tang dynasty who had three daughters but no sons. He marries the first two daughters to good husbands, but the youngest daughter wants her mate chosen by the goddess of good marriages. She throws a bouquet from a stage during a festival. A young beggar catches the flowers. The girl's father is appalled when the daughter insists on marrying the beggar. The marriage causes a long estrangement between the daughter and her parents. Though poor, the young couple lives happily until one day the gallant beggar subdues a fierce tiger. The emperor, impressed with his bravery, makes him commander of an army going to fight border bandits. The expedition lasts eighteen years. In her husband's absence, the strong-willed daughter lives in a mud cave, refusing to call on her father for relief from her poverty. Finally, the beggar-turned-general returns, honored by the emperor but greatly aged by his years of hard service. He finds that the years of poverty have turned his wife into an old woman before her time. Together, they weep. In a bittersweet climax, the stiff-necked father admits his error, and father and daughter are reconciled. In this way, tradition is mildly tweaked with the reminder that even a beggar impoverished by ill fortune may be a worthy man beneath his rags.

Puppet shows, performed by villagers or itinerant masters of the art, enthralled people of all ages. A variation on the usual puppet shows were the shadow plays at night. Hundreds of people gathered to watch the action performed behind a silk screen illuminated by a large gas lantern. As musicians and singers told the story, the puppeteers manipulated leather and wooden puppets to show the drama. Shadow horses, heroes, dragons, ships, demons, and gods performed the age-old stories of good and evil to the delighted crowds.

Mime players often performed for pennies on the streets, particularly at festival times. Such street performances could include half a dozen stories and take an entire afternoon as the actors, jesters, stilt-walkers, and musicians moved from corner to corner through the village. Costumes of symbolic meaning, extravagant facial makeup, and stylized gestures helped the audience identify characters and follow the plots in the traditional stories. The themes were always moralistic and served as reminders to the watchers of the importance and rules of proper conduct. As in many cultures, wicked stepmothers, heroic youngsters, doomed lovers, and ravenous wolves were popular characters.

A traditional story familiar to everyone recounted the tragedy of the great general Yueh Fei who served the Song dynasty. In his youth, his mother tattooed the four famous patriotic Chinese characters on his bare back. After a thousand painful nights, his skin bore the inscription *ching chong pao kuo* loyal sacrifice for the nation. Eventually, Yueh Fei rose to command the imperial army in the war against the Mongol invaders. He won many battles and might have saved China, but a traitor in the palace convinced the emperor that Yueh Fei wanted to overthrow him. The emperor threw Yueh Fei into prison where he died as the Mongols swept to victory. The emperor cast himself into the sea as Kubilai Khan established the Yuan dynasty.

The Moon Goddess often appeared in the plays because of her significance to the passing of seasons and the progress of the farming year. The Chinese lunar calendar is the oldest continuous record in history, dating from 2600 B.C.E. when it was promulgated by the legendary Yellow Emperor, Huang Di. There are twelve months in the year, each assigned an animal of the zodiac. Each year has a dominant animal in a cycle of twelve years. The difference between lunar and solar years is compensated for in the course of a complete cycle consisting of five, twelve-year cycles. Since the lunar year is shorter than the solar year used in the Western Gregorian calendar (a revision of the Julian calendar devised by the Romans based on the work of Egyptian astronomers), the Chinese Lunar New Year can fall anywhere from late January to the middle of February.

In the traditional Chinese outlook, the signs of the zodiac had considerable significance. According to ancient legend, Buddha summoned all the animals to him before he rose from earth to Nirvana. Only twelve came and he honored them by naming a month of the year after each. The character of each animal became part of a person's personality at birth: "the animal that hides in the heart."

In the pantheistic spiritual world of the rural folk, the deities of moon, sun, thunder, rain, earth, heaven, hearth, and stable all had their days of honor. Dragon Day fell in February and marked the traditional day for work to begin in the fields. In late March or early April, as the land turned green with spring, came Ancestor Time. For a week, people visited the graves of the recently departed to burn offerings of mock paper money. It was also a time of family reunions, as many grown children returned to the village to pay honor to their ancestors.

In May all China celebrated the life and work of the great third century B.C.E. poet Chu Yuan, who committed suicide rather than accept the victory of Ch'in Shih Huang Ti, the unifier of China and founder of the Chin dynasty. July was the Ghost Time, the unlucky month when ghosts were active. People avoided travel and never married in July. In mid-August, families gathered to enjoy the Moon Cake celebration, eating these confections under the full moon that heralded the beginning of harvest season.

Lunar New Year was the highlight of the year. Even the spirits of the recently dead were invited to the festivities marking the beginning of a new year. On New Year's Eve, relatives who had lost a loved one within the last three years walked to the graveyard to summon the soul of the departed. They returned home carrying a bright lantern in case the ghost had forgotten the way. Inside the house, children bowed and kowtowed to the loved one's photograph on a small altar. Widow and daughters offered dishes of his or her favorite foods. Kneeling before the altar, the family burned mock paper money and incense and prayed for moral guidance and good fortune in the year ahead. What many Westerners misinterpreted as ancestor worship was in reality a joyous spiritual reunion with the dead where the good and noble deeds of the departed were honored and children instructed on how to lead a moral life for the honor of the family.

Like Westerners at Christmas, Chinese villagers decorated their homes for Lunar New Year. They hung scrolls of red paper bearing couplets that expressed good wishes for visitors: for example, "May your business be as prosperous as water in the oceans; your wealth as great as water in the river."

Elaborate feasts began in every household late on New Year's Eve. By tradition, those who wished to enjoy longevity stayed awake past midnight—a task aided by the lighting of fireworks. Children waited in eager anticipation for New Year's Day, when they would don new clothes, kowtow to elders, and receive small packages of money for candy and toys. For the next fifteen days, people entertained neighbors and guests from other villages or went to enjoy the hospitality of others. In every house, guests bowed at the family altar to honor the departed. Only the very elderly remained at home throughout the festival, receiving the respects of frequent visitors. Newly wed couples in particular were busy travelers, repaying the gifts and kind wishes given them at their weddings. The largest occasion for them was a visit to the wife's parents' home to convey New Year's respects and to enjoy a memorable feast.

Families announced in advance the day they would be home to host visitors. Weeks of preparation went into the feasts. Two meals were offered on that day, the first a light meal of noodles served in a delicious soup, the second a grand feast of many dishes and delicacies. Each table had nine different dishes in addition to the soft bread made of steamed wheat flour. Though wine, beer, and whiskey were offered in abundance, the guests rarely drank so much as to become intoxicated. Chinese culture traditionally abhorred excess. Good talk, good food, and good friends were enough to make the day happy.

The Lunar New Year celebration concluded with the Lantern Festival. Children lit candles in bright silk lanterns and carried them outside on long, flexible poles. And though the days of celebration were drawing to a close, people were more relaxed than sad, reassured by this festival many hundreds of years old that life would continue much as it always had. The villagers connected to the past through veneration of their ancestors and to succeeding generations through their children who, giggling and singing, paraded the gaily bobbing lanterns through the streets.

CHAPTER 3

The Frustrated Scholar

THE QING DYNASTY FELL IN 1911, opening an era of cataclysmic change in China. I'm not sure how much my parents knew of the events of that dramatic year. In a country without an effective press, much less the electronic mass media of today, news spread slowly and unevenly. By the time it reached the ears of the villagers of rural China, the truth was usually corrupted by rumor and error. Most villagers simply did their work, raised their families, and hoped for the best. The mysterious and violent outside world would, they hoped, mind its own business and leave them in peace.

My father was an exception. He had enough education to have some sense of the wider world. He had approved of the self-strengthening programs of the progressive ministers and was an admirer of Dr. Sun Yat-sen. I think he must have waited eagerly for news. It is a pity that he could not share his interest in events beyond the borders of Zhou-bian village with my mother. She was an intelligent woman, and he could have taught her to read and write. With that to share, they might have been able to talk about matters great and small and become friends. But they were traditional Chinese people, and I doubt if it ever occurred to them that they might seek an intellectual companionship.

The fall of the Qing dynasty came quickly and with remarkably little bloodshed by the standards of Chinese history. Disgusted with the dynasty's corruption and weakness, many soldiers joined a revolutionary underground within the army. On October 10, 1911, an accidental explosion tore through a secret bomb factory in Hankou on the Yangtze. Fearing that a police investigation would reveal conspirators in the army, soldiers in the adjoining city of Wuchang mutinied. The mutiny spread rapidly to cities across China. Senior army officers refused to put down the rebellious soldiers, demanding instead that the dynasty adopt sweeping reforms. In Beijing, the mother and imperial regent of the infant emperor Puyi tried to save the throne by agreeing to surrender most of the dynasty's power to the reformist provincial governor Yuan Shikai. The revolutionary assembly gathering in Nanjing refused to approve

25

the plan. Instead, the delegates declared China a republic and elected Dr. Sun Yat-sen provisional president.

Negotiations between the two sides followed. Anxious to avoid civil war, Dr. Sun agreed to cede the presidency of the new republic to Yuan Shikai on the condition that the imperial family renounce all power. Senior army officers pressured the imperial family to agree. On February 12, 1912, Puyi abdicated. In January 1913, China held its first national election. Though it was an indirect election, plagued with many problems, it was the first attempt in China's long history to determine the will of the people. When the new parliament met in Beijing, Dr. Sun's Guomindang (Nationalist) party held the majority of seats. Yuan Shikai could not accept this challenge to his power, and he used the Guomindang's criticism of his financial program as an excuse to suppress the party. He fired all the pro-Guomindang provincial governors and sent his troops to destroy Guomindang strongholds. Dr. Sun was forced to flee abroad.

Yuan Shikai was unable to consolidate power. In 1914, with the Western powers distracted by the outbreak of World War I, Japan seized Germany's sphere of influence in Shandong province on the eastern coast. In 1915, Japan presented Yuan with the infamous Twenty-one Demands, which included the right of Japan to oversee the Chinese government and police force. Yuan cast about for ways to resist this aggression, but he needed a big loan from Japan to reorganize his government. Hoping to maneuver for a better deal once he'd secured his hold on power, he agreed to most of the demands. He died the following year, eighty-three days after crowning himself emperor. The Beijing government became a shaky coalition of Yuan's warlord generals. Some were no better than bandits; others were patriotic men who hoped to protect their provinces against their brethren and the Japanese until a new effort could be made to unite China. The warlord Chen Shu-fan, one of Yuan's followers, took control of Shaanxi province. He managed to maintain some measure of peace, but greedy officials and bandits plagued the villagers.

Mother was in her thirties by this time and busy raising her rapidly expanding family. After the birth of Wen-po, Father did not want any more children, but in those days birth control was little known in China. My mother bore two more sons and another daughter in the next decade: my sister Ling-yeh in 1913 and my brothers Wen-hui in 1917 and Wen-shuan in 1919. Wen-shuan became my father's favorite, but he disliked Wen-hui and treated him badly. Mother's stout defense of Wen-hui led to many violent arguments.

My older sisters, approaching marriageable age, helped with the younger children. My father devoted most of his attention to Wen-po, teaching him to read, write, and keep accounts. He read to him from the Confucian classics, and instructed him in the mandarin ideals of good government. In Wen-po he reposed his hope for immortality. Wen-po grew into a strong, perceptive youth who tried to serve as a conciliator in times of family tension. My mother leaned on him, often sending him on errands. When Wen-po was about twelve, Mother received word that her uncle in a nearby village had taken to his deathbed. She sewed him a pair of slippers to wear to his grave and then summoned Wen-po to deliver them. My father objected violently, fearing that a wolf or a tiger might attack Wen-po on the road. Mother dismissed Father's excuse and the two argued. My father lost his temper utterly and threw a heavy brick at her. It struck her on the forehead, opening a long gash that bled terribly. All my sisters were scared and crying, unable to do anything. My father simply stormed out of the house, dragging Wen-po with him.

My mother was offended, angry, and so wounded in body and spirit that she announced she did not want to live anymore. Fortunately, my mother's second brother, Wei Sze, came to our house at this fearful moment. He calmed her and helped my sisters bandage her. It was one of the few times this selfish brother, who was responsible for so much of Mother's unhappiness, ever did her a kind turn. By the next day the wound was infected, and the pain became excruciating. Mother lay in bed for many days, her face swollen and her heart despairing. Summoned at last by Father, a traditional healer could do little to arrest the infection. My mother's courage seemed broken, and she told my sisters that she could not see any good days ahead in her life. My sisters feared that she might commit suicide.

According to my brother Wen-po, our father seemed remorseful and afraid of losing Mother. But he never apologized to her. At last the injury began to heal, and Mother recovered some of her old physical and mental strength. A long scar would mar her forehead for the rest of her life, and I don't believe the scar on her already wounded heart ever healed. After two months, she managed to rise from her bed, but as Wen-po recalled: "A constant cloud of sadness filled the house. There was no happiness at all." Mother turned away from any further attempts at reconciliation with my father, devoting herself entirely to her children.

Wen-po recorded in his autobiography the outbreak of fighting in our province in 1920 when one of General Chen Shu-fan's lieutenants rebelled. Fighting continued for weeks, costing the lives of thousands of innocent farmers who were either impressed into the rival armies or were caught in the crossfire. Chen Shu-fan managed to suppress the rebellion, but in 1921 another paroxysm of bloody fighting swept the province. Undisciplined troops roamed the land, robbing, raping, and murdering. One supposed tax collector demanded fifty silver dollars from my parents or he would order his soldiers to burn the house. Though well-off in land, my parents were poor in hard currency like most rural folk. When they managed to raise only forty dollars, the tax collector beat my father. Wen-po recalled my mother, eyes streaming with angry tears, screaming at the soldiers: "You want our lives? Those we have. More silver we do not have. You may search the entire house as you please." Finally, the collector and his soldiers went away.

The fighting continued for months. A drought hit the area, destroying much of the harvest and adding more misery to the lives of the rural folk. Eventually, General Chen Shu-fan was defeated by General Feng Yu-shiang. General Feng was something of an odd figure: a Christian with a patriotic and liberal bias. But though he personally was more benevolent than many of the warlords, the government he established in Shaanxi province was riven with corruption. For the next few years Feng and the warlords Zhang Zuolin and Wu Pei-fu would dominate China north of the Yangtze. They maintained the shaky and largely ineffectual national government in Beijing. In competition with each other and fearful of Dr. Sun Yat-sen's growing Guomindang movement in southern China, they would continue to kowtow to the Great Powers, particularly Japan. Through loans, pressure, and threats, Japan's influence in northern China increased to new and dangerous levels.

Though our family was still well-to-do by village standards, my parents could not afford to hire a nanny, cook, or maid. The entire burden of running the house fell on the women of the family: Grandmother Chang Nan-sze, my mother, Chang Weng's wife, and the older girls.

Every day, the women of our household prepared three meals for about twenty people. Father, Uncle Chang Weng, and the hired hands rose an hour before sunrise to go to the fields. About two hours later, they returned to have a quick breakfast. The women had to rush from making breakfast to preparing the midday dinner that was the main meal of the day. In the afternoon, they had to sweep the floors, wash the pots and pans, and make wheat dough for the steamed bread that was a major staple in our part of China. All the while the younger children had to be cared for and the older girls instructed in the arts of the Chinese housewife. After perhaps an hour or two of spinning and sewing, the women would go to the kitchen to prepare the evening meal.

Since the climate of northwestern China varies from high summer heat to subzero winter cold, every family needed a variety of garments. The arduous task of making clothes began with the hand-spinning of thousands of bundles of cotton thread. Next the thread was hand-loomed into a coarse cotton fabric, which was dyed different colors depending on the age, gender, and personal preference of the eventual wearer. Tailoring and long hours of stitching by hand produced summer clothing that was light and durable for the work in the fields. Winter clothing required a double layer of fabric padded with cotton batting or loose cotton to preserve body heat.

Mother's oldest daughters began getting married in the early 1920s. We were among the richest families in the village, and Mother and the matchmakers had little trouble finding suitable husbands for the girls. Assembling a dowry was the work of many months. Every young wife was expected to bring to her new home most of the items needed to outfit her for years to come. Mother and the girls hand-stitched many sets of holiday and working clothes, much of it with cloth they had woven themselves. They made slippers, bed coverings, sleeping pajamas, and towels. They shopped for mirrors, cosmetics, and utensils. All were carefully stored for the grand day.

Chu-yeh was married to a young shopkeeper in 1921. He turned out to be a stingy man, much disliked in our family. About 1923, Koo-yeh married a well-to-do though uneducated farmer from a family friendly to Father. Unfortunately, the family soon fell on hard times because of illness and bad luck, losing much of its status in the community. In 1925, Reou-yeh married into another farming family. For her, marriage was particularly difficult because she had to nurse her overbearing mother-in-law, who had been crippled by a stroke. Still, all these marriages were reasonably successful, and my sisters were soon busy raising families of their own.

At this time in China, young wives rarely left their neighborhoods except during festival times when they would pay a visit to their parents' home. My mother missed her daughters, particularly her favorite, Reou-yeh, but at the same time their marriages relieved her of worry about their future. She had three sons yet to raise and a new daughter-in-law to train to the family routine.

Chong-er, the daughter-in-law who would brighten the next decade of Mother's life, came into the family through her marriage to Wen-po in 1922. The match was something of particular note to the village gossips since Chong-er at nineteen was six years older than Wen-po, who was only thirteen on their wedding day. Guests giggled and whispered, speculating on how the wedding night would progress between a grown woman and a shy boy. I imagine Wen-po blushing furiously as he lifted the red veil from Chong-er's face as the elders pronounced them married.

This lifting of the veil was usually the first sight that young couples had of each other. In traditional Chinese society, couples did not court but had their marriages arranged by parents with the help of the ubiquitous village matchmakers. But Wen-po and Chong-er had known each other since early childhood. Chong-er had taken charge of Wen-po when he was about six, choosing their games and making him run errands for her. He was almost slavishly devoted to her. Mother took note of the friendship and was impressed by Chong-er's looks, manners, and character. She secretly decided that eventually she would see them married. The families were already distantly related by marriage, and she approached Chong-er's mother when the time was right.

Chong-er's parents were agreeable to the match but insisted that the wedding must take place before Chong-er became an old maid of nineteen or twenty—a perilous position for any young woman in traditional Chinese society. Wen-po was not opposed to marrying Chong-er on some distant day after he'd become a man. But when Chong-er was nineteen the marriage couldn't be delayed any longer. The guests were invited, the feast planned, and the musicians hired. Villagers pitched in to help with decorating my parents' home and preparing the many dishes. Somewhere along the line, Wen-po and Chong-er were informed of the date of their wedding.

My parents spared little expense in celebrating the marriage of their eldest son. The entire village attended to share in the feast and to admire the gifts brought by the prominent guests. After the young couple knelt to thank their parents and the village elders for their upbringing, everyone offered warm wishes for a happy and prosperous life blessed with many children.

The speculation about the success of the wedding night continued well after the newlyweds were hustled off to bed. Wen-po did not want to go to the room with Chong-er, but my mother convinced him with her sweetest words into maintaining custom. No one was ever to know the intimate details of that night. Many years later on Taiwan, Wen-po told me of Chong-er's understanding and patience. He laughed when he recalled how in the early years of their marriage she kept candy and fruit in their room to lure him into bed. He smiled sadly: "I loved her always, even when, as a youngster, I was afraid to show it. She was the perfect wife to me, always gentle, patient, and wise. I would be buried at her side if it were possible." That it wasn't would be one of the tragedies of his long, eventful, and often dangerous life.

Moving into my parents' home, Chong-er quickly became my mother's closest confidant. She charmed everyone with her grace and cheerfulness. She relieved my mother and older sisters of much of the care of Ling-yeh, Wen-hui, and Wen-shuan, who were nine, five, and three at the time. Chu-yeh had already married and Koo-yeh and Reou-yeh were busy making their dowries. At first they may have been jealous of the place Chong-er so readily won in Mother's affections, but I think they soon came to appreciate that her presence meant they would not be leaving Mother to face life with our difficult father alone.

Chong-er developed some influence with Father, quietly mediating disputes in the household. She supported his efforts to give Wen-po the best education possible and was proud of her young husband's intelligence and accomplishments. The village one-room school taught only the ancient Confucian classics, and Father was forward-looking enough to realize that Wen-po would have to know much more to prosper in a rapidly changing China. He enrolled him in a boarding school some distance from our village. For the next half dozen years, Chong-er remained with Mother, working at her side as the weeks and months of the school term passed. When Wen-po needed money or clothing, Father made the arduous trek to the school.

For all that Chong-er or anyone else could do to ease the tension between Mother and Father, they still fought frequently. Feudal tradition condemned legal separation or divorce. Otherwise, I believe my parents would have divorced long before all the children were born. But in rural China, divorced women had almost no chance to remarry. Likewise, divorced men could not easily reverse their bad reputations, since few families would consent to marry a daughter to a divorced and probably abusive husband. So our parents stayed together, ostensibly for the well-being of the children, but at least equally to avoid violating social tradition. What a pity to live long years of marriage without mutual tender respect and intimate care for each other!

I think today my father would be diagnosed as mentally ill. Some of the stories about him hint that he may have regretted his long mistreatment of my mother but was unable to control his anger for long. Once when he visited Wen-po at boarding school to deliver winter clothes, Wen-po pleaded tearfully with him for kindness toward Mother. The next time Wen-po came home for vacation, Mother happily reported: "Your father was better toward me lately. You must have done well in school for your mother's sake."

Privacy is accorded little importance in close-knit Chinese society. In a rural village such as ours, everyone knew everyone else's affairs. Nor did my father take any care to minimize what others knew, frequently criticizing my mother in front of neighbors. These moments were particularly painful for her. But though the neighbors knew of our parents' bad marriage, they accorded both of them considerable respect as individuals. This was rather odd in my father's case. Although the husband was expected to rule his home in traditional Chinese society, wife beating was despised: a sure indication of a husband's inability to govern firmly and fairly without recourse to violence. But Father was an educated man and displayed both judgment and generosity outside the confines of the household. Though a brooding, shy man, he could become lively and involved when a matter grabbed his interest. He was an enthusiastic member of the village school board and a generous helper to all who needed his knowledge for such matters as contract writing, accounting, and land purchasing. Farmers from ten miles around came to seek his aid, which he provided to them without fee, though his inattention to his own farmwork cost him money.

Neighbors respected Mother for her kind heart, native intelligence, and sound judgment. Though she could not achieve a harmonious marriage with my father, she helped many other families. She was admired as a dutiful daughter-in-law, a loving mother, and a devoted friend. Neighbors often asked her to their homes to resolve quarrels and disputes. She had a keen understanding of the dynamics of family conflicts and the difficulties that could develop in child-parent relationships. She also had a persuasive and diplomatic manner. She quoted good examples of human harmony from folklore and life—a traditional Chinese means of soothing passions and settling disputes. Later, neighbors would confide in each other that our mother's intervention was "like a miracle of good medicine."

Though they had great difficulty in achieving peace in their own household, both my parents believed in the traditions of harmony, charity, and mutual cooperation that had prevailed in rural China for millennia. Hard times were about to test these traditions to the utmost. After several years of good weather and good harvests, a drought crept over northwestern China, drying up the crops. Rival warlords—some patriotic revolutionaries, some corrupt thugs—continued to fight each other and General Feng's regime. Roving bands of soldiers demanded food and money from the farmers. The soldiers dragged away many young men to fight in the battles of the warlords. Desultory fighting continued for years, sometimes exploding into bloody eruptions of violence.

In southern China, Dr. Sun Yat-sen had overcome great difficulties to establish a Guomindang (Nationalist) government with a capital at Guangzhou. The Soviet Union poured money into the creation of a Nationalist army and engineered an alliance between the Guomindang and the newly formed Chinese Communist Party (CCP). While the Nationalist army under General Chiang Kai-shek fought the southern warlords, Communist organizers prepared the way for further advances by fomenting discontent among rural farmers and city workers.

Dr. Sun died on March 12, 1925, and Chiang Kai-shek became the dominant member of the Guomindang leadership. In July 1926, he opened his campaign to unite China. Three Nationalist armies pushed north toward the Yangtze. Ahead of the armies, the Communist organized local uprisings. Some warlords joined Chiang; others were crushed in heavy fighting. By early 1927, the Nationalist armies had captured all of southeastern China and were advancing on Shanghai. But strains grew between the Communists and Chiang's conservative wing of the Guomindang. Chiang made his military base at Nanchang while the Communists and radical Guomindang leaders set up a government in Wuhan. The Communists took a leading role in the Wuhan government, pushing for radical economic and political reforms. The independence and radicalism of the Wuhan government threatened Chiang's domination of the Nationalist cause and put at risk many of his wealthy supporters.

In March 1927, as Chiang's troops approached Shanghai, an uprising led by Zhou Enlai established a Communist government in the city. The coup infuriated Chiang. He met secretly with leaders of the underworld Green

Gang, headquartered in the city's French concession area. On April 12, with the support of Western authorities, the Green Gang attacked the Communists. Chiang's troops joined in the slaughter of thousands of Communists and their sympathizers. Disguised as a Catholic priest, Zhou Enlai escaped to Hong Kong. Chiang set up a government in Nanjing and forced the Wuhan government to disband. In the countryside, his troops killed thousands of peasants who had joined Communist associations. Surviving Communists sought shelter in rugged Jiangxi province.

With the Communists on the run, Chiang began planning his conquest of northern China. General Feng sent word that he would cooperate with the Guomindang. Chiang's armies advanced into the north in the fall of 1927, defeating Wu Pei-fu and sidestepping a confrontation with the Japanese garrison in the Yellow River city of Jinan. The Manchurian warlord, Marshal Zhang Zuolin, who had occupied Beijing in late 1924, retreated beyond the Great Wall. A few miles short of the Manchurian capital of Shenyang (Mukden), bombs exploded under his train, killing Zhang and many of his staff.

The bombs had been planted by violent militarists in the Japanese Kwantung army, which protected Japan's interests in its sphere of influence in southern Manchuria. The plotters hoped that a crisis in Manchuria would cause the downfall of Japan's civilian government and bring the militarists to power. The dreams of the Kwantung officers failed to materialize. Resolute liberals in the Japanese government refused to be stampeded into mobilization. Zhang Zuolin's son, Zhang Xueliang, took command of his father's army. The "Young Marshal" proved a surprisingly competent successor despite a reputation as a playboy and a drug addict. He reassured the Japanese government while at the same time pledging loyalty to Chiang and accepting a seat on the Nationalist State Council.

By the fall of 1928, China was officially united for the first time since the fall of the Qing dynasty. However, Chiang's control was never complete. Warlords continued to control large areas, paying only lip service to the Guomindang government. The Communists were rebuilding in Jiangxi province. Corruption and inefficiency plagued the new government despite the best efforts of upright ministers. When a great drought devastated vast areas of China, the central government could do little to alleviate the suffering of the rural folk. Between 1928 and 1930, five million people starved to death and four hundred thousand peasants sold themselves or their children into servitude. Yet for all the weaknesses, faults, and failures of the new government, the establishment of the Chinese Republic represented a huge triumph for the forces of liberalism and reform. Given time to learn and build, the republic founded on Dr. Sun's vision might lead the long oppressed people of China into a new and triumphant age of prosperity and self-government.

My father no doubt applauded the victory of the Nationalists. My mother probably cared little if she understood at all. She saw life from the traditional villager's point of view. Life was full of labor. Sewing, cooking, baking, washing, cleaning, and carrying water and fuel required many hours. Animals, babies, children, husband, and aged relatives needed care. Often neighbors asked for help or counsel. But village life had its pleasures. People gossiped, told stories, sang, played with their children, enjoyed the social cup of tea, and relaxed outside their homes "fanning their troubles away" on the warm summer evenings. Mother believed deeply in the simple wisdom of rural folk, in mutual aid and cooperation, and in working toward the personal and social harmony and balance that lay at the foundation of Chinese tradition.

Westerners often have difficulty understanding Chinese attitudes toward religion. Like most Chinese, Mother saw no contradiction in honoring household gods and ancestors, finding solace in a Taoist view of nature, making an offering in a Buddhist temple, and living day to day according to the social contract devised by Confucius. In a sense, she was a fatalist who believed that much of an individual's life is predestined. But in another sense she believed in free will and the salvation of the soul, teaching her children that a divine hand protected those who loved justice and maintained good conduct.

The last years of the 1920s were particularly hard on Mother. Her parents and her beloved younger brother, Wei Ba, all died within two years, leaving her grieving deeply. She lost an ally when Grandmother Chang Nan-sze decided that she could no longer tolerate my father's bad temper. She insisted on the division of the family wealth between her two sons. Uncle Chang Weng set up his own household, and she moved in with his family. Soon after, Chang Weng's son, Pao-wa, died, prostrating his wife with grief. They might have adopted Wen-hui or Wen-shuan as custom provided, but Chang Weng purchased a young concubine to bear him another son. Though a common practice even in those years when concubinage was increasingly frowned on, it was a ridiculous expense for a farmer of modest means. I think the sorrow of losing a grandchild and her son's foolishness may have contributed to Grandmother Chang Nan-sze's death shortly after. Chang Weng's wife never recovered from the loss of her child and died within a couple of years.

My father became even more temperamental as the drought spread across our province. The declining harvests forced him to lay off most of his hired hands, though he himself was getting too old for heavy work. Wen-po was at school, and Wen-hui and Wen-shuan were only little boys. Finally, Father had to summon Wen-po home from school to help with the work. He secured him the position of teacher in the village school, but Wen-po taught only a few months before the village could no longer pay him. The fall harvest of 1928 had been poor, the winter dry. With little expected from the crop of winter wheat, people whispered of famine. In that fall of foreboding, Ling-yeh married a hardworking and decent young farmer, Nan Kou-chai, and settled in his village about two miles from ours.

In the early months of the New Year, Mother discovered to her great distress that she was pregnant again. Everyone was shocked. She was forty-five, her youngest child ten, and my father past sixty. My sisters and brothers were mortified, and my mother wept. My father was furious. With the crops burning up in the drought, he was not sure that he could feed the children he already had. How could Mother have been so careless, so disobedient to his wishes?

I was born on July 1, 1929, a most unwelcome addition to the family. Once again Mother had to take up the exhausting task of caring for a baby. Shortly after my birth, Chong-er gave birth to my dear niece and lifelong friend Sher-chen. My father brooded about the addition of two more children to the family just as famine was descending on the village. One morning when I was ten weeks old and my mother was in the kitchen preparing the noon meal, he slipped into the bedroom and placed a heavy blanket over me. I was tightly bound into a small bundle to sleep and quickly began to suffocate. Shortly afterward, my mother returned to the bedroom to change and feed me. She burst into tears when she saw that I had turned blue for want of air. She thought I was dead, but a moment later I revived. Mother never forgave my father. To hide the family's shame, my mother and siblings never mentioned the incident to neighbors. My father was chastened for a time, knowing how close he had come to suffering the outrage of the community and a disgrace that would bow his head for the rest of his life. Cut off from even the minimal affection of his family, he fell even deeper into his dark despondence.

By the fall of 1929, half the people in Zhou-bian village were on the verge of starvation. The catastrophe brought out the best in my father. Our family still had a large surplus of wheat from previous harvests. The poor neighbors came to Father and Uncle Chang Weng for help. My uncle was uncertain, but Father persuaded him to share. The next day, nearly fifty families came to our storehouse. Father and my uncle fed them all. Within days, our storehouse stood empty. Like our poor neighbors, we would share the hardships of the famine.

When the fall harvest failed, Father took Wen-po, Wen-hui, and Wen-shuan to the neighboring province of Gansu to look for work. Mother and Chong-er, crippled by their bound feet, could not make the journey and remained at home. They cared for me and my niece Sher-chen and wove cloth for sale to support us until Father could send money or food. Many people from Zhou-bian village joined the two hundred–mile trek to Gansu. Father no doubt took a leading part in the councils of the men. He was an elderly man now, respected for his age and wisdom, and though the road was hard for someone his age, I imagine him as animated and decisive in the collective struggle to survive.

In Gansu, Father and my brothers found little work. Father auctioned off the extra clothes they had brought from home. Wen-po worked as a street peddler selling fruits. Wen-hui and Wen-shuan, too young for regular work, made pennies running errands for shopkeepers. Somehow, they managed to earn enough to buy a hundred-pound bag of millet. They loaded the millet on a wheelbarrow, and Wen-po started off to push it the two hundred miles to Zhou-bian village. The effort of getting the millet to us so exhausted Wen-po that he fell ill. Chong-er and my mother put him to bed. He couldn't rise for a month, and during that time we received word that Father had sickened and died in Gansu.

For his years, Father was fit and in good health, so I have always suspected that hunger and exhaustion brought on his brief, fatal illness. In a sense he died for Zhou-bian village, giving away our surplus and his strength until he had no more to give. Though fate had denied him his scholarly ambitions, he demonstrated in the last year of his life a leadership and nobility of character in the best tradition of the mandarin civil servants. I have often wondered whether my father's sacrifice of the family's stored grain redeemed him in the eyes of God. His capacity for doing so much good as a neighbor but so much ill as a husband left my family deeply conflicted about his memory. I think beneath his anger he was a decent man whom modern psychiatric science might have helped. I was an infant when he died and have no memory of him. All I know I learned from my siblings and the few comments my mother made about him while I was growing up. She was proud of his selfless behavior in the time of famine and would mention it when she thought we needed reminding about the virtue of generosity. I don't think she ever managed to reconcile his good and bad sides. I remember her saying once, almost as if excusing him: "All husbands are fierce, stern, and mean toward their wives." Another time she said: "Your father was a good man in heart, but he did not know how to communicate with people." Beyond that, she rarely spoke of him, and we children avoided mentioning him lest we arouse her grief.

My brother Wen-po had a strong affection and deep respect for our learned father, and I wish I had known him so that I might have judged his character for myself. I confess that I retain resentment toward him for the way he treated my mother. Yet in my heart I love him for bringing me into this world. I also admire his devotion to the village he loved and his great generosity when he opened the family storerooms to his starving neighbors. Although he was, I think, a man of deeply disturbed character, he rose above his failings at that critical moment in his life to demonstrate a heroic charity. It is this aspect of his character I prefer to remember. I hope that the better part of his spirit, wherever it resides, may take some small pride in the son born so late in his life and under such difficult circumstances. Fate granted me the opportunity to pursue the life denied to him: the life of a scholar.

Sometimes as I write late in the night, laboring with my poor words to bring a greater understanding between China and my adopted land, I feel that my father, Chang Ying, watches over my shoulder and approves. Regardless of how unfairly he treated my mother, I love him as a prodigal son in America and as a Christian believing in forgiveness and salvation. I pray that his soul knows comfort and peace.

CHAPTER 4

Famine

I CAN IMAGINE THE BOYS STILL: their faces pinched with hunger, their clothes torn and dusty from the long journey, their eyes haunted with the loss of a father and the incalculable suffering witnessed along the road from Gansu. So in my imagination did Wen-hui and Wen-shuan return to Zhou-bian village.

In the great famine of the late 1920s and early 1930s, millions of rural Chinese abandoned their villages in a desperate search for food. It's hard to imagine how terrifying their decisions were. The rural folk knew next to nothing of the wider world, and their journeys were undertaken with little more knowledge than possessed by the youthful Marco Polo or the sailors of Columbus. So my brothers might have gone off to be lost forever from home and village. Instead, they came home to Mother and the family.

The family had almost no food, but Mother laid out what she could for her two starving boys. While they ate, Wen-po, Chong-er, and my mother talked. We must live or die as a family they decided, not break apart as so many households were doing. My father's body lay in Gansu, two hundred miles away. In ordinary times, his sons would have gone to bring him home. But we had no money or food, Wen-po was still sick, and Wen-hui and Wen-shuan were exhausted. My father's body must lie in a distant place until better times came. This was a terribly difficult decision. Chinese tradition calls for the burial of a man near his birthplace lest his spirit wander forever amid strangers under strange skies. So it is that traditional Chinese abhor sea voyages and long journeys by land for fear of dying far from home. For home is best, the village itself the giver of life. To be a revenant, an exile, a wanderer, a prodigal—as Wen-po and I would eventually become—was the hardest of hard fates.

The famine deepened. People collapsed and died on the streets. Some were strangers, some villagers whose strength had failed them only yards from their front doors. Every day people carried the dead to the edge of the village and buried them without coffins in shallow ditches. Wolves and wild dogs often dug up the graves, fighting over the putrefying flesh and strewing the sad remains of humanity in the fields.

My family desperately needed a means of obtaining food. Chong-er managed to borrow five silver dollars from a sympathetic aunt. Wen-po took the money and set out for the county market in Xing-ping City where he bought two bushels of wheat, lugging the heavy load the nine miles home on his back. While my niece Sher-chen and I played nearby, my brothers set about grinding the grain in a heavy stone mill. My mother and Chong-er took turns shaking the wooden winnowing box to separate the chaff from the flour. All the afternoon passed in grinding and winnowing. After the sparse evening meal, sometimes no more than a porridge made from the wheat chaff, the women kneaded the dough for the steamed buns called *mantou*. The dough fermented in the night, and the women baked the buns in the early morning in a steaming wok, the dough on a wooden lattice over the boiling water.

At first light, the boys would go into the streets with covered baskets of buns, peddling to those who had a penny to spend. Three times a week Wen-po would take the profit and make the exhausting trek to buy another two bushels of wheat. Unfortunately, we were too successful in our small business, and other families began imitating us. The result was the inevitable division of the trade into so many shares that no one could make a living. After a few good months we had to give up making *mantou* for sale. The boys looked for small jobs while Mother sought the aid of relatives. Wen-po told Chong-er and Mother that he would join the provincial army to help support the family. They wept bitter tears as he packed his few belongings.

All this while, fighting had continued between the warlords. The soldiers were as hungry as the civilians and they often extorted what little the villagers had. The commanders diverted for their own profit the thin stream of relief supplies arriving from the Nationalist government and missionary aid societies. The Christian warlord General Feng Yu-shiang was particularly reprehensible in sanctioning this practice, and—as a fellow Christian—I have always been particularly aggrieved at his behavior.

Feng had allied himself with Chiang during the reunification campaign. But after the Nationalist triumph in 1928, Feng and the Shanxi warlord Yan Xishan continued to rule their old territories while scheming to oust Chiang from the Guomindang leadership. Fighting soon erupted. Wen-po joined the army of the popular Nationalist warlord General Yang Hu-cheng, who was fighting Feng for control of Shaanxi. Though my brother had never trained to be a soldier, he proved exceptionally well suited to the life. He was strong, intelligent, decisive, brave, and of commanding personality. He was made a second lieutenant after a short period of training and given command of a platoon of men.

Shortly after Wen-po joined the army, Wen-hui wandered off in search of work and food. It would be nearly two years before we heard from him again. We were often hungry in those days. Mother and Chong-er wove cotton cloth for sale. Wen-shuan sought work as a day laborer. Wen-po was able to visit occasionally, bringing food and a little money. A couple of months after one of these visits, Chong-er discovered that she was expecting a second child. Her pregnancy was a difficult one. Often hungry and overtaxed by the cares of helping the family survive, she fell ill. Mother made her go to bed, nursing her as well as she could in those terrible times. Chong-er did not want Wen-po to hear of her illness since he could do nothing while in the army. Mother agreed, but the responsibility of keeping the news from Wen-po rested heavily on her heart.

With Wen-po and Wen-hui gone and Chong-er ill, thirteen-year-old Wen-shuan became Mother's greatest help. Together they trudged to the homes of relatives to ask for assistance. Mother's bent feet forced her to lean heavily on a cane and her son's arm. If they were given any food, Wen-shuan carried the basket on the long hike back.

In the late summer of 1932, Chong-er gave birth to a son, Xing-min. She was by then very ill and unable to breastfeed the baby. Mother found a wet nurse among the village women and redoubled her efforts to return Chong-er to health. She spent what little money she could raise on the best food available, though it was very expensive. When her daughters, themselves greatly taxed in supporting their families, criticized this extravagance, Mother answered tartly that daughters left home to be helpmates in another household while daughters-in-law came to be a crutch to an aging mother-in-law. Who then more worthy of extra care than her beloved Chong-er?

As a child, Chong-er had experienced severe intestinal pain. Her parents bought opium for her. The relief it brought planted the seed of addiction in Chong-er, but she resisted, only occasionally taking opium as an adult. But in her last months, she begged for relief from the pain. Reluctantly, Mother found opium pills for her. Chong-er wept nightly for her husband. Both women worried constantly about Wen-po, and when a letter or a little money didn't arrive on schedule, they became frantic with anxiety. Once my mother became so anxious that she went to the Buddhist temple where she paid to draw a message from the *I Ching*, China's mystical *Book of Changes*. The monk interpreted the message as meaning that Wen-po was sick and in danger and that she must make a contribution to the temple for his protection. Shaken, she paid to have a votive candle burned on the altar for a month. On her return home, she couldn't sleep and cried through the nights. But she kept the monk's dire warning to herself out of fear of upsetting Chong-er. Three days later, to everyone's great joy, a healthy, smiling Wen-po came for a visit. When the immediate celebration quieted, Mother told Wen-po and Chong-er of her visit to the temple and the monk's fraud. From that day to the end of her life, she never again stepped into a temple.

Wen-po's visit and his great pride in the beautiful son his wife had given him gave Chong-er an infusion of strength and my mother hope that her daughter-in-law might recover at last. But soon after Wen-po's departure, Chong-er slipped into her final decline. She died in her sleep on January 6, 1933. She was only twenty-eight. My mother would mourn her sweet Chong-er the rest of her days. She knew that Wen-po could not obtain another leave so soon after his last visit, and she kept the news of Chong-er's death from him for six months. She bought a fancy casket that had originally been built for a rich old man. The neighbors and her daughters tut-tutted at the extravagance, but Mother replied that Chong-er, despite her short life, had brought the family honor by producing a son and a daughter. She deserved a beautiful resting place, and Wen-po would appreciate the fact that his wife had been richly buried when he at last stood at her grave.

My mother was a person of uncommon good sense, but she may have let her emotions get the better of her in the case of Chong-er's casket. The carpenter, who had his own family to support in these hard times, was enraged when she could not make the agreed payments. He visited the house daily to demand money, yelling insults that all the neighbors could hear when Mother, her tiny grandson in her arms, begged for more time. My little niece and I hid in a corner, terrified of the angry man at our door. Several times he caught Wen-shuan outside the house and beat him as a warning to my mother. She was deeply grieved by the carpenter's rudeness, particularly since in better times he had been one of the family's hired men, who were always treated kindly by my father. I don't believe her conscience rested until she managed to raise the money to pay him some months later.

My first memories come from that winter. I remember watching my mother bathing her small, twisted feet in warm water in the morning before rewrapping them and setting about the day's chores. I was horrified at her misshapen feet with the broken toes bent under the sole. I shed tears, fearful that my niece Sher-chen would grow up with such twisted painful feet. Mother told me not to worry, that most girls were spared the torture of foot binding in this new, if troubled, China. I was relieved but achingly sorrowful that my mother had to limp her way through every day on her pitiful "lotus" feet.

During the day, when she could spare a moment, Mother told me stories or gave me a saying to memorize. The emphasis was nearly always the same: that we must be kind and charitable, remembering the sacred rule expressed by Confucius centuries before Jesus uttered the same sentiment: "Do not do to others what you would not want them to do to you."

I was still a very little boy, but Mother expected me to be "a good little uncle," remembering that I must share her attention with Sher-chen and Xing-min now that their mother was gone. I did my best to live up to her wishes. I protected Sher-chen, and she looked up to me, always obeying and never talking back. Together we looked after Xing-min as he learned to walk and began joining our games. Our many hours together produced a bond that has lasted many decades. Whenever I visit China, they greet me with joy and entertain me with great kindness.

The drought lifted briefly in the summer of 1933. But, alas, the promise of better times disappeared under clouds of ravenous locusts. Everyone old enough to wield a flail rushed to the fields to drive the insects away. But it was impossible. Nearly the entire fall harvest was destroyed. The loss left many people utterly hopeless. Many wandered away from the village, never to return. Others gave up and died. Some people lost their reason, and others drowned or hanged themselves. Somehow our family managed to carry on under Mother's leadership.

My mother was nearing fifty. Giving birth to many children and ignoring her own needs in the famine made her older than her years. But she was endowed with great willpower and carried on even as her body begged her to lie down and accept fate as so many in the village already had. Often she could feed us little for days on end. When we were all on the point of starvation, she would go to a friend or relative to ask for help. She was a proud woman, the widow of an educated and prominent man, and begging came hard to her. But she would rise and, putting her personal dignity aside, go to seek aid for the four children in her care.

Her oldest brother, Wei San, traveled the area selling cotton seed and oil. He had a large family of his own, including five children, two daughters-in-law, and a wife who was an opium smoker. But he was generous and never hesitated to give us aid when he could. Sometimes Mother would take us all to meet Uncle Wei San in one of the village marketplaces. He would buy us a meal and then purchase several loaves of bread for us to take home. I remember he would pat me on the shoulder and tell me to be a good boy so that someday I could go to school and bring the family honor. We loved him deeply. Mother did not want to hide anything from Wei San's wife, whom she liked despite her addiction to opium. But Wei San feared that his wife would insist on restricting his charity to home. Later we found out that his wife had known all along of the help he'd given us but said nothing in order to spare Mother's feelings.

Wei San could not always help, and Mother and Wen-shuan walked many miles to seek the aid of other relatives. She always hesitated to go on these trips, both because she hated to beg and because the walking hurt her feet terribly.

Sometimes she would delay too long, hoping for some money from Wen-po or for some other good fortune to come our way. But if nothing arrived, the children would cry and whimper through the night as their stomachs twisted with hunger. Once I remember my little nephew crying all through a dismal afternoon for a bite of food. It was then Mother heard the voice of a cousin hawking *mantou* in the street. She gathered Xing-min in her arms, sure that good fortune had sent her cousin our way, and went out to ask him for a small piece of bread for her grandson. To my mother's great shock, her cousin answered her harshly: "Sister, these are days of terrible famine. No one can help or trust anyone else. Go away! I cannot help your grandson."

Deeply humiliated in front of the crowd of buyers, Mother crept away, the bawling Xing-min clutched to her chest. Many in the crowd grumbled since Mother was known as an honest and generous person who had helped many of them in times of need or domestic conflict. But her cousin had bread to sell and many mouths needed filling; the villagers continued to buy from him. Back inside our house, Mother wept bitter tears. She vowed never to see her cousin again. A few minutes later, a merciful neighbor woman knocked on our door and handed through a bit of bread for the infant. Later, when the famine lifted, Mother would decide to forgive her cousin since they had known good times and friendship as youngsters. But he was embarrassed by his behavior and always avoided her.

Thanks to my mother's careful selection of their husbands, all her daughters were better off than we were during the famine. They had men at home and their own extended families to give them aid. Moreover, thanks to Mother's willingness to break with tradition, their feet were unbound and healthy, making it possible for them to work beside their husbands. All my sisters gave us food or small sums of money, with or without the approval of their husbands. Since Chu-yeh's in-laws were particularly well-to-do, Mother went to their village for help after Chong-er's death and the angry carpenter began beating Wen-shuan over the money owed him for her casket. But Chu-yeh's husband made her and Wen-shuan stand in front of his desk in the family store like the humblest petitioners. Before she could finish her request, he leaped to his feet. "You squandered your money foolishly on an expensive casket for a mere girl! I won't pay for your folly!" Customers and store workers turned to watch as Mother stood horrified by this breach of the ancient custom that dictated respect for elders and mothers-in-law in particular. But Chu-yeh's husband was unremitting in his anger: "And I won't give you food either. This is a terrible time of famine. No one should expect sympathy and charity from anyone. There's no free lunch at mealtime. Now you may leave my store!"

Mother was even more humiliated than when her cousin had refused her wailing grandson a piece of bread on our street. If Chu-yeh's husband wouldn't or couldn't help pay the money owed the carpenter, he could have said so in private in any number of respectful ways. Then he might have offered Wen-shuan and her a simple meal to strengthen them for the journey home. That was the very least she had a right to expect as a mother-in-law. Chu-yeh was terribly grieved when she heard of the incident. She was a gentle, easygoing person, much loved by all of us though we saw her rarely. She sent a message to Mother apologizing for the incident and, shortly after, a basket of food taken from the family's storeroom without her husband's knowledge.

Although Mother would eventually seek a reconciliation with her son-in-law, he always avoided her after this incident, not even coming to our house at Lunar New Year to give his respect to the family's ancestors as tradition demanded. The business in his store fell off after better times returned, and I have always thought this was in part because of his loss of community reputation after his shameful treatment of my mother. He eventually went bankrupt and had to work for other men.

On the same trip that brought her such humiliation in her son-in-law's store, Mother visited a friend of Wen-po's from their time together at school. Wen-po had told her to go see Chang Feng-li if she had nowhere else to turn. She didn't know Chang Feng-li, and she didn't want to put her son under an obligation to a friend. But now it seemed she had no other choice but to visit the stranger whom Wen-po had insisted was a man of uncommon generosity. And he was, far beyond anything we could have hoped for. His family owned a rich lowland farm with water nearby to irrigate the fields even in this time of drought. He ran the family store. On hearing Mother's name, he immediately told her and Wen-shuan to sit while he sent for food. He insisted on delaying any talk of business until they had enjoyed their best meal in many months. He explained that he was still a young man and not rich, but that Mother was welcome to ask him for help any time her extended family could not render aid. He readily counted out money to pay the enraged carpenter, relieving Mother of a terrible worry. He gave her enough additional money to buy food for two months. Then, brushing away her thanks, he ordered a basket of food prepared for them to carry home. Mother was nearly beside herself with gratitude, but he assured her that he was delighted to help the family of his friend "as an honor and happy commitment." He only asked that Mother have a letter written to Wen-po, assuring him of Chang Feng-li's friendship.

Necessity forced Mother to ask for Chang Feng-li's help a number of times after this. He always did what he could. Often in later years she would remind us of our debt to him: "Any generosity in time of poverty is ten times more valuable than one hundred acts of generosity in times of plenty. If you are able, you must always repay more than you borrowed. We can't do that for Mr. Chang Feng-li. We owe him too much. But we can give him all the honor we can." Every New Year she would send one of her sons the ten miles to Chang Feng-li's home to salute him for his generosity. Today, I still remember him in my prayers. Though I became a Christian and believe that salvation is best achieved through Christ's message, I have never known anyone more deserving of Heaven than Mr. Chang Feng-li. In the terrible years of the famine, he was our family's savior. But his greatest favor to us lay yet some years in the future, when he would open his door and risk his life to save Wen-po from capture and probable execution by the Communists.

For all the help my uncle Wei San, my sisters, Mr. Chang Feng-li, and other kind relatives and friends gave us through the years of famine, my family could not have survived without the sale of most of the family's land. It was extremely difficult to part with land that the family had owned since the time of my great-grandfather Chang Jing-shue. My mother sorrowed that she could not be a better custodian of the family wealth. Wen-shuan, who never wanted to be anything but a farmer, was nearly heartbroken as buyers took possession of our acres.

By tradition, clan members had first opportunity to buy family lands, but in our case all of our immediate clan families were as impoverished as we were. Only outsiders had the money to pay even a minimal price for the unproductive, drought-stricken fields. This brought the evils of landlordism and the exploitation of hired farmworkers to our area for the first time, replacing the older system of individual small farms that had done so much to foster village harmony in our area. Well before the famine ended, our family had lost all but a few acres surrounding the family cemetery. These Mother refused to sell. We would not sell the graves of our ancestors to survive; rather, we would survive on even less or starve in the attempt.

Looking back I find it difficult to forgive some of the relatives who were selfish and unkind when Mother requested help during the famine. But I remind myself that Chinese society was under extreme pressure. While millions starved in the great famine, generals, imperialists, and ideologues continued to fight each other. In Shaanxi, the loyal General Yang Hu-cheng had reduced Feng Yu-shiang's power considerably. But General Yan Xishan continued a firm grip on Shanxi province to the east. While Chiang and the warlords faced off in northern China, the Manchurian warlord Zhang Xueliang expanded his territory and began a dangerous series of confrontations with the Japanese Kwantung army. Chiang acquiesced to Zhang's territorial expansion and encouraged the baiting of the Japanese, even though the Nationalist government was in no condition to take on yet another conflict.

Besides the restive northern warlords, Chiang faced the continued challenge of the Communists in southern China. After Chiang's crushing attack on his Communist allies in Shanghai in 1927, the CCP had rebuilt in mountainous Jiangxi province. Chiang wanted to launch a new campaign before his rivals grew too strong. But his plan was interrupted by a disaster in Manchuria. On September 18, 1931, the restless officers of Japan's Kwantung army set off bombs on the railroad line outside the Manchurian capital of Shenyang. Blaming Zhang Xueliang for the blasts, the Japanese militarists launched a devastating assault on his army. Zhang called for help, but Chiang decided to appeal to the League of Nations. He ordered Zhang to fall back to the Great Wall, ceding Manchuria to the Japanese. Chiang's unpopular decision, though soundly based on military reality, brought heavy criticism from intellectuals and popular protests in many cities. Japan set up the puppet state of Manchukuo, recruiting the former child-emperor Puyi as nominal chief executive. The League of Nations named a commission and held hearings in February 1933. By a nearly unanimous vote (Thailand abstained), the League condemned Japanese aggression. Japan quit the League, never to return. Without American participation or any effective means to counter aggression, the League could do no more as fascism and militarism propelled humankind toward a new world war.

Many factors besides political turmoil contributed to the pressures on the traditional way of life in rural China. Modernity in all its myriad forms was stressing age-old systems. What is remarkable to me is not that these traditional systems began to show strain but that they held up at all. Though significantly weakened, Confucian traditions of lawfulness and local cooperation survived. When the famine finally began to lift in Shaanxi province in the fall of 1934, these traditions reestablished themselves, continuing through my childhood. Too many people had died or wandered away for the village to recover fully in the short time before war and revolution would end traditional village life. But I am grateful that in the next few years I was able to store up memories and lessons that would carry me through the rest of my life.

CHAPTER 5

The Good Student

THE GREAT FAMINE COST OUR family most of its wealth and social position. We were no longer one of the leading families in Zhou-bian village but only one of the many poor families that made up the majority. We no longer hired farm laborers to work for us. Rather, my brother Wen-shuan had to work for other families. My mother had managed to hold on to the few acres surrounding the family cemetery, but we no longer owned a horse, mule, or ox, nor plow, wagon, or mill. All these had gone in the famine, sold for a small part of their worth. So every morning before dawn Wen-shuan trudged off to work on another man's land—land that had once been ours. Behind his impassive face and quiet manner, he burned with ambition to restore our fortunes as landowners and respected farmers. He would labor many years, his strong back bent to the service of others, before his dreams would come briefly true.

My prodigal brother Wen-hui returned that lean harvest season and was welcomed with great rejoicing. He had changed in his two years of wandering. He was still cheerful: teasing the younger children and laughing often. But he seemed to have learned some secret about human nature or fate that he could not put into words. Nor would he tell us how he had managed to survive. We supposed that he'd worked menial jobs, begged when he had to, perhaps even joined one army or another in the fighting between warlords.

Mother worried about Wen-hui, concerned that his good spirits hid a restlessness that would lead him to wander away again. Her second son had always been equipped with a quick, shrewd intelligence. He enjoyed people and knew how to attract them. Growing up, other boys had learned that Wen-hui always got the better of a trade for marbles, a kite, or a ball, but they were unresentful, liking him for his good humor and generosity. He never had Wen-po's maturity, habit of careful thought, or air of command. Nor did he have Wen-shuan's reliable stolidity, his appearance of taking strength and practical, if slow, wisdom from the earth itself. There was about Wen-hui something quicksilver, something of the eternal street peddler forever in search of a sale or a trade.

49

Wen-hui had always irritated our father. Perhaps Father saw in him too much of the quick-witted younger men who consistently outtraded him in the market and then laughed about it behind his back. Father did not make friends easily, though many respected him, nor did he find it easy to deal with others unless his advice on law or his skills in writing were called upon. In Wen-hui he saw a boy of intelligence but with no particular love of learning who might nevertheless prove far more successful at achieving wealth than his scholarly, retiring father. Perhaps our father's irritation came most of all from his worry that in pursuit of a deal Wen-hui might take too great a risk and run afoul of hard men who would exact a heavy price for being outwitted.

In those days Mother defended Wen-hui from Father's angry words and cuffs. But I think she secretly shared her husband's concerns about Wen-hui. She had worried constantly during the years we'd had no news of him. Now that he was home, she was determined to channel his energies toward worthy goals. She was, however, far too wise to think that she could change his character. Wen-hui was a natural salesman, and there was nothing wrong with that. Hadn't Great-grandfather Chang Jing-shue, "the screeching-wheel man," become wealthy and brought the family honor after starting as a simple peddler? What Wen-hui needed were the skills to make him more than a street hawker. She suggested he go to school, and Wen-hui readily agreed. Though he'd had only scant schooling in the past, he'd been an apt enough student. Now he would deploy all his intelligence and energy to be an exceptional student—one to whom his father's spirit might render grudging respect, even if Wen-hui's interest lay in the tools of commerce and not in law and Confucian analectics.

On hearing of Wen-hui's desire to attend school, our half sister, Bei-yeh, offered to take him into her household. She had always liked her half brother despite their difference in age of thirty years. She made the excuse that Wen-hui could tutor her son Nan Tong-wa, who was close to his age but slower to learn. I think behind Bei-yeh's generous and unexpected offer was her fervent desire to demonstrate her gratitude for my mother's care and friendship. Bei-yeh had been a jealous and uncooperative stepdaughter after our parents' marriage. Her temper hadn't changed much by the time she left home to marry. But some years later, when she was herself a young mother, Bei-yeh had become desperately ill. Mother moved into her home, nursed her, and cared for her children. They had been good friends ever since. Now Bei-yeh had a chance to return a favor.

Wen-hui lived with Bei-yeh's family for a year. He made rapid progress in school, learning in months what other students took years to master. When our meager resources could no longer support him in school, Mother secured him an apprenticeship with a shop owner in Xing-ping City. Wen-hui was soon managing the store's accounts, using both hands to work the abacus, an uncanny skill that attracted great admiration from customers.

Wen-po and eventually Wen-hui were able to send a little money home, but most of the responsibility for maintaining the family fell on Wen-shuan and my mother. Wen-shuan continued to spend most of his days working for others, though he was laboriously trying to get our own land back in production. Mother spent her spare hours weaving the rough cotton cloth used to make farmers' clothing. What we didn't need ourselves, she sold.

With the return of better times, the village could at last afford to hire a schoolmaster. I was seven when I first went to school. Sher-chen stayed at home with Mother and my nephew Xing-min. I remember my sorrow at parting from my constant companion. By this time city girls were being encouraged to attend school but not country girls like Sher-chen. I missed her desperately in the first days at school, though I knew all the village boys who were my classmates.

After the terrible famine, nearly every family wanted to push at least one boy ahead in the world. A literate young man could obtain a better living and help his family survive hard times. As a result of this enthusiasm for education, sixty of us crowded into the single room of the village school. Some of us knew a few Chinese characters already or were outwardly bright and promising. We were pushed to the head of the class while those of less accomplishment or ability filled the lower places. The order changed a good deal in the first few weeks as we began the laborious task of learning the thousands of Chinese characters required for literacy. Those with quick memories moved up; those without fell back. Mr. Lu, our teacher, executed this traditional ability ranking with ruthless efficiency, playing no favorites and taking no account of age. A number of older boys found themselves humiliated by their low positions in the class. Some of the slower or less motivated boys quit school. The rest of us plowed ahead.

We sat at square tables against the walls of the room. Before us we laid out our inkwells, paper, and brushes. We learned by rote memorization with no explanation of meaning or content. When Mr. Lu observed an error during one of his constant patrols, he would reach over to demonstrate the proper formation of a character with a few quick strokes. He rarely spoke and we rarely asked questions.

Our days were divided into three parts: morning recitation of our lessons, quiet practice of our characters, and Mr. Lu's presentation of the lesson we were expected to learn for the next morning.

Except for the Lunar New Year celebration, we attended school seven days a week from after harvest to spring planting. I walked with friends the mile to school every morning and then home at noon for a long lunch hour. On nice fall and spring days, we often dawdled on our way back, arriving just as Mr. Lu was ringing his handbell to warn us that the switch stood in the corner for those who took too long.

Though I enjoyed school and found a fascination in learning the beautiful Chinese characters, the afternoons often dragged. With a meal on our stomachs, it was hard to stay awake. When Mr. Lu had his back to us, we would whisper or communicate with signs. Occasionally, a few of us would break into giggles, but the hilarity passed off quickly when Mr. Lu turned his stern gaze on us.

If the day was fine, on our walk home, we would play tag or hide-and-seek. We were filled with boyish good spirits and proud of our status as favored children among the majority who had no opportunity to go to school. On the whole, we didn't lord it over these less fortunate children. Our positions were too fragile, such a display of pride unseemly. I do recall that we teased one older boy who had tried school briefly before dropping out to labor in the fields. But he ended that quickly with a demonstration of just how much a dirt clod could sting when launched by a strong and accurate arm.

At home, Mother had Sher-chen busy learning the duties of a housewife. Sher-chen and I both thought Xing-min got off easy. In truth, he was a little spoiled. When I sat down to do my homework, Mother would encourage him to sit beside me to learn a few characters. But he rarely had the patience, preferring to run about making mischief. After supper Mother would give the three of us an hour or so to play together before I had to return to my studies and Sher-chen to her chores. I never taught Sher-chen any characters nor did she express any interest; village girls simply did not learn to read and write. Looking back, I regret adhering so closely to tradition. She was a bright girl and would have learned rapidly. Even a few hundred characters committed to memory might have eased her way as a young woman in the tumultuous years to come.

I worked hard to learn my lessons, often repeating them to Mother, who would listen critically though the content was unfamiliar to her. Mr. Lu believed that high volume aided memory and expected us to bellow out our lessons at morning recitation. He was a thoroughly traditional teacher, demanding absolute obedience and conformity. We addressed him as *Lao-sze* (old master), the honorific for all teachers in China below university level. He was a neat man in his late fifties who, like his father, had been a teacher all his life. He could recite the major Confucian classics by heart and held to the old ways with the conviction of a true believer. Though a stern man, he was not an unkind one. He assigned the more accomplished pupils to help the slower ones. He rewarded good work with a solemn nod, would nudge a dozing student rather than switching him, and often dismissed us a few minutes early on a lovely afternoon.

Eventually, I think most of us became quite fond of him despite his formal reserve. He went home every day for lunch but often stayed the night at the school. Though the patriarch of his large household, he was apparently considered too old and too scholarly to be of much use in the daily routine. He didn't seem to mind, and we would see him in the evenings sitting contentedly on a bench by the schoolhouse door, smoking his pipe. At those times, we could approach to have our fortunes told. His eyes would twinkle and the fortunes would always predict wealth and happiness.

A cold northwest wind from Mongolia often chilled us on our way to school on winter mornings. We rarely had much snow, but the fierce wind day after day depressed bodies and spirits. On those days, the schoolhouse was always chilly, the wind seeking out every crack to get in among us. We burned smokeless charcoal in pots on our desks, the small heat only barely keeping the ink in our inkwells from freezing. Mr. Lu had a slightly larger *kang* on his desk, its fuel provided as part of his salary.

I recall one particularly bitter afternoon as we huddled in our padded coats, dismally copying out characters in our freezing misery. Mr. Lu watched us from his desk, probably as gloomy as we were. After some time, he rose, called us to pay attention. "Come into the center. Put your *kangs* on the outside of the circle and sit close."

Mystified, we complied. He placed his chair in the gap in the circle and set his own *kang* in the center. He opened a volume of the famous classical novel *The Three Kingdoms* by Luo Guanzhong and began reading us one of the stories about the three patriotic friends who had united to save the embattled Han dynasty: the aristocratic Liu Xuande, the fugitive Lord Guan, and the pig butcher Zhang Fei. We were enthralled as his modulated, expressive voice pulled us into the story, forgetting our cold, forgetting even our wonder that our strict teacher would take such a liberty with our daily schedule.

When I came to visit him in my high school years, I never mentioned that afternoon, afraid that its recollection might embarrass him. He always greeted me with great kindness. In remote Zhou-bian village, he hungered for companionship and would keep me as long as he could, asking about my classes and the news of the outside world. He was a good man, truly deserving of the title *Lao-sze*.

Mother remained my most important teacher, always encouraging me to live an upright and useful life. The hard years had aged her, and she sometimes wept silently, recalling the suffering we'd known in the famine. She was determined that we should prepare ourselves as well as possible for the next cycle of bad times. She abhorred gambling, opium, tobacco, whiskey, and all extravagances and vices. Daily she drummed into us the importance of honesty, respect, hard work, frugality, and gratitude—the Confucian values that she, though illiterate, had absorbed as an intelligent and careful observer of the Chinese way of life. In a sense, she shared some of our late father's loneliness. Many good and intelligent people lived in Zhou-bian village, but even the village elders had no more wisdom than Mother had gained in a half century of life. When confronted by a difficult decision, she had no one to turn to who was any wiser than she was. Many of the village women were incurious, satisfied with the mindless rhythms of daily life. But Mother still wanted to understand life on a deeper level, and she sometimes brooded for many hours.

In those times, we were quiet, careful not to disturb her, because—like many intelligent people—she could be very sharp when her thoughts were interrupted. Most evenings she made a point of telling us an instructive tale. The family slept on a large, baked-mud bed that was heated from below with a small fire in the winter. Wen-shuan and I slept at one end, Mother, Sher-chen, and Xing-min at the other end. Mother was very protective of her grandchildren, never allowing Wen-shuan or me to criticize or discipline them. They were, she reminded us, growing up without a mother and deserved extra consideration. If either one cried about the least scrape or disappointment, Mother would immediately sympathize, shedding tears herself as she remembered their lost mother, her beloved Chong-er. In those emotional moments, she would also apologize to Wen-shuan and me for being less than a fully attentive mother to us. We would assure her that she was the best of all mothers and was doing exactly right in showering her grandchildren with affection.

As the little ones snuggled close to her on our bed, she would begin her storytelling. She might start with a gentle story from China's vast store of legends and myths. Few of these stories are known in the West, but virtually every theme and most of the plots in the Brothers Grimm have their counterparts in Chinese folklore. There is, for example, a tale very much like *Red Riding Hood*, in which three little Chinese girls do away with a hungry wolf. (The American writer and illustrator Ed Young did a delightful adaptation of the story in his picture book *Lon Po Po*.)

Mother might next sing a soft, drowsy song. She was very musical, and we enjoyed listening to her sing songs from Shaanxi opera. We knew these songs from listening to her many times but rarely joined because it was more pleasant to listen. As Sher-chen and Xing-min began to doze, Mother would go on to a story of village life or the history of our family that would illustrate some moral she wanted Wen-shuan and me to absorb. She would tell of her wise, thrifty, and upright grandmother. Or of her hardworking cousin and his wife who had made a small farm prosper to the extent that he had been able to buy more land and become wealthy. This revered relative went to the fields even in old age when he could afford to sit by and watch others work. The entire village hailed them as a model couple for young people to imitate.

Another story told of our selfless great-great-great-aunt, who had lived more than a century before. She had been widowed at twenty-two after a brief but wonderful marriage—so wonderful that she chose not to remarry although many men admired her beauty and character. Instead, she devoted herself to raising her widowed brother's four motherless children. Her self-sacrifice meant she would never have children of her own to care for her in old age and to honor her memory after she died. She lived to be ninety, raising not only her nieces and nephews but also their children and grandchildren. When she died, the entire village turned out to praise her worthiness, and the imperial magistrate ordered that the inscription on her gravestone compare her to Kuan-yin, the Chinese goddess of mercy and compassion. So it was, Mother told us, that the greatest honor sometimes came to those who labored daily at humble tasks.

We enjoyed all Mother's stories though they were often heavily didactic. Occasionally, Wen-shuan, or Wen-hui if he were home on a visit, would persuade her to tell a ghost story. As in many cultures, Chinese parents used ghost stories to frighten children into good behavior. The great paradox is that most children love ghost stories. I was an exception, and ghost stories scared me very much, though I would not let on to my brothers for fear of being teased. Mother knew this but saw no particular harm in giving me the occasional fright. So every so often she'd give in to my brothers' wheedling and tell a ghost story, even if it meant setting aside her chosen theme for the night.

If my brothers teased too much, she might follow the ghost story by repeating with great relish one of her favorite stories: the time our great-grandfather Chang Jing-shue allowed the villagers to wreak a terrible punishment on an unworthy son. This true story related how a young man in our village had disobeyed and mistreated his widowed mother for many years. Everyone criticized his behavior, and the clan elders—our great-grandfather among them—chastised this cruel and dishonorable son. Yet he was incorrigible and persisted in abusing his mother. Other young men saw how he successfully ignored threats and blandishments, and they began to be less respectful to their elders and less willing to labor for the common good. Finally, the sad widow died, her heart broken with the shame of having raised such an unworthy son. At her graveside, her son seemed unmoved, sneering at the weeping of the village women and anxious to be off to waste his time drinking and gambling with his unwholesome friends. The crowd grew restless. A few people shouted epithets and criticisms at the young man, hoping to shame him into showing an appropriate grief. Still he sneered, and the crowd began to look to our great-grandfather, Chang Jing-shue, to render a judgment. When it seemed that the entire village was united against the son, Chang Jing-shue raised his hand for silence and then shouted: "Let us bury this bad son with his martyred mother as a lesson to all children who would abuse and disrespect their elders." Immediately the crowd surged forward, pushing the young man into the grave beside his mother's coffin. There, despite his pleading and wailing, they buried him alive.

News of this harsh punishment spread quickly, and Chang Jing-shue was hauled before the imperial magistrate. Despite the threats of the judge, he refused to renounce his actions or to blame the death of the young man on others. He was sent to jail without trial and suffered there for three years before his sons managed to sell enough of the family's land to buy his freedom. The corrupt judge and his friends profited from our great-grandfather's loss of freedom and wealth. But Chang Jing-shue and his sons set about rebuilding the family's fortune. They received much help from people who saw him as a hero who had upheld the village's honor and the traditional code of respect for elders.

Though Wen-shuan and Wen-hui might at first object to hearing this oft-told story, I think we were all moved each time we heard of our great-grandfather's courage in the face of certain punishment. Would we have as much courage to take the side of right conduct no matter what price we would have to pay?

I do not blame my brothers or my mother for my fear of ghosts or dark places that persists in my character even today. I was an impressionable child with an active imagination. I had seen Chong-er's body and the bodies of many villagers who died in the famine. When I was about seven, a boy in our neighborhood disappeared late one summer evening. The village men searched through the night and for days afterward. His mother, a wealthy widow, was beside herself, refusing all comfort from the village women. Rumors spread that the child had been kidnapped by bandits and was being held for ransom. Finally, his body was discovered floating in a deep well. When the men drew his body up into the daylight, his mother went crazy with grief. The men carried the body to the widow's house and laid it in the bedroom and then went to squat in the shade, smoking and talking in low tones as men in many ages have done while waiting for their women to prepare a body for burial.

The village women, my mother among them, offered to help the widow wash and dress her son for the grave. But the widow refused, forcing them out into the street and closing the door against them. For many days, she refused all entreaties to open the door. Inside the stifling house, the body decomposed until the whole street smelled of putrefying flesh. Most of us schoolchildren had to pass the widow's home every morning, but we were too terrified unless accompanied by a parent or an older brother. Finally, some of the village men summoned courage and pushed their way into the widow's home. Ignoring her pleas, they wrapped the body in a shroud and carried it out for a decent burial.

I do not know if I was there. I think Mother would have ordered me to stay home if she'd known the men were about to take action. Yet I can remember in every detail watching the burial party leaving the house, the men's faces gray and nauseated with the horror of dealing with a corpse so badly decomposed. Perhaps I did not see, except in my imagination, the wild face of the hysterical mother as she tore her hair and clutched at the men, begging them to let her keep her son. Yet again my memory recalls every shriek of her terrible grief. So perhaps I did watch, drawn to the scene by that strange attraction people have for sights of great tragedy and suffering. The ancient Greeks spoke of catharsis, of the purging of emotions and the restoration of balance through participation in tragedy. It is not an entirely Western concept, having in it much that is Chinese and indeed universal in the human experience.

The death of my schoolmate produced an empathetic reaction that made me all the more vulnerable to my vivid imagination. Times were still very hard in Zhou-bian village, and not long after this incident Mother and Wen-shuan went again to seek the assistance of our kind friend Mr. Chang Feng-li. I was left at home with my niece Sher-Chen to care for her little brother Xing-min. Before Mother and Wen-shuan were gone many hours, the weather turned stormy. Our neighbors hurried their children indoors and hastily barred doors and shutters. The wind blew down the empty street, scattering debris and lifting little whirlwinds of dust. We recalled that the widow's son had been a boy of an impish temperament, prone to rough teasing and occasional bullying. The imperial magistrate had yet to make a determination on the cause of death and there were whispers that perhaps he had been murdered, pushed in by other boys or perhaps grabbed and pulled down into the well by some malevolent spirit who made its home in the dank depths. As the clouds dropped low and dark over our village, it seemed entirely plausible to me that the ghost of the drowned boy might choose this hour to walk the streets in search of playmates or victims. I said as much to Sher-Chen, hoping she would laugh and tease me out of my fears. Instead, she fell under the spell of my imaginings.

Frightening as we found the street, we could not go inside for fear of the shadows accumulating in every corner as the storm snuffed the last of the afternoon light. We remembered the cold, pale body of Chong-er stretched on our bed waiting for burial. She had been a kind and good woman who loved us all dearly. But perhaps she missed her children and nephew too much. Perhaps her ghost would come to snatch us away to the land of the dead. So we huddled in the doorway, terrified by our fantasy as the first drops of rain hit the hard-packed dirt of the village street and a feral dog loped past, throwing a yellow glance over his shoulder at us three children. Eventually, Xing-min, who had better sense than his older sister and his uncle, insisted on going inside for something to eat. We took him in, fed him quickly, and then put him to bed.

We waited, casting frightened looks into the dark corners, until he fell asleep. Then we rushed out the door into the pelting rain.

Mother and Wen-shuan found us sleeping in the doorway, our clothes and hair soaked from the storm that had passed off to the east, leaving behind a clear, star-strewn sky in the hours before dawn. The rain had caught them halfway home from Mr. Chang Feng-li's. Worried about us, Mother wanted to continue, but the rain became too heavy, the way too dark and hard for Wen-shuan with the heavy basket and Mother on her twisted, painful feet. They took shelter at the home of my uncle Wei Sze. When the storm passed on, they again took to the road, hurrying as fast as they could over the last miles to Zhou-bian village.

Clucking with a mixture of anger, sorrow, and relief, Mother gathered us up, and Wen-shuan carried us to bed. I can still remember the strength of his arms around me, the safety this quiet teenager brought to my life in the absence of father and grown brothers. In the way of older brothers, Wen-shuan could be impatient and snappish with me, but now he was gentle, hushing my whimpered explanations. Mother built a small fire beneath the mud bed, and we drifted off to sleep as she crooned a lullaby.

The incident upset Mother greatly, and she resolved to instill better sense in me. Ghosts had not been the danger on the rainy street but one of the hungry wolves or tigers that lived in the mountains not far away. Our part of Shaanxi was still very wild and these beasts were known to carry off a child in times when the wild things too suffered from famine. Mother undertook to explain to me that ghosts were very rare and only bothered those children who were afraid of them. Perhaps she was trying to tell me that she didn't really believe in ghosts at all, though that ran contrary to widely held beliefs in the China of that time. I'm afraid that for once she failed to convince me. Though I became in adult life a political scientist and a firm believer in modernity and rationality, my boyhood fears remain with me, and I continue to have a horror of dark places, graveyards, and tales of the supernatural.

In truth, I think Mother was deeply conflicted on the subject of ghosts. I remember an incident when Xing-min woke one night crying for his mother. My mother hushed him and, when he'd drifted back to sleep, I could hear her whispering to Chong-er: "Daughter-in-law, why do you not leave this house and let your children sleep without bad dreams? You have a different place now. You don't need to worry; I will care for your children. Now, go. Be at peace."

The years passed. I became an excellent student. Mother did not have the education to understand many of the things I learned, but she kept me at my homework until I was done, no matter how insistently a sunny afternoon and playmates called from the street beyond our door. Mother remained deeply committed to the value system of our small village, but I think she was beginning to grasp how small a part of the world we inhabited. Our old schoolmaster, though sincere and kind, knew only the traditional subjects. Mother was progressive enough to understand that I had to acquire a much more varied knowledge to survive as an intellectual in a rapidly changing China. She began talking of my going away to school. Exactly how she would pay for such an expensive undertaking she didn't know yet, but she was preparing us for a parting.

In the meantime, I had my daily lessons to learn. I learned hundreds and hundreds of Chinese characters and spent long hours committing passages from the Confucian *Analects* to heart. Even with my talent for school, I found the memorizing difficult. The language was antiquated and hard to follow. (Imagine a class of American boys trying to read, memorize, and explain long passages of Chaucer's *Canterbury Tales* in the original Middle English.) I suspect some passages confused even Mr. Lu, though he labored manfully to teach us. I felt particularly sorry for the less able boys who were frequently whipped for making errors in recitation. Worse was the public humiliation of bungling a passage. Village families were competitive about the progress of their children in school, and every student knew that word of a poor performance would soon get back to his parents. A few boys, unable to do the work, dropped out of school when it became apparent that the material was utterly beyond them.

Mother woke me at dawn every school-day morning. On cold mornings, like mothers everywhere, she might have to call several times before her son crept from beneath the warm quilt. Getting ready, I would recite my passage for the day in a loud voice, Mother smiling encouragement if I did well or frowning if I stumbled. Occasionally, I would ask her to wake me an hour early if I had a particularly difficult passage to memorize. Villagers did not own watches or clocks, but Mother was inordinately good at judging time by the position of the sun, moon, and stars. But even she could make an error on a cloudy predawn. One morning, she rose too early, hustling me out the door hours before dawn. In the street I realized that not a single soul was stirring. I pounded on our door, but Mother had returned to bed and—for perhaps the only time in her life as a parent—fallen into a deep sleep. My fear of ghosts grabbed hold of me, and I rushed next door to a schoolmate's house. I pounded on the barred door until his father shouted for me to go home. I scuttled back to our door and pounded harder. Still my mother didn't hear. I looked about in terror, imagining that I saw ghosts flitting among the shadows, every second creeping closer to grab and drag me away. I flung myself at the door, pounding, screaming, and crying. Finally, Mother raised the bar and pulled her "angry monster baby boy" inside before I could wake the entire neighborhood. She chided me for getting so upset, but I only howled that she shouldn't have pushed me into the street where ghosts and wolves lurked. At last she calmed me enough to take me back to bed. My behavior would no doubt bring comments from the neighbors in the morning, but for the moment she ignored all that, rubbing my back and humming softly. At first my fear, anger, and humiliation were too great to let me sleep, but eventually I dozed off. I awoke in full daylight, the hour for school already passed. That morning Mother took her cane and hobbled to school with me, where she apologized to Mr. Lu for my tardiness. I assume he eventually heard of my tantrum in the night, but he never mentioned it.

The personal losses in Mother's life continued to accumulate. In 1935, her once-quarrelsome stepdaughter, Bei-yeh, died. They were separated by only a few years in actual age and had grown more like sisters than stepmother and stepdaughter since their reconciliation. Now Bei-yeh was gone and with her another link to all the might-have-beens in my mother's life.

In 1936, my sister Reou-yeh moved back home with her three children after her abusive husband and her difficult, crippled mother-in-law both died in the last year of the famine. Of her daughters, Mother had always been closest to Reou-yeh and greatly regretted choosing her an ill-tempered husband. She welcomed her daughter home, hoping that they might spend many happy days together. It was not to be. Reou-yeh was herself in failing health and could do little to help around the house. Mother was in her midfifties, an age when most Chinese women could enjoy grandchildren and some leisure while younger women did most of the hard work of running a household. Instead, she had a sick daughter, two sons, and five grandchildren to care for.

Patient, quiet Wen-shuan ate, slept, and went out to work the land that had come down to us from our ancestors. It wasn't his nature to exert the authority of a surrogate father over his younger brother, nephews, and nieces. So Mother bore all the responsibility. She carried on: patient, loving, efficient, and wise, concerned always with both our physical well-being and our moral development. A year after moving home, Reou-yeh died of an undiagnosed cause. Perhaps a single visit to a doctor might have saved her life, but we had neither money nor the chance to seek medical treatment for her.

Her lonely father-in-law took her children to live with him in another village. Within a couple of years, Reou-yeh's eldest son, Kai-sheng, married a woman six years his senior. She was a thoroughly wonderful person who cared willingly for her young husband, his siblings, and Reou-yeh's aged father-in-law. Her selflessness won praise throughout the village. She and Kai-sheng used to visit us at New Year's to do my mother honor.

In these years, war continued to convulse large areas of China. Chiang Kai-shek attacked the Communists repeatedly, eventually forcing them to abandon their base in mountainous Jiangxi province in southeastern China. On October 16, 1934, the Red Army broke through the ring of Nationalist forces and began its long retreat into China's remote northwest. Under almost daily attack by Nationalist troops and planes, the Red Army crossed twenty-four rivers and hundreds of streams, eighteen mountain ranges (some rising as high as 16,000 feet), and great swamps where a single misstep meant death. In October 1935, after 6,000 miles and 370 days of almost constant movement, the Red Army set up a new base at Yan'an, 200 miles north of Xi'an. Some 80,000 of the original 100,000 soldiers had fallen from the ranks on the Long March, but the Red Army had survived.

The Long March brought Mao Zedong to the forefront of the Communist leadership. Mao pressed for a new style of revolution. Marxist-Leninist doctrine dictated the radicalization of the urban proletariat first, but Mao called for an agrarian revolution led by the rural peasantry. This profound change in philosophy would eventually lead to Communist victory.

Xi'an became the natural staging point for Nationalist attacks on the Communists. But while Chiang mustered his forces for a renewed offensive, many leaders called for peace and the formation of a united front against the growing Japanese threat beyond the Great Wall. In October 1936, the Japanese breached the Great Wall and invaded Suiyuan province. Unmoved by popular demonstrations calling for a united front, Chiang refused to make peace with the Communists. The "Young Marshal" Zhang Xueliang and General Yang Hu-cheng decided on a drastic course of action. On December 12, 1936, elements of Zhang's army overran Chiang's headquarters outside Xi'an, killing several bodyguards and capturing the Generalissimo. In another culture such a coup would have led to the immediate execution of the deposed leader. But Chinese politics function under very subtle rules of force and accommodation. Three weeks of complicated negotiations followed as Zhang and Yang tried to nail together an anti-Japanese united front. Zhou Enlai flew from Yan'an to Xi'an on December 16 to express the Communist view that only Chiang had the power and prestige to lead a united front. But Chiang refused to accept leadership until he was released and flown to the Nationalist capital at Nanjing. To guarantee Chiang's safe passage, Zhang volunteered to accompany him. In Nanjing, Zhang was arrested, court-martialed, and sentenced to ten years in prison. Chiang commuted the prison sentence to house arrest, but extended the term indefinitely. (In 1990, Zhang was finally released by the Nationalist government in Taiwan, spending the last decade of his long life in Hawaii. He died in 2001 at the age of 101.)

Chiang delayed formation of the united front with qualifications and petty objections. Meanwhile, the Japanese readied for a full-scale invasion of China. As the spring of 1937 turned to summer, China lay woefully unprepared for a conflagration unmatched since the arrival of the Mongol hordes seven centuries before.

CHAPTER 6

The Tiger

WORLD WAR II BEGAN IN China on July 27, 1937, when Japanese garrison troops from Beijing's international zone stormed the famous Marco Polo Bridge, ten miles west of the city. Chiang Kai-shek responded to the capture of Beijing and its port of Tianjin by attacking the Japanese garrison in Shanghai. His plan turned into a strategic disaster. Three months of savage fighting cost the Nationalist army 250,000 casualties, 60 percent of its best troops. Chiang retreated to Nanjing and then up the Yangtze to Wuhan, the industrial heart of central China. Entering Nanjing on December 12, the Japanese began a seven-week orgy of looting, rape, and murder. Estimates put the death toll between 100,000 and 300,000 in the infamous Rape of Nanjing.

Two Japanese armies moved on Wuhan, one army up the Yangtze from Nanjing, a second south along the railroad line from Beijing through the crucial railroad hub at Zhengzhou near the old Song capital of Kaifeng. In a desperate attempt to stave off the northern threat, Chiang ordered troops to blow up the Yellow River dikes below Zhengzhou in May 1938. The resulting torrent flooded three provinces, eleven cities, and four thousand villages; left two million Chinese homeless; drowned tens of thousands; and cost the Nationalists a large measure of support among the people—all for minimal military advantage. Fighting raged around Wuhan through the summer and fall. The Nationalist army suffered another 200,000 casualties before Chiang ordered a retreat into Sichuan province where he established a new capital at Chongqing.

By the end of 1938, the Japanese controlled nearly all of China north of the Yellow River, central China as far inland as Wuhan, coastal China as far south as Swatow across the strait from occupied Taiwan, and the great port of Guangzhou. But the conquest came at a heavy cost in casualties. When well led, Chinese soldiers fought with a skill and bravery that compensated for their lack of modern equipment. In April 1938, General Li Zongren lured the Japanese into a clever trap at Xuzhou between Nanjing and Kaifeng, killing 30,000 of

Japan's finest troops. Having achieved their immediate strategic goals in China, the Japanese divided their conquests into several puppet states. But these flimsy governments couldn't field effective armies, forcing Japan to deploy nearly half its army in China throughout the war.

Calls continued for an effective united front against the Japanese. The Communists made concessions, placing their forces under the general command of the Nationalist government and agreeing to suspend radical land reform and the formation of rural soviets. Aid from abroad came up the fragile Burma Road or over the Himalayas by air. The terrible manpower losses suffered in 1938 forced the Nationalist government to adopt a policy of forced conscription whose frequent brutality shocked Western journalists and military advisors. Of the 14 million men conscripted into the Chinese army between 1937 and 1945, one man of every ten died from hunger, disease, or exhaustion before reaching combat.

In the late summer of 1937, Wen-po learned that his provincial-defense division would be transferred to the Nationalist regular army for the fight against the Japanese. Many of the provincial officers objected. In the provincial army they had prestige and power, but in the regular army they would fall under the authority of graduates of the Nationalist military academy, a humiliation many refused to accept. Scores of provincial officers tendered their resignations, but Wen-po resolved to lead his men into battle against the Japanese. He would not let others do his patriotic duty, and he was determined to prove that his skill and courage were the equal of any academy-trained officer's.

I still remember the excitement of the neighborhood children when Wen-po's sergeant came striding down our street. The children followed him, shouting questions. Was he a general? Had he killed many of the "short bandits" (the popular term for the Japanese)? Was the Generalissimo his friend? He answered good-naturedly. No, he was a sergeant, not a general; he had yet to kill any of the "short bandits" but would soon; and he didn't know the Generalissimo, but he did serve under Chang Wen-po, the best captain in the provincial army. One of my friends pushed me forward: "Here is the captain's brother, Wen-wei." The sergeant shook my hand gravely. Would I do him the honor of escorting him to my mother's home? He had come to take her to Xi'an to see Wen-po. Swelling with pride, I scampered ahead to our door.

Mother was very excited by Wen-po's invitation to a holiday in Xi'an. She packed a bag and gathered up Xing-min. Sher-chen and I hung around her, begging to be included. But she said that we would have to wait until Wen-hui came for us in a few days. Until then, we were to obey Wen-shuan, not troubling him too much when he came in tired from the fields.

None of us understood that Wen-po was summoning his family to Xi'an to say good-bye before he went to fight the Japanese—a fight that might well cost him his life. All wars inflict disproportionate casualties among junior officers, and this was particularly true in China's war against the Japanese. Chinese troops were patriotic but often poorly trained and poorly equipped. Sometimes one old rifle served to arm three men, each man taking it up in turn as the man before him fell killed or wounded. Under such dreadful handicaps, junior officers had to expose themselves constantly to issue orders and inspire their men. Other officers might resign to avoid such danger, but not Wen-po.

A week later, a smiling, excited Wen-hui picked us up. We walked the nine miles to Xing-ping City where we boarded the train for Xi'an. Sher-chen and I had never been on a train before, and we rode with our noses plastered to the window to watch the world passing at such a phenomenal speed. The big city of Xi'an overwhelmed us. We had never seen so many people, so many shops, so much hubbub. We clung to Wen-hui's sides, afraid that we would be swept away upon the rivers of people and commerce. There were many soldiers in the streets, the new recruits not yet in uniform. Thousands of refugees from eastern China camped along the edge of the roads and in the side streets. They spoke outrageous dialects that seemed foreign and threatening, though they looked like the people we'd known all our lives. Perhaps by some terrible oversight no one had noticed these foreigners. Perhaps they were Japanese! I whispered my fear to Wen-hui. He laughed. "No, they just aren't from near here. Don't worry; they are sons of Han like us."

We joined Mother, Xing-min, and Wen-po at the small hotel where he'd rented rooms. He greeted us with every effort to be kind and jolly, though he was unused to the company of small children. Wonders accumulated in the next few days. He took us to see the great city gate assigned to him to defend. Unlike many of the ragged, frightened recruits we saw being marched through the streets, Wen-po's men looked tough and well armed, confident in their training and their captain. I saw the sergeant again, who showed me Wen-po's motto emblazoned on the company flag: "Only readiness to die in battle wins victory and life."

Wen-po took us to a motion picture the next evening, where we sat amazed at this wonder so much more realistic than any shadow play. Mother giggled when the heroic young officer and the valiant peasant girl promised eternal love in a scene so intimate that I think she was actually quite shocked. We quailed when the wicked "short bandits" invaded the village and cheered when they were sent fleeing by the enraged farmers. Mother and Sher-chen wept when the gallant young officer died, but Wen-hui and I sat manfully dry-eyed through the scene.

Sher-chen, Xing-min, and I went to bed exhausted at the end of each day while the adults stayed up late talking. I noted that Mother became more somber as the days passed. I inquired why of Wen-hui, but he told me to wait until

Wen-po had time to explain. I was yet too intimidated by my eldest brother to press him, but he soon chose a time to explain matters to us: He was going to fight the Japanese. He would be in danger, but China needed her soldier sons to risk their lives in this time. He would write often and return someday with presents for us all. Until then, we were to help Mother as much as we could, remembering her painful feet and saving her exertion when we could. He finished by teaching us a patriotic song, which we belted out with great enthusiasm.

Circumstances had kept Wen-po from the intimate role he might have played in the upbringing of his children and youngest brother, but all that week he took every spare minute to be with us. He read a book of patriotic poems with me, impressed at my ability to memorize quickly. He lauded me, told me I must study hard in school to bring the family honor. "I'll take care of driving the Japanese into the sea; you get high marks in school. Is that a fair division of the work?"

I glowed. "Yes, eldest brother. Drive them into the sea quickly, and then come home. I'll read to you every night."

He smiled. "Yes," he said. "Someday you must do that for me. I am like Mother; sometimes my head hurts, and it would be soothing to lie with my eyes closed while you read to me."

On our last night together, Wen-po took us to a Muslim restaurant where we ate under the illumination of electric lights. Mother was fascinated with electricity, commenting that the bulbs were so bright that just that evening she'd spied a perfectly good needle lying on the tile floor of the hotel lobby. Sher-chen had picked it up for her, and she would take it home, expecting it to be her lucky needle. The dinner was a huge success, enjoyed thoroughly by everyone, though I noted Mother stare a time or two with deep sadness in her eyes at her two eldest sons. I was old enough even then to guess that she was wondering if either of them would survive the war.

Wen-hui took Sher-chen and me back to Zhou-bian village the next day. Mother and Xing-min stayed on another two weeks with Wen-po. In later years, she often recalled the difficulty of saying good-bye to him when he put her on the train for Xing-ping City. She wept, inconsolable despite his assurances that he would write often and return home safe. She, of course, knew these were the words spoken by soldiers all through the ages, meaningless except in the love they expressed.

Mother wept through the two hours it took for the train to reach Xing-ping City, where she was greeted by Wen-hui. She was still red-eyed but self-possessed by the time they reached home. She had done her weeping; it was time to get on with things.

Wen-po and his company proceeded from Xi'an to Hubei province, where they fought vainly to hold back the Japanese advance on Wuhan. For the next two years, he and his men would fight the Japanese in Hubei and adjoining Hunan province.

In central Shaanxi province, we lived surrounded by the competing forces of war. Xi'an was the main Nationalist base for controlling Shaanxi south of the Wei River. A few dozen miles north of the river, Nationalist control faded away, leaving the northern third of the province under Communist control from their base at Yan'an. Japanese-occupied territory lay several hundred miles to the east, leaving our area well outside the immediate zone of fighting. But everyone knew the situation could change in a matter of days if the Communists and the Nationalists clashed or the Japanese decided to resume their march inland.

On the whole, we were very fortunate. Though we worried about Wen-po on the front near Wuhan, we lived peacefully. The great famine had passed, and we usually had enough to eat. Wen-po and Wen-hui sent money home regularly. Wen-shuan had our land in production again, and we could see a time coming when we would again be a family of respected independent farmers. I was a schoolboy, bringing home excellent grades and expected to win the family honor in the future.

In 1939, at the age of ten, I started boarding school in Xing-ping City at the same school Wen-po had attended. It was hard being away from home, but I was honored to be in a fine school and determined to excel. War was working great changes in the area. The flood of refugees from eastern China doubled the population of Xing-ping City to some two hundred thousand. Half the students in my school were refugees, mostly the sons of the urban middle class. A few girls of progressive parents attended classes with us. Though quiet and keeping to their own group, these girls had a wonderful effect on me, demonstrating that girls could be just as bright, studious, and talented as boys. I had tremendous admiration for my wise mother, so shrewd in matters of the human heart. Several of my aunts, nieces, and sisters-in-law were clever, intelligent women. But what a disadvantage to have no education! I resolved that when it came my time to marry I would seek a modern and literate young woman for a wife.

The girls were day students living with their parents while the boys lived in the school dormitories. The school had about a hundred boys in fifth grade and another hundred in sixth. In a separate school but sharing some facilities were another three hundred boys in seventh, eighth, and ninth grades. About a third of us slept in wooden beds in a long, open barracks. The rest lived six or eight to a dormitory room. The dormitories were unheated, and we spent winter nights curled up under thick, padded quilts. We kept our extra clothing and a few personal items beneath our beds.

Our days began early, a bugle rousing us from sleep at 6:00 a.m. in the winter, 6:30 a.m. in the summer. We washed in warm water, a great luxury and one of the few concessions to comfort in the school. Our beds made and our rooms cleaned, we assembled on the parade ground to salute the flag and to sing the Nationalist anthem. Rather unfortunately, the words had been set to *Frère Jaques*, causing Westerners who did not understand the powerful sentiments of the Chinese words to smile condescendingly on hearing the anthem.

> Guomindang
> follows Dr. Sun's Nationalism,
> Democracy,
> and Livelihood of the People.
> Create a republic
> to usher in a universal peace.
> We are the vanguards
> of the republic,
> devoted to the fulfillment
> of Dr. Sun's goal of revolution.

After twenty minutes of calisthenics to warm the body, we trooped in to a breakfast of porridge, wheat bread, and tea. Classes began at 8:30 a.m., changing every half hour. We studied a modern range of subjects: history, language, science, geography, social science, and mathematics. I was well equipped in language, having studied hard in the village one-room school. I was considerably less prepared for anything involving mathematics, since I'd never been taught more than simple tallies until a few months before my entrance exams, when Wen-hui hired a tutor for me.

Our lunch was usually bread, tea, and noodles with vegetables. Once a week we had fried rice and turnip soup as a treat. We had a chance to study or nap after lunch and then attended less taxing classes in the afternoon. During music period, we learned patriotic, anti-Japanese songs. In art class we painted, drew, and learned mapmaking. We enjoyed basketball, ping-pong, British football, and a variety of games during an hour-long exercise period. When classes ended we had an hour to play games, read, or relax before the flag-lowering ceremony and a plain supper of more noodles, vegetables, and bread. After supper, we had another hour to relax, followed by a study period of two or three hours before lights out.

Our teachers were kind and knowledgeable. I was particularly fond of Mr. Gao Chong-sze, our homeroom teacher in sixth and seventh grade, who flattered me as his "number one" student. (Not until years later would I learn that he was one of the chief Communist organizers in Xing-ping City.) Another of my favorite teachers, Mr. Deng Ming-san, once paid my board when Wen-hui could not raise the money. Fortunately, the schools were public and very reasonably priced.

I'll confess that I was a bookworm and rarely inclined to spend my leisure hours in sports, games, or languid conversation. I enjoyed learning and burrowed into my studies with pleasure. I was rarely teased for my studiousness. One of the saddest things I have ever seen in America is the bumper sticker: "My kid beat up your honor student." In China, honor students truly were honored, and I enjoyed the respect and admiration of nearly all my classmates. I was sought out for help on difficult lessons and was happy to help those less academically gifted.

But, of course, I was also a boy and quick to have a fit of giggling or silly amusement. I remember once when someone got the idea of tying thread around our penises and waiting until we nearly burst before urinating. The wait and the length of urination were carefully recorded, the winner awarded a paper star in honor of his achievement. It was a prize I did not win. Another time, I recall we painted black circles around the eyes of a napping student and then howled at his expression when he awoke to find us laughing at him for no apparent reason. In junior high school, we discovered that by placing our ears against the wall we could overhear the gossip of the girls in the adjoining latrine. We, of course, were quick to share any gossip we learned with the other boys, particularly if it indicated that a girl liked one of the boys.

On my part, I became friendly with a willowy girl named Du Chun-fang, who seemed to me to personify all that was wonderful in the young Chinese female, an opinion confirmed when she demurely let me know that she liked me too. Though there was nothing even approximating Western dating during my youth in China, we were soon identified by others as sweethearts. We would remain so for many years.

In junior high the classes were longer, the work more demanding. We began the study of English in seventh grade. None of our teachers actually spoke English with any fluency, and we attacked the problem of learning this vastly strange language by memorizing its arcane grammatical rules. The entire concept of a phonetically based writing system utterly befuddled us. Since our teachers couldn't illustrate adequately, they took refuge in a labyrinth of moods, cases, tenses, clauses, complements, and phrases patrolled by a wild assortment of transitive, intransitive, dependent, independent, and parenthetical beasts, all prepared to gobble down the unwary student. Most of the students decided they would not try to penetrate the innermost secrets of English but would content themselves with learning only enough to pass. But those of us who hoped to go on to a highly regarded high school and then to university persevered in our attempts to master English through brute memorization of the rules.

Once or twice a week, our teachers would call a Boy Scout meeting during the recreational period following supper. The program emphasized patriotic virtues and encouraged us to do a good deed each day. We took outings and organized cleanup projects around the school. We trooped into the countryside to inform the peasants about Japanese atrocities and the courageous resistance of our armies. We took pride in our scout uniforms and awards, which seemed to give us some shared identity with the millions of soldiers fighting to save China from the "short bandits."

Altogether, our lives were planned to the point of regimentation with the daily schedule posted six weeks ahead. We were closely supervised, and misbehavior was quickly and firmly punished. The dormitories were crowded and cold, the food monotonous. Yet we didn't seem to notice our discomfort. Our education stressed the traditional virtues of thrift, respect, self-discipline, honesty, and particularly patriotism. We all believed that we were soldiers in the war against the Japanese though we carried books and slates, not guns and grenades.

Wen-hui visited often to pay my fees and to see how I was getting along. He was always cheerful and a great hit with my teachers and fellow students. Wen-shuan visited every now and then to bring me food and clothes from home. He was uncomfortable in the city and embarrassed by his peasant attire and manners around the school. While the gatekeeper let Wen-hui in with a bow, he often made Wen-shuan wait outside while he verified that the student Chang Wen-wei was expecting such a humble visitor. Wen-shuan rarely stayed inside the school compound for long, but he was always anxious to see that I was in good health and had enough to eat and wear. In these concerns he could be almost motherly, tut-tutting about a small tear in my clothes and offering to fix it, though my fingers were far more nimble with a needle and thread than his big, chapped farmer's hands.

The school year started in September. We had a month off at Lunar New Year and a two-month summer holiday. During the five years I spent in boarding school in Xing-ping City, I attended classes six days a week and went home only once a month from Saturday evening to Sunday afternoon. The family always made much of my visit. Mother would wash my clothes while Sher-chen and Xing-min waited on me. Coming in from the fields, Wen-shuan would smile his quiet smile, lay a hard, calloused hand momentarily on my head, and then go to wash up. Mother would serve my favorite foods at supper while Xing-min and Sher-chen plied me with questions about school. Wen-shuan, as was his way, rarely spoke, but he'd listen to every word, pride shining in his gentle eyes for this little brother who would one day be a scholar and a servant of the people. All my loneliness at school, the tears I shed beneath the covers, all the work and memorization, seemed a very small price to pay as my family enveloped me in their love.

Later Mother would tell me the accumulated gossip from the family and village since I'd last been home. When all was told, we would tell stories or sing until long after our usual bedtimes. The next morning our humble village would always seem born afresh to me—the best, the luckiest place on earth to be born. The hours would pass all too quickly, and I would fight to keep sadness at bay as my time to depart approached. Mother would bustle about, suppressing her own sadness. When it was time for me to start the long walk back to school, she would present me with a package of my favorite foods and tell me again of her pride in me. She'd watch from the doorway until I reached the village gate and turned to wave a final time.

We were very fortunate to live far from the active combat fronts where thousands of Chinese soldiers were dying every day. Wen-shuan was exempt from conscription as a farmer and the only adult male at home. Wen-hui was a member of the home-defense militia in Xing-ping City and was likewise spared great danger unless the Japanese decided to advance in our direction.

Wen-hui was beginning to make a good living as a traveling salesman, but Mother worried that he might fall in with disreputable company in his travels. Wen-hui had always been the least restrained and most fun-loving of us brothers. He was fond of late nights with his friends, much to the disgust of Wen-shuan, who had a puritanical streak. Mother decided that the time had come for Wen-hui to marry and settle down. Wen-hui was not at all opposed to marrying, but he wasn't about to let Mother and a matchmaker choose his bride. Mother acquiesced to his involvement and they screened several candidates. Our family no longer had wealth or social position, but Mother and Wen-hui were able to publicize his splendid abilities in business and his bright prospects. Their salesmanship worked, and a friend of Mother's allowed that her granddaughter might be a good match.

By chance, Wen-hui knew the girl's brother and, with his help, was able to observe his prospective bride from hiding. How aware Ma Li-chun was of his inspection I don't know, but I suspect her brother alerted her. Wen-hui was much taken with her, and he and our mother began a campaign to convince the girl's parents of the suitability of the match. The girl's brother and grandmother became our allies, exerting pressure on Wen-hui's behalf. Reou-yeh, in the last months of her life, visited the girl's parents to plead her brother's case. Eventually, everyone was convinced, and Wen-hui and Ma Li-chun were engaged in 1937. They married in 1939 to enjoy a happy though sadly brief marriage.

Ma Li-chun moved into our home in Zhou-bian village. Having another woman in the house was a great relief to Mother. Ma Li-chun was a domestic and hardworking girl. She took over the cooking, sparing Mother many hours on her twisted, painful feet. Mother's eyesight was failing, and she was grateful when Ma Li-chun offered to sew our clothes. Mother devoted her newfound leisure to weaving, a craft she'd always enjoyed above the other housewife's chores. Except for poor Reou-yeh, Mother had not enjoyed the company of another woman in the house since the death of her beloved Chong-er. Ma Li-chun was a quieter, less effusive woman than Chong-er but likewise kind and cheerful. The two women developed a deep affection for each other. Ma Li-chun was soon pregnant, and Mother looked forward to the arrival of a new grandchild. But the baby died, and a time of joy turned into a time of mourning.

Often in my mother's life, there seemed more incidents of tragedy than joy. Though the strains of the famine had weakened some of the bonds within our extended family, we remained close to Mother's older brother, the generous, hardworking Wei San. Though he had a large family of his own, he always took time to talk to me whenever we met. In parting he would pat my shoulder, telling me to work hard at my studies so that one day the family could brag of the village boy who had become a famous scholar and magistrate.

I treasured his affection and gentle counsel, so it was a terrible shock when he died suddenly when I was twelve. I was walking home from school through my uncle's village when I met a boy I knew. "Wen-wei," he said, "you must tell your mother that her brother Wei San is dead."

For a moment, I couldn't breathe. "How? Are you sure?"

He nodded sadly. "Yes, his heart stopped. I'm sorry."

Instead of hurrying home, I ran to my uncle's house. From outside, I could hear the weeping and wailing of women and little children. I entered quietly to see my uncle, so vital in life, laid out pale and unmoving. Perhaps it was only my imagination but there seemed a lingering expression of surprise on his face, as if death had come so suddenly that he'd had no time to comprehend its arrival. Despite my intention to do the manly thing by rushing home to break the terrible news to Mother, I collapsed in a corner, weeping uncontrollably and unable to leave his side.

Not until hours later did Mother arrive, her face ashen with shock and grief. She helped the family prepare Wei San's body for burial, cooked for the family, and cared for the bewildered grandchildren. She didn't break down until the funeral when she was overwhelmed with grief, bitterly bewailing that she'd never paid back our uncle for all his many kindnesses to us during the famine. Wen-shuan in his awkward way and I in my boyish one tried to assure her that Uncle Wei San knew how much she loved and respected him and that he loved and respected his brave, strong sister in return. We all missed him terribly.

About this time we received a letter from Wen-po, telling us that he had been wounded but was recovering in a hospital in Hunan province. After the fall of Wuhan in October 1938, Wen-po's division withdrew to the vicinity of Tung-ting Lake, a hundred miles south of Wuhan and halfway to the important city of Changsa. Wen-po and his company were assigned to hold a low mountain peak overlooking the strategic Kang Wang Bridge at the northeastern end of the lake. Attacked repeatedly for days, they held against bombers, tanks, artillery fire, and massed infantry assaults. Two-thirds of Wen-po's 150 men died in the fighting, but the survivors fought on under his leadership. He did not rest for days, staying in constant touch by field phone with his superiors. Finally, the Japanese fell back and the company was relieved by fresh troops. The survivors of Wen-po's company trudged down the mountain. It was at that point that an exhausted, careless soldier stumbled, accidentally discharging his submachine gun. Several bullets tore into Wen-po's midsection.

Under other circumstances, Wen-po might have been left behind as too grievously wounded to survive. But the regimental colonel would not abandon the young officer who had fought "like a tiger." Four soldiers carried the cot bearing Wen-po for three days. At a crude military hospital in Wukang City, doctors removed several bullets and a dozen feet of his intestines. One bullet lay too close to his spine to remove, and he would carry it the rest of his life. For days he lay unconscious. The colonel's description of him spread, and by the time he awoke, he was "Tiger Chang." He lay for weeks in mortal danger of infection. He made arrangements for sending his small savings to Mother and resigned himself to death at a young age. But his wounds began to heal and, after many months, he was discharged from the hospital.

It was with great pride and joy that we in Zhou-bian village read his letter recounting his recovery and assignment to the military college in Wukang, a branch of the famous Huang-pu Military Academy. This was a great distinction for a junior officer with little formal education and indicated that his superiors recognized him as a man of exceptional ability who might one day command thousands rather than mere scores of men. For the next two years, he would study his profession as his wounds healed.

Wen-po wrote home often to reassure Mother that he was no longer in danger. But the wartime mails often went astray and months sometimes passed without a letter from him. Mother would pine for news, the worry pinching her face and stomach and robbing her of sleep. She would rejoice when a letter arrived. Wen-hui or I would read it to her if one of us chanced to be home. Otherwise, she would send for the village schoolmaster. The relief revived her, and she would talk of the day when she could gather all her surviving children about her in safety.

Incompetence and corruption in high places and Chiang's continued vendetta against the Communists plagued the Nationalist cause despite the dedication and competence of thousands of officers like Wen-po and the determined heroism of millions of common soldiers. In 1940, the Communists stirred a hornet's nest when the Eighth Route Army launched its ambitious

100 Regiments Offensive to regain territory lost to the Japanese in northern China. The offensive won the CCP prestige in a time when Nationalist forces were showing little aggressiveness, but the Japanese struck back savagely, instituting the "Three Alls Policy": Kill all, burn all, destroy all. Japanese troops leveled an estimated 150,000 homes, killed thousands of villagers, and enslaved thousands more as forced laborers.

In the Japanese victories Chiang saw an opportunity to strike at his Communist allies. The Communist New Fourth Army was recruiting south of the Yangtze in Jiangxi province where the CCP had enjoyed wide popular support before the Long March. The territory was nominally Nationalist, and Chiang demanded that the Communists withdraw north of the river. When the Communists were slow to comply, he attacked, killing thousands as a punishment for their "insubordination." After six days of fighting from January 7 to 13, 1941, a cease-fire was arranged, and the Communists withdrew across the river. However, the united front was largely a fiction after the New Fourth Army Incident.

Personal losses continued to mount for my mother. My sister Koo-yeh, Mother's second daughter, died in childbirth in December 1941 at the age of thirty-six. I had not seen much of this serious, quiet sister in a number of years. She had married a farmer even more reticent than she was. His large extended family fragmented under the pressure of business difficulties, bad luck, and the onset of the great famine. After that she ruled her own household with an iron fist, dominating her husband and imposing a miserly thriftiness on him and their four children. During the famine, she had been reluctant to assist us, announcing that she must be sure to care for her own family first. She always treated my mother properly, but there was little warmth in their relationship. We younger children were uneasy and even a bit frightened around her. Yet she was daughter, sister, and aunt, and we mourned.

I think that Koo-yeh's death, coming so soon after Uncle Wei San's, served to remind Mother of her own mortality. She was determined to see her marriageable sons secure while there was still time for her to arrange the choice of brides. Wen-po put her off, saying he had no desire to remarry so long as the war continued. Wen-shuan, however, was anxious to marry. Finding him a wife presented a real challenge for Mother. Where Wen-hui was smiling and outgoing, Wen-shuan was so shy that he gave the impression of unfriendly grimness. Actually, he was the kindest of men and more than ready to be a dutiful husband.

By chance, Mother discovered a girl who met all her high expectations. She knew the girl's mother, another widow and a distant relative, but had never known that she had a daughter. Visiting the opposite end of our village one day, Mother came upon her friend and a young woman in affectionate conversation. With a slight hesitation, Mother's friend introduced her daughter, Sun-sze. Later Mother pressed for an explanation. Her friend explained that she had been married and divorced very young, leaving behind an infant daughter in her former husband's house in another village. Divorce was very unusual and quite shocking in China, so she kept that part of her past hidden when she married a nice older man in our village. They lived together in perfect harmony for a decade before he died. His loss left her deeply depressed, and she became almost a recluse until the daughter from her first marriage began visiting and got her involved in life again. She was very proud of her intelligent, pretty daughter and hoped that she could find her a husband of wealth and good prospects, perhaps a university student.

When my mother suggested that Wen-shuan would make a good husband, the woman hesitated. She knew Wen-shuan had a reputation for hard work and honesty, but he had no education and only a few acres. But Mother persisted and the woman weakened. She knew that my brothers, sisters, and I enjoyed high regard in the village, but I think it was Mother's reputation as an exceptional mother-in-law to Chong-er and Ma Li-chun that finally convinced her. Married to Wen-shuan, Sun-sze would have a kind mother-in-law who would allow her many visits home and would often invite her mother to visit. Both young people were anxious for the match, and Wen-shuan and Sun-sze were married in 1942. It was a wonderful marriage that would produce three sons, three daughters, and much happiness through some very bad times in China.

The arrival of a second daughter-in-law under the family roof presented a new challenge to Mother's skills as a psychologist. Though they would eventually become friends, the two young women were not initially a good fit. Ma Li-chun, the wife of the quick-witted, ebullient Wen-hui, was a quiet, steady girl who needed time to form opinions and words. Chang Sun-sze, the wife of the reticent, slow-thinking Wen-shuan, was a witty, talkative girl, quick to say what was on her mind without much consideration. Such opposite personalities were bound to rub up against each other in much the same way Wen-hui and Wen-shuan had their differences over the years. But Mother remembered her own experience as a young bride in the home of Grandmother Chang Nan-sze and the unfair treatment she'd received from her sister-in-law, my uncle Cheng Weng's wife. She would not allow the same bad feeling to permeate her house. She was careful not to favor one daughter-in-law over the other. Wen-hui and Wen-shuan naturally and properly sided with their wives when complaints came out in "pillow talk." Then Mother would call all parties together for reconciliation. I think she enjoyed the subtle maneuvering immensely, and the two young women soon adapted to the household and each other.

The changes wrought by the war reached even peaceful rural hamlets like Zhou-bian village. Beggars came through daily, mostly good, honest people who had been driven from their homes by war. Mother remembered being forced to beg during the great famine and gave what help she could. Acting troupes, often made up of left-leaning students, stopped in the village to perform anti-Japanese plays. Wounded and crippled soldiers sought shelter among the rural folk. Officials, many of them reassigned from occupied eastern China, made surveys, inspected roads, and tried to reassure the people of the eventual triumph of the Nationalist cause.

My family had risen from the poverty of the great famine to become an example of healthy adaptation to the changes in Chinese society. Mother was widely applauded for the success of her sons and the successful marriages of her daughters. People praised her for her light touch and skillful psychology in maintaining household harmony among people of drastically different temperaments. She was considered progressive for allowing her sons a large role in choosing their brides. Looking back, it seemed that Mother had always been a bit daring. Traditional, yes, but not in an unexamined way, as she had demonstrated decades before when she'd been among the first village women to stop binding their daughters' feet.

After two years of advanced training, Wen-po joined his division on the Yunnan border with Vietnam, commanding a battalion as a lieutenant colonel. For the next two years, he would fight Japanese agents, opium smugglers, and their French allies from the puppet Vichy regime in Vietnam. Motivated by patriotism and a passionate hatred of the opium trade, Wen-po frequently put himself at great personal risk. He mounted ambushes, often with only a squad or two of soldiers. He once captured three Frenchmen who had ridden horseback into his area on an opium purchase. Though the incident sparked a diplomatic protest to Chongqing from Paris, he refused to curtail his policing. In his autobiography, he recounted entering a smugglers' camp masquerading as a buyer, only to be recognized by an ill chance. Before he could be disarmed, he drew his pistol and shot his way out. Such deeds of derring-do enhanced his reputation as "Tiger Chang."

Despite the bravery of the Chinese foot soldier and the dedication of honest officers like my brother, the Nationalist cause continued to falter under the uncertain leadership of Chiang Kai-shek. Western aid supported only a small percentage of the cost of the Chinese war effort. Under orders from Chiang's government, Nationalist troops enforced heavy taxes on the rural people. The confiscation of foodstuffs in a time of famine in southern China led to thousands of needless deaths. In comparison, the Communist army in the north seemed humane, paying for all the food it took and providing relief to the farmers by forcing rent reductions on landlords. American advisors suggested several plans for sending Western military aid to the Communists, but Chiang argued vehemently against strengthening the CCP.

While powerful men and great nations struggled, my family in central Shaanxi continued to live comfortably if frugally. In the spring of 1944 I achieved one of the great ambitions of my life when I graduated from junior high school at the top of my class, becoming one of only six students in the province granted admission to Xi'an's most prestigious high school without having to take the entrance examinations. Tired, dusty, and triumphant, I reached Zhou-bian village. Above me, a rocket blossomed against a clear evening sky as my family, friends, and neighbors began celebrating the honor brought home by the studious village lad. I was slightly embarrassed as I drew closer, but then saw my mother balanced on her cane and her twisted feet in the crowd at the village gate, her eyes shining with pride. This was as much her triumph as mine. Weeping with joy, I went forward to greet her. The waiting crowd drew me in, applauding, laughing, slapping me on the back as I passed through the gate into the heart of my village and the unreserved love of kind people.

Major Chang Wen-po, 1942.

Generalissimo Chiang Kai-shek and Brigadier General Chang Wen-po, 1948.

Chang Wei-sze in Beijing, Sept.1948, with her grandson Xing-min at left, her son Wen-wei at right.

The Chang family in Shanghai, December 1948. Left to right: Ma Li-chun, Wen-wei, Mother Chang Wei-sze, Wen-po, Sher-ping, Li Lin-fen. Chang Wei-sze is wearing a black headscarf.

Chang Wen-hui in uniform as a quartermaster lieutenant in Manchuria, 1947.

On Taiwan in 1952. Back row: Li Lin-fen, Wen-po, Wen-wei; front row: Sher-yan, Sher-ping, and Xing-kou.

Chang Wen-sze, a few months before her death in July 1955.

The grave of Chang Ying and Chang Wen-sze, Zhou-bian village, Shaanxi province, 1973.

The graduation class of 1944 from Xing ping Junior High School. Graduating at the top of his class, Wen-wei is in the front row, standing at far left.

Major General Chang Wen-po (standing in khaki uniform) guiding Chiang Ching-kuo, son of Chiang Kai-shek and future president of the Republic of China, on an inspection trip of Little Quemoy Island, 1948.

Chang Wen-wei as a cadet on Taiwan, 1952.

Chang Wen-wei training at officer candidate school, 1952.

David W. Chang on admission to Southwestern College (later Rhodes College), Memphis, Tennessee, 1953.

David W. Chang as a graduate of Southwestern College, June 1955.

David W. Chang (second from left) and a friend visiting Miss Lillian C. Wells (center) and family near her retirement home in Morristown, Tennessee, 1953.

David W. Chang flying a kite during spring vacation from Southwestern College, 1954.

David W. Chang and his brother Major General Chang Wen-po, with their wives and families in Taiwan, 1970.

David W. Chang with his recently published book Zhou Enlai and Deng Xiaoping and the Chinese Leadership Succession Crisis *in 1984 at the University of Wisconsin, Oshkosh.*

David W. Chang with Dr. Chien Fu, foreign minister of the Republic of China, in Taipei, 1976.

David W. Chang delivering an address to the Nan-ting conference of scholars in Washington, D.C., 1999.

CHAPTER 7

The Wise Mother

THROUGH THE SUMMER OF 1944, I enjoyed the interest, even the adulation of the village people. Mother bragged to the other women of the great career I would have as a government official once I'd finished my education. I tried to explain to her that my success was hardly assured at fifteen and that I had to excel in high school to gain admission to a university where I would spend several more years in study before earning a degree. She brushed away these cautions; I was her brilliant youngest child, sure to win the family and his mother such honor that years after her death people would point to her grave and say: "Here rests the worthy woman who gave birth to the great magistrate, Chang Wen-wei. Blessed be both their names."

My mother's inordinate pride in me was understandable. Patriotism runs very deep in China. Traditionally, mandarin officials were seen not as tools of the rulers but as servants of the people. That I might assume such an esteemed position—though *mandarin* was no longer the term—filled my mother with the profoundest happiness. Other parents in the village envied her good fortune in having such a scholarly son, but it was not a destructive jealousy but an example of the pride that in times past had caused villagers to take up collections so that a poor but bright boy might spend years studying the Confucian classics in preparation for the imperial examinations.

Though she was a traditional village woman, Mother did not cling to outmoded practices. When she began speaking of a wife for me, I let her know that I expected more say in the choice than even my brother Wen-hui had enjoyed. She readily agreed to this, though she took pride in her past success in finding good wives for her sons. As the village's best student and a young man with a promising future, I was attractive to many parents with marriageable daughters. I often felt myself under inspection when I walked through the streets of the village. Older men and women drew me into conversation. Occasionally, I'd hear the giggles of girls peeking through the cracks in shutters and doors. I found the attention pleasing, a sign that I had earned respect and status in the village. But I knew that I could not marry a village girl. My education and life in the city were leading me onto paths that a village girl would have great difficulty following, hard though she might try out of love and obligation. The differences in education and intellectual interest had been deadly for my parents' marriage, and my father had only a small part of the education I would obtain as a university student. My partner in life should be a modern woman who could read, write, and share fully in the challenges of my life as a patriotic intellectual in a changing China. Though Mother was not equipped to understand much in my intellectual life, she understood that my education was making me very different from the average village lad. So, when the matchmakers called to sing the virtues of this or that village girl, she sent them away disappointed.

One day, however, a matchmaker came to our door on a different errand: a match not for me but for my niece Sher-chen. To my surprise the young man proposed was my junior high classmate, Nan Pu-chao. To the best of my knowledge he had never seen Sher-chen, but he must have gotten a glimpse of her during one of our walks home from Xing-ping City. Without letting me know how deeply his chance sight of Sher-chen had affected him, he went home and spoke to his parents about her. They hired a matchmaker to make discreet inquiries into the circumstances of our family and, having received a satisfactory report, were now making an offer.

Mother was an old hand at negotiating marriage contracts and let slip no indication of how she greeted the petition as she listened impassively to the matchmaker. Once we were alone, Mother quizzed me about Nan Pu-chao. I had only good to say about him. He was several years older than I was, not an unusual circumstance in Chinese schools, and a serious if not particularly gifted student. He was decent and hardworking, the son of an educated man who taught school and owned a prosperous farm. Altogether, I could see no reason why he shouldn't make a good provider and devoted husband for Sher-chen.

Mother considered this information with her usual good sense. Wen-po was far away, fighting Japanese raiders and chasing opium smugglers on China's southern border with Vietnam. So it fell to Mother to arrange the best possible match for her granddaughter. Pu-chao seemed ideal, and she sent word of her tentative approval to the match. Complications soon arose, however. Both Pu-chao's parents died of a rampant infectious disease. The loss so devastated Pu-chao that his older brothers worried about his mental and physical survival. An early marriage to Sher-chen seemed the best cure, and the older brothers begged Mother to sanction the union before Sher-chen reached the traditional age of eighteen. Mother put them off and fell to pondering. Sher-chen had grown into a healthy, lively, and confident young woman with a quick intelligence despite her lack of education. Mother had taught her the skills of mediation and psychology as well as the traditional skills of the housewife. If any girl of fifteen could manage marriage and life in a strange household, it was Sher-chen. After thorough reflection, she called Sher-chen and me to her.

We sat with teacups steaming in front of us, for green tea is many things to the Chinese: comfort, a restorative for the body, and a stimulant to conversation, careful thought, and wise decision. "Granddaughter," Mother began, "you are still young. Are you ready to love and care for Pu-chao as his wife? Or would you prefer to wait? You are very dear to me and do not need to leave this home at your first opportunity."

"I am afraid of losing him, Grandmother. But you know best if I am ready."

"He is a good boy. I like him. But if he won't wait, or his brothers won't let him, there will be another chance for you in a few years."

"I am afraid that Fortune would not smile so warmly on me next time. But you know best, Grandmother."

Mother turned to me. "What do you think, youngest son?"

"Pu-chao is a good man. And I don't say so only because he is my friend. He is kind, studious, and comes from a good family. If Sher-chen feels she is ready to be a wife, I won't object. But you know best, Mother."

We talked on in this manner for some time. Always Sher-chen and I deferred to Mother's wisdom. It wouldn't have occurred to us to do otherwise, both because tradition dictated such respect and because we were entirely confident in her judgment. After she had examined every aspect of the issue, patting things into place as if she were preparing dough for baking, she announced her decision: "I think then that you should marry, Sher-chen. I will mourn for losing you but rejoice more for your luck in becoming such a good man's wife. And he will be very fortunate in you."

"Thank you, Grandmother," Sher-chen said, a wide grin spreading across her face despite the seriousness of the moment. She reached out to take the old woman's hands, bowed low over them.

"Wen-wei, you must write Wen-po," Mother said. "I will tell Wen-shuan and Wen-hui. I don't think anyone will object." She got her feet under her and pushed herself up on her cane. Sher-chen jumped up, bouncing with excitement. Mother made a shooing motion. "Go, Granddaughter. Go. Tell Ma Li-chun and Chang Sun-sze, then run and tell your friends."

Sher-chen ran off and shortly we heard the cries of joy and congratulations from the two young wives, whom I suspected had listened breathlessly to the entire conversation from around a corner. I extended an arm to help Mother walk. "Let's stroll in the street for a few minutes," she said. "I need fresh air."

"Your feet don't pain you too much?"

She shrugged. "As much or little as always."

"Sher-chen is very happy. I think you made the correct decision."

She shuffled along beside me. "Yes, very happy. I wish a grandmother could guarantee such happiness always. But every girl must learn a wife's sadnesses on her own."

"Pu-chao is a good man. And you were wise to give Sher-chen a say in this matter."

"Yes. It was never fair for any girl or boy to be married against their wishes. It has taken me a lifetime to learn that. I, who was married to a very difficult man. You'd think I might have understood that earlier. But I suppose the truths closest to us are often the easiest to miss."

Time would prove the rightness of Mother's decision. Young married life would not be easy for Pu-chao and Sher-chen. Soon after their marriage, Pu-chao's brothers argued bitterly, eventually deciding to divide the farm though it would cause a further decline in the family income. Without enough money to continue his schooling, Pu-chao joined the army in the last months of the war. On his discharge he returned to school on government aid, gaining enough qualifications to become a schoolteacher. They were separated again when he was drafted into the Communist army during the Korean War. In the decades that followed, they got by on his small teacher's salary while enduring the turmoil caused by Mao's attempts to destroy traditional Chinese culture. Through it all their mutual affection never wavered.

Wen-po had also fallen victim to the wiles of matchmakers. In Yunnan, the wives of other officers introduced the dashing bachelor colonel to a small, pretty girl from a good family. Though he had told Mother that he would not marry so long as he was exposed to the dangers of combat, he was thoroughly enamored of Li Lin-fen. A wedding was soon arranged.

I read Wen-po's letter announcing his news to Mother on the eve of the Moon Cake celebration in August. I hesitated when I reached the dramatic sentence: "Most honored Mother, please rejoice with me that I have taken a new wife, Li Lin-fen, who looks forward eagerly to greeting you with all the honor due a mother-in-law."

I looked at Mother, wary that her face might betray anger for not having been asked permission or given any role in the selection of a new wife for her eldest son. For a long moment she sat impassive; then she spoke: "It is a pretty name. I'm glad your brother has taken a wife. No man, not even a soldier, should be without a wife." Later that night, when we were all in bed, I heard her murmuring softly. I could not pick out the words, but I believe she spoke to Chong-er's spirit, imploring her to rejoice that the husband she had left a widower so many years before had at last taken a wife.

Wen-hui helped me to carry my possessions on the hike to Xing-ping City and the train trip to Xi'an. It was a trip I'd made only one time before, and I was wide-eyed with excitement as we steamed down the valley toward the ancient capital. For a village lad like me, wartime Xi'an was a place of dizzying turmoil. The city was heavily garrisoned with men and military equipment against a Communist move south of the Wei River or a Japanese move up the Yellow River from the east. American airplanes of General Claire Chennault's 14th Army Air Force buzzed the city at low altitude. Military trucks grumbled in long, slow lines. Motorcycle messengers raced alongside the convoys, weaving in and out amid bicycles, pedicabs, pedestrians, and beasts of burden. Unlike Wen-shuan, who would have grimaced in discomfort at the crowding and the uproar, Wen-hui loved the city. "What do you suppose Mother would say if I came home with a motorcycle?"

"She'd brain you with a lump of coal for wasting money," I said.

He laughed, stretched his arms wide as if to embrace the hubbub. Then we shouldered our burdens and set off. After the leisurely pace of Zhou-bian village, most people in Xi'an seemed hurried, desperately intent on accomplishing something beyond the normal cycle of daily routine. I'm sure that was only a naive village boy's impression and that most of Xi'an's residents were carrying out their routines with the unhurried but deliberate pace of people accustomed to traditional cycles. Yet in this birthplace of so much of China's history, one had the feeling that something new had crept in, some sense that the time might not, after all, turn in cycles but rush blindly toward some unknowable future like a locomotive without an engineer. Or so it seemed to me.

Because of Japanese bombing raids, Xing-kuo (National Reconstruction) High School had been relocated five miles south of the city at the foot of Chung-nan Mountain. Dormitories were dug into the soft earth of the mountain, each housing thirty-five students. We were strictly regimented under the control of army officers and army regulations. We were not in school to enjoy ourselves but to prepare for the immense task of rebuilding China. Yet the rigorous conditions and rules were not as burdensome as a peacetime reader might expect: we were all patriotic, particularly the students from occupied China. Half the student body and two-thirds of the teachers were refugees from eastern China. Daily we wrestled with the problems arising from different dialects, customs, and backgrounds. Good humor was our salvation. I, for one, found the sophistication of the easterners fascinating. I'd always seen myself becoming a county magistrate; now I began dreaming of a position with the central bureaucracy or the diplomatic corps. Visions of great cities and distant foreign lands blossomed in my imagination.

The curriculum was far more challenging than anything even hinted at in my earlier schooling. The teachers at Xing-kuo High School expected us to achieve a proficiency in science and mathematics that would later make my similar courses in American universities seem easy. We studied English, history, business, and a range of other subjects with nearly equal intensity. Fortunately, I found that my study habits could accommodate the increased demands, and I continued to earn marks at or near the top of my classes.

Once a month we were allowed to go into Xi'an to visit friends and to seek some wholesome entertainment, usually a picture show or an opera. I'm afraid that released from the supervision of the military officers at our school we were a boisterous lot. But the Chinese have always indulged a certain level of youthful good spirits among students, and our shenanigans were rarely harmful.

My friend Du Chun-fang attended a girls' high school in the city, and I visited her on my every visit to town. She had matured into a pretty young woman, and I began to see her as more than a companion. We shared long walks in the city parks and many confidences until it seemed natural enough to fall in love. But love between traditional Chinese young people, even in the relatively liberated 1940s, was something requiring careful, patient nurturing. We were far too shy to succumb to a sudden passion that would hurl us into each other's embrace. Rather, we experienced a slow realization of the depth of our mutual affection and began speaking of marriage.

I returned to Zhou-bian village only at Lunar New Year and for summer vacation. After my time in the environs of a great city, I was sometimes frustrated and impatient with the provincialism of the village and my family. But I soon forgot this sense of apartness as I slipped back into the family routine. Mother would store up the news: sometimes gossip for my entertainment, sometimes matters of great concern that she wanted to talk over. That first night home we would lie in the dark talking for many hours after the others had fallen asleep, exhausted with the excitement of the homecoming celebration.

Mother could be lighthearted and funny, telling of the foibles and misadventures of the village folk. Then she would turn serious, relating in minute detail matters of concern to our family. Wen-shuan and Wen-hui were of such opposite personalities that they were often at odds. Most of the farmwork fell to Wen-shuan while Wen-hui carried on his profession as a traveling salesman. Wen-hui had helped finance the rebuilding of our farm and felt that his financial contribution and his status as an older brother put Wen-shuan under an obligation to defer to him and heed his advice. Wen-shuan bridled under these expectations. Though marriage had settled Wen-hui considerably, Wen-shuan was still irritated with his brother's dislike of farmwork and his fondness for gambling and carousing with his friends. The sisters-in-law, Wen-hui's Ma Li-chun and Wen-shuan's Chang Sun-sze, sided with their husbands, often maintaining a frosty distance long after the men had quit arguing.

Mother was an excellent psychologist—perceptive, patient, and sympathetic—but her closeness to the situation in her own home often made the right course of action difficult for her to discern. During our late-night conversations, she would carefully lay out all sides before asking my opinion. I was still very young and felt greatly honored by her confidences. She would listen carefully to my opinion, accepting with grace any perception on my part that might contribute to the resolution of the problem. When my suggestions were wrongheaded, she would gently demonstrate why. From these lessons in human psychology, I learned as much from my illiterate mother as from any of my scholarly teachers at school.

Within a day or two, Mother would tell me to call a family meeting. The adults would gather (I was now considered one, though only in my midteens), and we'd set about finding a solution to family tensions. Mother would have me summarize the issues, a role that she saw as part of my training as a future government official. Others would speak and gradually she would maneuver the disputants into positions where compromise could be made without loss of face. She was never dictatorial, always achieving her ends with subtlety and consideration for everyone's feelings. In our great respect for her, we listened, hardly realizing at first how delicately she restored family harmony.

It would take me many years and much more experience with the world to fully realize that each time I made the journey from Xi'an to Zhou-bian village I crossed more than distance but also generations in time. Xi'an and my school had entered a new era of rapid change and moral relativism while Zhou-bian village and my home—for all the changes wrought by famine and war—still functioned according to the age-old rules of rural life. While I am too much the believer in progress and modernity to mourn the passing of much that typified life in the old China, I feel blessed that in the years of my adolescence I was privileged to learn from those older traditions. My mother took great strength from the rural principles of kindness, justice, mutual assistance, and respect for age, education, the land, and the past. Though the history of her time forced many changes in her life, she remained steadfast to those principles and a shining exemplar of traditional virtues. From her I learned the joys of family and hard work, when to speak and when to listen, the difference between courage and expediency, and, most important of all, how to discern between right and wrong, honor and shame.

The defeat of Japan came with startling rapidity for the Nationalist leadership. Cut out of the inner councils of the major Allied powers, Chiang's government was unprepared for the atomic bombing of Hiroshima on August 6, 1945, and the Soviet invasion of Manchuria two days later. After a second atomic bomb destroyed the port of Nagasaki, Japan announced its surrender on August 14.

Communists and Nationalists scrambled to reoccupy territory conquered by the Japanese. On paper the Nationalist army had a huge advantage, outnumbering the Communist People's Liberation Army 2.7 million to 1 million and holding an even wider margin in modern military equipment. But in any prolonged conflict, an army can be only as strong as the economy that supports it, and China's economy was in need of critical care and a peaceful period of recovery.

In the immediate aftermath of the Japanese surrender, American aircraft transported 110,000 of Chiang's best troops to reoccupy the major cities. Meanwhile, the Communists took control of vast areas of rural China, particularly in Jiangsu, Hebei, Shandong, and Shaanxi provinces. Soviet forces occupied Manchuria, stripping the factories of large equipment and turning over immense caches of arms to the local Communist resistance. Nationalist forces arriving by sea and air had to deploy according to instructions from Soviet commanders. The pro-Nationalist resistance under the Young Marshal's brother was driven into making an alliance with the Communists when Chiang refused to release the Young Marshal from arrest and insisted that they disarm. In forced marches, 100,000 Communist soldiers of General Lin Biao's Eighth Route Army pushed into Manchuria. Meanwhile, Wen-po's regiment was transferred from southern China to Manchuria with the rest of the Fifty-second Army Corps, traveling by sea from the Vietnamese port of Haiphong.

Soviet forces withdrew gradually through 1946, leaving Nationalist forces controlling the cities of Changchun and Shenyang (Mukden) and the Communists occupying most of the countryside and the major city of Harbin. President Harry Truman sent General George Marshall to China as his special envoy in December 1945. Marshall labored through 1946, eventually brokering an agreement between the Nationalists and the Communists for the formation of a pluralistic government based on Dr. Sun Yat-sen's principles of nationalism, democracy, and socialism. The agreement lasted only weeks. In November, when Communist forces refused to acknowledge Nationalist authority in Manchuria, Chiang launched a major offensive from Beijing north along the railroad corridor to Shenyang. The Nationalist thrust ran into heavy resistance from Lin Biao's army, many of whose members were Manchurian and willing to fight fiercely on their home soil. Chiang rushed reinforcements north. China's future might well depend on the result of the fighting in Manchuria.

In January 1947, General Marshall announced the failure of his mission, relegating the United States to the sidelines for the rest of the war. The failure to achieve a negotiated peace contributed to the radicalization of the Communist political campaign in northern China. The CCP turned from land distribution and rent reduction to outright confiscation and punishment. Pent-up anger against the wealthier members of village society led to outbreaks of violence and another blow to the traditional way of life.

Lin Biao, the great Communist general, restructured his forces in Manchuria into a conventional army that could fight the Nationalists toe-to-toe for control of the cities. In early 1947, he attacked Siping, midway between Harbin and Shenyang, with an immense army of 400,000. Nationalist troops supported by air power beat back the attack. Undiscouraged, Lin Biao launched assaults on the railroad corridors linking the cities held by the Nationalists. Morale in the Nationalist forces was already shaky. A high percentage of the Nationalist soldiers were southerners with little desire to fight on what they considered foreign soil. Numerous units were poorly trained, armed, fed, and the common soldiers treated brutally by arrogant officers. When Lin Biao's tactics threatened to isolate these already disheartened units, many of the soldiers quit the ranks and fled to the safety of the cities. They left behind large stocks of munitions that further strengthened Lin Biao's army.

Still, it was not military reversals but economic crisis that doomed the Nationalist war effort. Between September 1945 and February 1947 the Shanghai wholesale price index—a measure of the deteriorating value of the national currency, the *fabi*—rose from 100 to 3,000. Workers could no longer feed their families, and Shanghai alone experienced 1,716 strikes in 1946. Chiang pressed ahead with his military campaign while his economic advisors tried desperately to find the means to keep the economy functioning long enough for the Nationalist armies to achieve a decisive battlefield victory.

Chiang seemed incapable of understanding the people's mood or undertaking the reforms that even at this late date might have revived the Nationalist cause. While millions starved in a countryside ravaged by war, drought, and flood, China's ruling elite lived in luxury. The war against the Japanese had been patriotic, the people willing to rally behind nearly any leader so long as he fought the invaders. But the Communists roused no similar hatred among the rural folk. After nearly four decades of revolution, invasion, and civil war, the people wanted peace no matter what party claimed victory in this latest struggle.

Mother began experiencing serious health problems in the winter of 1946. She was troubled by ferocious headaches and suffered intensely. I finally convinced her to get treatment at the Protestant hospital in Xi'an. She stayed in Kwang-jen Hospital for several weeks, resting and receiving medication for high blood pressure. Wen-po sent money for her care, and I visited daily. Meanwhile, it was spring harvest season at home, and Wen-shuan and Wen-hui sorely missed her help running the household. But I refused to let her check out of the hospital. I argued with my brothers, holding my ground against both of them. Mother herself told me to delay her return so that she might be spared the hard work of harvest season. This was uncharacteristic of her, and I began to sense that she was far more tired and considerably more ill than I had originally imagined.

During her time in the hospital, missionaries spoke to Mother about Christianity. Mother was by nature a skeptic, but she was attracted to the idea that the Son of God would humble himself to walk among the people and then give his life as a sacrifice for the salvation of their souls. When she was released, she carried the message of Christianity back to Zhou-bian village and spread it among the village women. Over and over she recited the passage she had carefully committed to memory in the hospital: "For God so loved the world, that he gave his only begotten Son, that whosoever believeth in him should not perish, but have everlasting life" (John 3:16). Though her rendering of the story of Christ's sacrifice was at best unsophisticated, she held firmly to her belief in him for the rest of her life.

Wen-hui followed Wen-po to Manchuria in January 1947 to become an army quartermaster with the rank of second lieutenant. He had to find a wide variety of supplies, including Mongolian ponies. On the side, he was able to continue his private trading. He sent small sums to me to help pay my educational expenses. I would then take or send the balance home to help the family. My two oldest brothers enjoyed a special bond, and Wen-po was happy to see Wen-hui doing well. Wen-po brought Li Lin-fen and later his son, Xing-min, to Shenyang to live with him. That spring, Li Lin-fen gave birth to a daughter, Sher-yan. Wen-po visited the hospital wearing his new rank of brigadier general.

During the Lunar New Year's holidays of my last year in high school, I told Mother of my blossoming friendship with Du Chun-fang. With some hesitation, I revealed that we'd spoken of getting married once I was well on my way to a university degree and that I'd even been inspected by her parents and found acceptable. Mother was delighted with my news. Not that she didn't expect some say, perhaps even a veto, over my choice. I was, after all, hardly more than a boy in her eyes and her youngest and most precious child for my late birth and near asphyxiation at my father's hands. She quizzed me on my visit to the home of Chun-fang's parents in Xing-ping City. I had to admit that it had been something of an ambush. On our arrival, I'd found the entire family assembled: parents, grandparents, aunts, uncles, and cousins. I was subjected to a thorough, though polite examination. Apparently, I passed, because Chun-fang seemed very happy afterward. I asked her why she'd not given me warning of the ordeal beforehand. She smiled. "I was afraid that you'd prepare too much. You're much more charming when you're caught off guard." Whatever resentment I might have felt for the surprise melted in her teasing compliment and loving look. Mother laughed at the story and pressed me for an opportunity to inspect this girl who'd taken my heart. I put her off with the excuse that I needed to pass my university entrance exams before arranging a visit.

Though I couldn't have guessed it, this was the last time I'd celebrate the Lunar New Year in Zhou-bian village. As civil order broke down under the stress of the civil war, bandits once again roamed the countryside. Wen-shuan and I discussed the situation. He was determined to stay on in the village, farming our land, but we decided to move Mother, Ma Li-chun, and her small son, Min-sheng, to Xing-ping City. I found them a small house and we made the move before I returned to my studies in Xi'an.

An urgent telegram summoned me a few weeks later. I caught an evening train from Xi'an to Xing-ping City, arriving to find Min-sheng desperately ill. I hurried to the Xing-ping Health Center for something to cool his fever. Among Chinese folk unaccustomed to Western medicines even a few aspirin tablets could have a profound effect. But at midnight no one came to the door of the health center. I stood in the chill night, pounding again and again, but it was no use. By the time I returned home, Min-sheng was slipping away. He died before dawn. He had been a bright and lively child, a light of great promise in our lives in the dark days of the war. His loss devastated us all.

Mother refused to let Ma Li-chun inform Wen-hui in far-off Manchuria of his son's death. Rather, Mother, Ma Li-chun, and Sher-chen would journey to Manchuria to tell him the news. They would make a home for him and Pu-chao, Sher-chen's husband, who had recently been released from the army and had enrolled in the university at Shenyang. Ignorant of the true situation in Manchuria, I approved of the plan and wrote to Wen-po and Wen-hui. Wen-po was appalled. The war had turned against the Nationalists, and he couldn't have two women besides his own wife to worry about, especially when Mother was in her midsixties and nearly crippled by her twisted feet. He forbade the move. Sadly, I wrote Wen-hui the news of his son's death.

In May of 1947 I graduated from high school at the top of my class. I visited my family in Xing-ping City and Zhou-bian village, enjoying their welcome and praise. Du Chun-fang had graduated from the girls' high school in Xi'an and was soon to undertake her first teaching job. We were both very busy with our plans for the next few years, and again I ducked Mother's invitation to bring Chun-fang for an introductory visit. A friend and I took the train for Shanghai where we would take the college entrance examinations. The great city overwhelmed me with its size and activity, but I managed to do well on my exams despite the distractions. I was offered admittance to Chao-yang University Law School in Beijing. I bought a ticket on a coastal steamer and sailed for Tianjin, the port of Beijing.

I had no time to go home, so I wrote to Chun-fang, asking her to visit Mother on her own. No doubt she was somewhat intimidated on first meeting Mother, who was easily old enough to be her grandmother and possessed great force of personality. But Chun-fang had the charm and self-assurance to withstand Mother's scrutiny. Mother was immediately delighted in her. They became fast friends, enjoying each other's company despite their differences in age and education. In her days off from teaching in Xing-ping City, Chun-fang often visited Mother.

I settled in at Chao-yang University, anticipating a quiet year in which I could make a good start toward my law degree. The reality became quite the opposite. Wen-hui and Ma Li-chun had hatched a plot to bring her to Manchuria without Mother. One morning, Ma Li-chun announced that she was going to visit her parents. Instead, she boarded a train for Xi'an and then an airplane to Beijing. Shortly before her arrival, I received a telegram from Wen-hui, telling me to meet Ma Li-chun at the airport and take her to the railroad station where one of his subordinates would be waiting to accompany her to Shenyang. I was astounded at their audacity and wondered if they had somehow convinced Mother to remain behind. Before I could leave for the airport another telegram arrived, this one from Mother, ordering me to put Ma Li-chun on a plane back to Xi'an. Family discipline and maternal authority were to be obeyed and God help anyone who disagreed.

I was always anxious to help my mother or my adored older brother in anything possible. But I think I can be forgiven for feeling a little put upon as I stared at the two conflicting telegrams. Was I expected to thwart the reunion of a young couple that had recently lost a child? On the other hand, how could I disobey Mother? She had always been our rock, our support in every sense, our kind but firm general, judge, cheerleader, and guide. To go against her will was almost beyond my comprehension.

Yet I did. The next morning I put Ma Li-chun aboard the train for Shenyang in the company of Wen-hui's bashful subordinate. The journey would take them through territory actively disputed by Communist and Nationalist troops. In an ambush, Ma Li-chun could die. Or she might be taken off the train and held for ransom. But for all her risks, it was I who must face Mother's wrath. And wrathful she was. In her eyes, Wen-hui and I had violated all the traditional rules of respect and obedience owed a parent. Du Chun-fang wrote me of Mother's distress. For weeks she raged and wept, refusing to eat and unable to sleep. We thought we knew our mother well, but nothing prepared us for the extent of her anger, depression, and shame.

In January 1948, Wen-hui and Ma Li-chun went to the steelmaking city of Anshan to visit Wen-po, Li Lin-fen, their infant daughter, Sher-yan, and Xing-min, Wen-po's son from his marriage to Chong-er. As ill luck would have it, only a few days later Wen-po and his troops were transferred to Shenyang to help defend the capital from an imminent attack. The Communists attacked

Anshan instead. Wen-hui and his wife took refuge in a steel mill from the shelling. When the city fell, they tried to make it through the streets to a hospital where Li Lin-fen, Sher-yan, and Xing-min were hiding. Somewhere in the chaos reigning in the streets, Wen-hui and Ma Li-chun became separated. Eventually, Ma Li-chun made it to the hospital, but Wen-hui never arrived.

For several days they searched. Some friends said that he'd been taken prisoner; others said that they'd seen his body in the street. Finally, the women and Xing-min made their way out of the city and started the trek by foot to rejoin Wen-po in Shenyang, sixty hard and dangerous miles away. Sher-yan was only ten months old, and Xing-min carried her every step of the way on his back.

The mystery of what happened to Wen-hui became one of the most painful questions in my life. I revered Wen-po, whose authority over me was almost that of a father over a son. I respected Wen-shuan for his strength, competence, and quiet devotion to our family. But I adored Wen-hui with his sparkling eyes and ready laugh. Even as a young husband and father, he had always managed to find the cash for my school tuition. When the news of his disappearance reached me at the university in Beijing, I wept and prayed that he'd only been taken prisoner.

Wen-po sent Ma Li-chun, Xing-min, Sher-yan, and Li Lin-fen—who was about to have another baby—south by air to Beijing as the fighting in Manchuria worsened. When they unpacked at the apartment I'd found, they handed me fifteen small gold bars, the accumulated savings of Wen-po and Wen-hui. The joyous color and the buttery feel of the gold gave me no pleasure. Instead, I felt a great weight descending on me. Though I was hardly more than a boy, Wen-po had entrusted me in his absence with the well-being of his family and the wife of Wen-hui. The gold bespoke responsibility that I was far from sure I could carry.

My fearful first reaction must have shown in my face because a while later, when Li Lin-fen was busy changing the baby and Xing-min was reading a newspaper, Ma Li-chun pulled me aside. "Don't worry, brother-in-law," she whispered. "Li Lin-fen can look after her baby and the one she'll have soon. I'll do the cooking and housework. You do the thinking. We'll be fine."

I smiled gratefully at her. She was not a girl of quick intelligence, but she had a wonderful sympathy for others. "How about Xing-min?"

"He's a teenager. He'll eat and get in the way."

We laughed, causing Xing-min to look up from his newspaper. "All right," I said. "I'll do my best to think."

She tapped my forehead with a knuckle, as if sounding my head for hollow spots. "Wen-hui says you're the best of all the brothers at thinking. Don't worry about Li Lin-fen. She's a good girl. I like her very much, funny accent and all. She'll help."

Her reassurance helped chase away my fears, and I began to take pride in the trust Wen-po had placed in me. In the following days, I plied my nephew and sisters-in-law with questions about Wen-hui, but their reticence warned me that they might know or at least suspect more than they were willing to say for fear of upsetting Mother and me. I stopped asking questions, preferring to hope for the best.

Two weeks later Li Lin-fen gave birth to her second daughter, Sher-ping. We were all delighted. The apartment was now more crowded than ever, but we managed. Li Lin-fen was up frequently in the night, but she maintained her usual quiet good humor. Ma Li-chun, who had lost both her sons and more recently a husband, was a great help, although a couple of times I caught her weeping quietly while holding Sher-yan or Sher-ping in her arms. But she was a strong, country girl, and she dealt with her sadness by pitching into the heavy work with her usual energy.

I am proud that I managed as the head of the family in those months. Xing-min was a great help to me, always willing to run an errand or listen to my doubts. Ma Li-chun and Li Lin-fen were hardworking, cheerful, and uncomplaining. They were unfailingly courteous and helpful to each other, though the differences in dialects and backgrounds made it difficult for them to establish great intimacy. Li Lin-fen was a quiet, pretty girl, who had been orphaned young and raised by a great aunt. I had a good ear for dialects and soon learned to understand her heavy Yunnan accent. She was reticent by nature but talked readily enough to me. Her difficult childhood had given her a strong sense of self-preservation, and she was an ideal military wife. She loved Wen-po deeply but accepted that they must be parted for long periods. She would carry on in his absence, survive, and wait for his return and better times.

Not long after Sher-ping's birth, I received a disturbing letter from Du Chun-fang. Mother had lost her voice. A local doctor had examined her and noted a growth on her vocal cords. He prescribed traditional treatment, but no amount of herbal preparations seemed to help. Fortunately, I had Wen-po's and Wen-hui's savings. Knowing that they would agree to the expenditure, I immediately sent money to fly Mother to Beijing.

We put on our best clothes and happiest expressions to greet her at the arrival gate. We expected that she would be both ill and in a sore humor for the recent disrespect shown her authority by Ma Li-chun's journey to Manchuria. But Mother arrived in good humor. She had enjoyed her first airplane flight, particularly the sight of the miniature farmers and draft animals at work in the fields. She spoke in a rasping whisper, but otherwise seemed quite normal, if tired and showing her years. She assured Ma Li-chun that she'd entirely forgiven her daughter-in-law's disobedience, committed as it was out of love for Wen-hui. She welcomed Li Lin-fen to the family as another woman of equal status, thus releasing her new daughter-in-law from many of the traditional obligations imposed by mothers-in-law. She complimented Xing-min on his manly appearance and cooed over the newest additions to the family, Sher-yan and her newly arrived sister, Sher-ping. Then she took my arm and, leaning her weight on me, we set off into the great city of Beijing.

I had arranged for Mother to see Beijing's leading throat specialist, Dr. Liu Rui-hwa of Medical Union Hospital. I checked her into the French hospital, which was cheaper than Medical Union Hospital, and made her comfortable. When we were alone, she asked about Wen-hui. I lied, telling her that we had definite information that he was a prisoner. She seemed satisfied with this, and I told myself that I was justified in lying so that she could concentrate her energy on getting well.

Dr. Liu diagnosed Mother's condition as papilloma, a benign tumor of the throat membrane. Though benign, the tumor was growing, and he would operate as soon as possible. The first operation was a seeming success, but the general anesthetic was very frightening for her, and breathing, eating, and drinking were exceedingly painful for several days afterward. I lived at the hospital, serving as her nurse during my weeks of summer vacation from the university. I changed her sheets, bathed her, helped her get on a fresh gown, and combed her hair. She was a modest woman and much preferred my personal care to that of strangers. For me, it was a pleasure and an honor. I had no income to help pay for her treatment, but I could in this way show my gratitude and love. Few times in my life have I felt so personally gratified as I was in those weeks of service to my mother, my eldest two brothers, and their families.

Mother was in good spirits on her release from the hospital, her voice by no means recovered but much stronger. She teased me that her old lullabies would now more likely keep me awake than put me to sleep. I, of course, told her that she would be singing like a bird again in a matter of weeks. I took her on sightseeing trips about the city. She gazed in wonder at the Forbidden City, the Summer Palace, and the Temple of Heaven. She had, of course, heard of these monuments of China's imperial past, but until she saw them they had seemed but the settings of fairy stories. It still hurt her to talk much, and I had to divine her reactions from her changing expressions. But at the Forbidden City, she murmured: "And this was where the emperor lived?"

"Yes."

"And it was forbidden for common people to enter?"

"That's true."

"But we can enter now?"

"Into most of it, yes."

"My, my. Me just like an empress. My, my." She giggled.

She had a different reaction to the magnificent Temple of Heaven, built in the fifteenth century without the use of a single nail. She gazed for a long time at the startlingly blue roof. "It is the color I imagine Heaven to be. I suppose one day soon I will find out." Like every child hearing a parent speak so, I made light of her comment, but there was no doubt that Mother, for all her inexhaustible will, had begun to grapple with her mortality.

Unfortunately, Mother soon began to lose her voice again. Dr. Liu examined her and told us that the tumor was growing back. He would have to employ a different technique, paring away a portion of the growth every couple of weeks and then applying a careful dose of radiation. As many as a dozen repetitions of this procedure over an extended period would be necessary to eliminate the tumor entirely.

Until this conference, I had supposed that my time as de facto head of the household would last only a few weeks, that as soon as Mother was able, she, my sisters-in-law, and my nephew and nieces would go to Xing-ping City where living was cheaper and the war more distant. Now I realized that I would have to look after them for many weeks, perhaps months to come. I will admit that the restriction on my freedom and the interference with my studies occasionally made me glum and irritable. But I was a good Chinese boy and accepted the responsibilities thrust on me by tradition and difficult times. Painfully aware of my need to make the best possible bargain, I searched out and purchased a small house for us. Here, I hoped, we could ride out the coming storms.

Wen-po sent Mr. Chao Yi, a retired army sergeant, to help us. Chao Yi had been Wen-hui's confidant, helping him set up as an army contractor in Manchuria. He became a loyal friend to all of us during the months in Beijing. He was a calm, kind man, who had learned wisdom in the school of life. Whenever I needed to unburden myself, he was ready to listen.

By the spring of 1948, the Nationalist cause tottered on the edge of dissolution. Lin Biao's forces surrounded Shenyang and Changchun in Manchuria. In April, Marshal Zhu De, commanding all Communist forces, ordered his other brilliant deputy, General Peng Dehuai, to attack Luoyang in Henan province. The capture of the city severed Xi'an's railroad connection to the east. Peng moved against Kaifeng and the critical railroad junction at Zhengzhou where the main line east and west crossed the north-south line between Beijing and Wuhan. The Communists captured Kaifeng in June, withdrawing after a week in the face of heavy Nationalist reinforcements and air strikes. Nationalist losses numbered a shocking 90,000 and gave proof of the effectiveness of Communist forces in conventional fighting.

In July, Nationalist troops fired on student demonstrators in Beijing, killing fourteen and wounding more than a hundred. It was a sign of a government growing desperate. Inflation soared out of control. In the year between June

1947 and July 1948, the Shanghai consumer price index rose almost 10,000 percent. A bag of rice that cost 12 yuan in 1937 cost 63 million by August 1948. Such increases were insupportable, and the Chinese economy became a barter economy by the fall of 1948. That autumn Lin Biao conducted a brilliant campaign in Manchuria, routing the Nationalist army and capturing Shenyang and Changchun. Pu-chao, Sher-chen's husband, escaped by air to Beijing after the university in Shenyang closed. He stayed with us for a few weeks, hoping to resume his education in Beijing, but the Communists seemed victorious everywhere and he decided to go home to Sher-chen while travel was still possible.

The Nationalists suffered staggering losses in Manchuria. Of 400,000 Nationalist troops in the province, only 20,000 escaped. My brother Wen-po and his division were among them. Evacuated by ship, they landed in Shanghai to take new positions in defense of China's largest city. Wen-po was promoted to major general and assigned as deputy commander of the Second Division, Fifty-second Army Corps, one of the elite forces in the Nationalist army.

The military triumph of the Communists in the north put me in a difficult position politically. Like many of my fellow students, I no longer counted myself a loyalist to the Nationalist cause. I remained a firm believer in Dr. Sun Yat-sen's program of nationalism, democracy, and socialism, but those principles had long been subsumed within the Guomindang party by militarism, corruption, and rule by the gun. Nor was I by any means a Communist since I saw how strongly Marxist doctrine conflicted with much of the best in Chinese culture. I still hoped that a third force might emerge, led perhaps by Dr. Sun's widow, Soong Ching-ling, who had courageously represented her husband's program against the corruption of the Nationalist cause.

In a time of sweeping arrests and frequent executions, I determined that quiet neutrality was the only remotely safe course. To anyone who asked about my politics, I explained that I was too busy with my studies and caring for Mother to adopt any position. It was my intention to remain in Beijing with Mother as the new shape of China emerged from its difficult birthing. After all, I was a student-scholar dedicated to the mandarin ideal of service to China. As in all past dynastic transformations in China, the new regime, whatever its character, would need people like me to carry on the functions of government in peacetime.

A message from Wen-po abruptly ended my determination to remain in Beijing. I was to obtain transportation any way I could and bring the family south to Shanghai absolutely as soon as possible. I was appalled by the prospect. Mother was very ill, her second course of treatments only just begun by Dr. Liu. To move her would be to risk her life. Yet sending the rest of the family south while we remained in Beijing meant being cut off from them for years, perhaps forever. That loss in itself might deprive Mother of all desire to live.

If Mother had been healthy, I might have dodged responsibility by submitting the decision to her judgment. But that was not possible in these circumstances. Moreover, I had received orders from my eldest brother and was bound by tradition to obey. Although I was by now the most educated person my family had ever produced, a modern young man with an immodest opinion of his intellectual capacity, I was at heart still a village boy. Confucian tradition demanded obedience to an older brother; I must obey.

I told Xing-min and Mr. Chao Yi of Wen-po's orders. Chao Yi volunteered to stay behind to sell our house, rejoining us later in Shanghai. When I objected that it would be very dangerous to delay, he smiled. "I'm an old man. The Communists won't pay any attention to me."

Obtaining tickets for the journey proved very difficult. Communist troops were already probing Beijing's suburbs and a great battle might begin any day. Thousands of people were willing to pay nearly anything to escape. I had the gold bars from Wen-hui and Wen-po but how was I to negotiate a remotely fair price on the black market? Fortunately, a college friend came to my assistance. He was from Tianjin, the seaport servicing Beijing, and had friends on the Tianjin police force. Through them he was able to negotiate the purchase of four third-class tickets on one ship and two second-class tickets on another for the sea voyage to Shanghai.

We rode the train to Tianjin only days before the Communists broke the rail line, cutting Beijing off from the sea. We rented a room at the Harbor Hotel and waited until two of the policemen came with the tickets and received their payment. For several days longer we waited, watching from the window the turmoil on the docks as civilians fought to get aboard rusty ferries, and Nationalist soldiers wrestled precious guns and supplies onto leaky freighters. It was not yet total chaos, but panic lurked just below the surface, ready to break through once the Communists began shelling the port. Finally, our first ship arrived. I bundled Li Lin-fen, the two little girls, Ma Li-chun, and Xing-min aboard. I feared that at the last moment some ticket agent looking for a bribe might insist that the baby must have a ticket, but no one did.

For another week, Mother and I waited. Artillery boomed in the distance. Every morning on rising I expected to see the harbor empty of ships, disconsolate crowds on the docks searching the horizon in vain. At last our ship nudged into the pier. A hotel porter, whom I tipped generously, helped me get Mother aboard through the pushing crowds. A few people gave space when they saw the sick woman, but most were too frightened to notice her. At last we were aboard, taken by a kind crewman to our second-class cabin. We were exceedingly fortunate to have it. Every space on the small coastal steamer was soon crowded with families. Many had no food and were "starving their way to Shanghai," four or five long days away. Once the ship was under way, the corridors became fetid with vomit and human waste. Air hung hot, lifeless, and stinking. The toilets overflowed and drinking water had to be rationed. Trying to find some fresh air, I encountered the captain on one of the bridge wings. He was a heavyset, aging man who in his prime might have looked piratical but now seemed merely careworn and tired. I asked him how many passengers were aboard.

He shrugged. "Who knows? We lost count below second class. Four-fifths of the rest have forged tickets. Too damned many, that's certain. What I worry about is fire. Some old gal decides she's going to cook in some corner and catches a crate or a bale of something on fire. How could we get a hose through those packed passageways? There'd be a panic."

My mind settled peevishly on the matter of bogus tickets. "How do the owners make money if so many people ride with faked tickets?"

The captain snorted. "The bastards made enough money a long time ago. Now they're in Taiwan or Hawaii enjoying it. We won't go north again, and this time I took off as many people as I dared. Perhaps there will be a small reward for me in Heaven. The owners can rot in Hell." He lumbered off to look after his ship as we wallowed south toward Shanghai.

Our ship docked in Shanghai in the first week of December 1948. We were plucked from the crowd on the dock by a friend of mine from high school in Xi'an, now a university student, and taken by pedicab to a hotel where he had reserved a room for us. Mother was exhausted by the voyage and the press of the pierside crowd. While my friend sat discreetly near the door, I made her comfortable and encouraged her to nap until Wen-po and his family arrived. But she couldn't. I sat beside her, holding her hand. "How long has it been since we saw him in Xi'an?" she murmured.

"Ten years," I said. "Almost eleven."

"Ah," she said. "It feels like a hundred. I suppose he is much changed."

"Yes," I said. "I suppose he is."

"And I," she said, "I have become an old woman."

"Not so old, Mother. You've been ill and the voyage has been hard. You'll feel better and younger here."

She smiled, said a little dreamily, "Almost eleven years. My, my."

"I was only a little boy when we saw him in Xi'an."

She squeezed my hand. "You're still my little boy. Just a much taller one. Now help me up. I'll sit in a chair. I don't want him to see me lying in bed like some ancient crone."

I protested, but she insisted, and I helped her to her feet. At that moment we heard voices in the hall, followed by a firm knock on the door.

My friend opened it to reveal a short, muscular man with a close military haircut and a baby in the crook of an arm. Wen-po hesitated for the briefest of moments and then stepped inside, trailed by Xing-min and Li Lin-fen, carrying Sher-yen. Wen-po handed Sher-ping to Xing-min and then bowed deeply to Mother. "Dear Mother . . ." he said, his voice thick with emotion.

Mother held onto my arm, her face streaming with tears. I felt a shudder go through her, as of some long-tightened spring unwinding. After ten years and countless nights of worry and weeping, here she was with her firstborn son again, and he was safe, a great man, a general, but most of all safe. She let go of me, hobbled forward. He gently took her arm and guided her to a seat. He paused only for a moment to acknowledge me with a grave nod. "You have done well, Wen-wei. Welcome." He sat then beside her, started to talk softly, apologizing for all the years he had not seen her, for not letting her come to Manchuria because of the danger. She wept, told him of her worries, of how desperately she prayed that Wen-hui might still be alive, might yet come home to her. I sat a bit apart, stunned into silence in the presence of the man I remembered only with softened details, like a sepia photograph, but who sat now only a few feet from me, his reality stern in its very intensity: my beloved brother, the hero, the warrior, the man called "Tiger Chang."

The years had worked changes on us all. A decade of fighting the Japanese, opium smugglers, and Communists had turned Wen-po from a fresh-faced captain into a hard-bitten campaigner, used to the ways of command and terrible responsibility. Mother had changed from a vibrant, energetic woman in her midfifties to an old, deathly ill woman approaching seventy. Her eyes could still warm with deep love or snap with irritation, but illness, pain, and fatigue ruled her now. I had grown from an awkward village schoolboy into a young man of education, confident and perhaps even a little overproud of my achievements.

Every so often, Wen-po would glance my way, and I could feel him assessing this stranger who was his brother. Later we had a chance to talk alone while Mother rested. He thanked me again for managing the journey from Beijing.

"I'm sorry I could not greet you on the dock, but I have many responsibilities now."

I had been slightly miffed that he hadn't been there to greet us, but his apology mollified me. "I understand," I said. "Everything went well."

He smiled then and I could feel the magnetism that made men want to follow him. "You arranged the whole journey like a military operation. I could probably have you made an officer, once you've had a little training."

I smiled, shook my head. "No, I am going to be a civil servant of the people, perhaps a government minister. One of the men who tells men like you what to do."

He laughed. "Yes, but when did China last work so? The mandarins have passed into history."

"No, just changed their name."

"Ah, is that all?" he said dryly, and I caught a hint of the skeptical attitude all professional soldiers seem to have toward civil servants.

I became serious. "I truly believe Dr. Sun's teaching that to serve the people should be the goal of an educated man's life. That is what I work for, eldest brother."

"Yes, I know," he said. "I only hope these difficult times will give you the opportunity." Abruptly he changed the subject. "Tell me about Mother."

I laid out the details of Mother's medical condition and what lay before us as a family in support of her recovery. Much to my surprise, Wen-po insisted that I continue to manage the family's affairs. I was, he argued, far more familiar with Mother's condition and could supervise her treatment much better. Moreover, his duties often called him away for days at a time and distracted him with cares during the small time he could spend at home. He would lend me his advice, but for now, at least, I must remain as the functioning head of the family.

I was pleased with his confidence in me, though the task ahead seemed as overwhelming as getting the family from Beijing to Shanghai. I secured an apartment for the family and purchased a supply of wheat flour, rice, candles, and first aid materials. With those immediate necessities met, I set about getting Mother under the best possible medical care. To her great good fortune, Dr. Liu's former professor, Dr. Albert M. Dunlap, had a large practice in Shanghai. I sought him out with Dr. Liu's letter of introduction.

Dr. Dunlap had come to China many years before to teach and practice medicine. When I met him, he was in his late sixties, a gentle, courtly man with kind eyes. He put me immediately at my ease, asked about the health of his old friend Dr. Liu, and then listened as I explained Mother's condition. He asked a few questions, and then agreed to take her under his care. I had to explain that we had little money left by this time, but he waved a hand, assuring me that he wouldn't charge more than we could afford. I asked if he intended to remain in China if it appeared that the Communists were going to win.

He smiled, rather grimly I thought. "Oh, I expect they'll win soon enough. Chiang is scuttling off to Taiwan with as much loot as he can carry. It may take the sacrifice of your brother and the army's best soldiers, but Chiang will save himself and his cronies. But I'll stay to see how the Communists make out. It will be interesting."

Dr. Dunlap's comments came as a slap of reality to me. In recent months I had been so caught up in Mother's treatment and the challenge of getting the family to Shanghai that I'd had little time to evaluate the political future of China. The Communists were victorious in the north; would they carry the south with similar dispatch? Or did the Nationalists retain sufficient reserves of manpower, money, and will to resist successfully? The government-controlled press was little help, daily reporting or predicting immense victories that would turn the war into a Nationalist triumph: The great Generalissimo Chiang Kai-shek was executing a brilliant strategy worthy of Sun Tzu. Overconfident, the Communists were rushing ahead to a destruction as complete as the armies of Napoleon in the Russian snows or Hitler's legions at Stalingrad.

It was all nonsense, of course. But though Dr. Dunlap's comments brought home to me that even Shanghai must eventually fall, I still believed that Mother would have enough time to recover before that fearful day. As I walked back to our apartment, I felt relieved of a huge burden. Dr. Dunlap had agreed to take Mother as a patient, and no one in China, not even Dr. Liu, could give her better care.

Mother took to Dr. Dunlap immediately. She did not fear Westerners and had made friends with several of the Western staff during her hospitalization in Xi'an. She had long ago put aside the racial prejudices and superstitions of her rural upbringing in favor of a humanism that believed in the innate goodness in all people. That she had achieved this state of philosophical grace in the midst of so much suffering in her personal life and so much upheaval in her society was a stupendous achievement. Mother and Dr. Dunlap could not converse directly since she understood neither his English nor his passable Mandarin. But though they had to communicate through me or a nurse who spoke the Shaanxi dialect, they established a bond as two people of similar age who, for all their radical differences in education and circumstances, had both witnessed much of life's chaotic interplay between good and evil, courage and tragedy. They had become wise people and recognized each other as such.

Despite Mother's health problems, China's desperate plight, and our mourning for Wen-hui, the early months of 1949 were some of the happiest I'd ever known. We all lived in the apartment I'd bought, relishing the warmth of a loving family while much of the world outside crumbled. Mother seemed a little better. Wen-po and I got on wonderfully, often talking until dawn on the nights he could spare from his duties. The young women and children were safe and happy. Li Lin-fen looked after her little daughters. Ma Li-chun enjoyed cooking for the rest of us and doing the daily marketing in the company of Mr. Chao Yi, who had rejoined us after his own perilous journey south with the proceeds of the sale of our house in Beijing. Xing-min and I resumed our studies. I enrolled in the law college of Soochow University, happy to be preparing for the future even in this time of trouble.

Mother visited Dr. Dunlap's office every couple of weeks to have the tumor pared back a little more. He found that he could work on the tumor without administering a general anesthetic or giving her undue pain. She was delighted, bravely holding down her tongue with a depressor while he reached into her throat with his instruments. Following each of these procedures, she would spend a few days in the Shanghai Radium Hospital for radiation treatment.

We all followed the news as well as we could. In the early months of 1949, there was a brief revival of hope for a negotiated peace. Within days of our departure, Lin Biao's Communist army had forced the surrender of Tianjin. With the loss of Beijing in the offing, Chiang resigned as president, turning over the office to his vice president, the successful general Li Zongren. On January 31, the Nationalist commander in Beijing bowed to Lin Biao's overwhelming superiority and surrendered. Li Zongren opened negotiations with the Communist leadership. He hoped to find some compromise in the Communist demands, but his room to maneuver was severely limited by Chiang's continued presence as chairman of the Guomindang party. For two months, the sides exchanged messages but were unable to make progress. With all their preparations in place for an invasion of southern China, the Communists issued an ultimatum in April. Chiang refused to let Li accept and the war resumed, the Nationalist forces again under the direction of Chiang.

The Communist armies drove south, smashing all opposition. Thousands of Nationalist troops took ship from Shanghai for Taiwan, which Chiang was preparing as a final bastion of resistance. My brother's army corps was selected to cover the evacuation, a grim honor for some of the army's finest troops. Wen-po made his headquarters in a large concrete fort in the port suburb of Wu-song where the Yangtze enters the East China Sea. On April 23, the Communists captured the Nationalist capital at Nanjing, 170 miles west of Shanghai. On May 10 we heard fighting in the western suburbs of Shanghai.

Wen-po and I discussed the probable future. The Nationalist commander of Shanghai, General Tang Enbei, bragged that he would make Shanghai another Stalingrad, but Wen-po dismissed this as bluster. Shanghai would fall. If he survived the battle, he supposed he would be evacuated to Taiwan. He shook his head. "I shouldn't have remarried. Li Lin-fen is a fine wife and I love my two new daughters, but I am a soldier and this fight is far from finished. I thought it would be by now. I thought the Americans would stand by us and that we'd defeat the Communists. I never thought we'd end up chased like rats and have to scuttle off to Taiwan to save our miserable skins."

"Perhaps the Americans will help us soon."

He sighed. "Then why have they waited so long? If they had only used their big bombers on the Communists, sent their smaller planes to support our infantry, I think we could have won. I know my corps was never defeated."

"But why did the Americans abandon us?"

He shook his head. "Communists in their government? Too much corruption in ours? Just too much death in the last few years? I don't know. I do know that they don't respect the Generalissimo anymore."

We talked late into the night. Wen-po was reluctant to denounce any of his superiors, but he spoke with great bitterness about the Nationalist disaster. It was a soldier's perspective, short on economic and political factors and long on the failures of military strategy and American military support. At last we turned to the immediate problem of how our family would survive. Xing-min and I had already told him that we had no intention of leaving China, that we'd stay to care for Mother and to continue our education. I added that I had made a commitment to Du Chun-fang and intended to fulfill it.

Wen-po bowed to this decision but continued to ponder on how best to protect Li Lin-fen and his little girls, finally deciding that they would be safest with me. "The evacuation is going to be very dangerous, very chaotic. They will be in great danger throughout. I may not survive this battle, and then they will have no one to look after them in Taiwan. They will live in poverty, perhaps starve. Even if I do make it to Taiwan with my men, the Communists won't be long behind. They'll invade and Li Lin-fen and the girls will be at even greater risk. If we can't stop them at the beaches, there may be a slaughter like nothing we've had in all the bloody history of China."

"But suppose you do stop them at the beaches?" I asked.

"Then the war will go on. Perhaps we'll keep a toehold somewhere on the mainland, a place that we can use as a staging area for a campaign to recover the country. Or maybe we'll have to make an amphibious landing somewhere. But we'll come back. I will come back, even if it's to fight as a guerrilla in the mountains. And how will I care for my wife and daughters then? I see nothing to do but leave them with you until Mother is well. Then you can all go back to Zhou-bian village. It will be many years before there is fighting in Shaanxi again."

For a time we sat in thought. The village of our birth seemed very far away, life there, for all its poverty and labor, almost idyllic. I was not entirely happy with the great responsibility Wen-po's decision imposed on me, but it was entirely in keeping with traditional family ties. Our father had educated Wen-po in the Confucian principles, and Wen-po would remain a profound believer all his life. I had more education and a more skeptical nature, but I likewise accepted that I must put family obligation above any consideration for myself. Wen-po expected it of me, and I expected him to ask. I would, in fact, have seen it as a breach of tradition and mutual regard if he had not given me the responsibility. So my answer was short and unequivocal: "I will do my best, eldest brother."

The battle for Shanghai lasted two weeks. Wen-po's duties kept him at the defenses in Wu-song. Every couple of days his driver would come to our apartment to see if we needed anything. On one occasion, Mother insisted that I return with him to see if Wen-po was truly all right. With a loaded basket of his favorite Shaanxi food, I took my seat beside the nervous driver. The crash of artillery and the whine of warplanes grew louder as we neared the outskirts. I'd never felt so exposed in my life as we crossed the strip of open country separating Shanghai from Wu-song. Columns of smoke rose from burning buildings at a dozen points on the landward horizon. Out to sea a drifting haze of smoke and now and then a gray silhouette outlined a warship firing inland. We crossed under the guns of the Wu-song defenses, halting at a guard post where the driver hurriedly explained my identity. The guard waved us on, and a few minutes later we bumped to a stop in front of the bunker housing Wen-po's headquarters.

Coming in from the bright daylight, all seemed dim inside the bunker. Blinking to adjust my vision, I was taken aback by the number of prone figures sprawled about the room. The driver approached a trio of officers studying a wall map. Wen-po tilted his head to listen, then turned to stare at me with surprise and then anger. "You shouldn't have come!" he snapped. "It's dangerous here."

"I'm sorry," I said. "Mother insisted."

He brushed this aside. "Mother is an old village woman who doesn't understand these things. You should know better."

I hung my head. He steamed for a minute, and then turned to say something quietly to the two officers with him at the map. They nodded and went off to find corners to sleep. Wen-po led me to a table. "Well, let's see what's in the basket."

"It isn't much, but Mother worried you might not be eating properly."

"I'm not. But it's lack of time, not lack of food." He found a package of steamed rolls and began eating ravenously.

"Why are all these men asleep?" I ventured.

"We do our fighting at night. We sleep during the day if we sleep at all."

"Do you sleep?"

"Now and then. I don't need much." He seemed to make a tremendous effort, managed to turn his thoughts from duty. We talked for twenty minutes about family affairs before he wiped his fingers and rose. "I must be at my work. It's too late for you to go home tonight. Just stay out of the way and hope for the best."

With dusk, the sleeping men roused to eat a hurried supper. I sat unnoticed in a corner as most of the young officers hurried out to take command of positions about the defenses. Other men took seats along a bank of field telephones. I asked a man nearby about the phones and he explained that their lines stretched to the artillery batteries and infantry positions around the defenses. "Those three lines connect to the radio shack in another bunker. Radio gives us contact with the air force and navy." He spoke with obvious pride: "The Tiger designed our defenses in fields of interlocking support. Given enough reinforcements and ammunition, we could hold here for weeks against the whole Communist army."

There was indeed something almost feline about my brother's grace as he prowled behind the phone operators as the dusk deepened and the phones shrilled with increasing frequency. Just after full dark an artillery shell fell nearby, shaking the bunker. A half dozen more rounds followed. It seemed every phone was ringing. At the maps on the walls, men began marking impact areas and infantry probes. Our own artillery went into action. Through the seeming chaos of noise, my brother strode, his voice hard, commanding, but rarely louder than necessary. Several times he disappeared into the night to observe the fighting.

I sat in my corner, my feet drawn in so I wouldn't trip any of the hurrying men. Outside the night reverberated with war. I suppose I should have considered significances, taken the opportunity to reflect on the nearly forty years of war since the Revolution of 1911 and all the thousands of battles fought over the bleeding ground of my tragic country. But I was too awed, terrified, repelled, and fascinated by the immediate experience to do more than watch.

After interminable hours, dawn came, the firing easing gradually until there was only the occasional thump of a mortar in the distance. Wen-po accepted another cup of tea from a soldier who had all night scurried about with a steaming bucket. He issued a few more orders and then came to sit on a stool near me. His face was streaked with sweat, his eyes red-rimmed, but he seemed not so much exhausted as peacefully fatigued like an athlete after an intense contest. "And that, little brother, is a normal night for us. Nothing special, just artillery and infantry probes trying to determine how strong we are and if we're going to fight or crack when they hit us hard. They will do that soon." He stared at me for a long moment. "And you are not going to be here. It is a joy to see you, but your duty is with the family no matter what Mother says. Simply tell her that I forbid you coming here again. And don't let her send Xing-min in your place. She usually manages a way to get what she wants. But not in this. I forbid it."

"Yes, eldest brother."

He leaned over, rested a hand on my shoulder. "But I will remember the supper you brought me the rest of my days. Not what we ate, though it was a good change from army rations, but for the company I ate it in. Now have a cup of tea and whatever you can find for breakfast. Then my driver will take you back. It should be safe for some hours."

"You should sleep."

"Of course," he said. "When I have a moment."

On May 15, a truck pulled up to the apartment house, and a young officer hurried to our door. All wives and children of officers were being evacuated, he said breathlessly. Li Lin-fen had ten minutes to gather her children and belongings. I tried to interrupt to tell him that Wen-po and I had decided on a different plan. He shook his head. These orders came from the highest authority and could not be disobeyed. Li Lin-fen rushed about, managing to gather most of her meager possessions. She bid Mother a hurried farewell, giving her just time enough to caress the two little girls a final time. Weeping, Mother pressed a thin gold bracelet into Li Lin-fen's hand. Then the three of them were gone in the care of the young officer.

The brief peace we'd enjoyed in Shanghai had entirely vanished. Daily, the sound of guns grew closer. Classmates of mine who lived in the western suburbs slept in our living room. I went to visit Dr. Dunlap to learn if his plans had changed. He assured me that he would continue his practice in Shanghai as long as a Communist government allowed. In turn, I assured him that we also intended to stay in Shanghai. We parted, wishing each other luck in surviving the next few days.

At this point I don't think most of us appreciated how radically Communist rule would change China or how brutally Mao and his deputies would pursue that transformation. I believed that the Communists were Chinese patriots first, dedicated Marxist-Leninists a distant second. Though a Communist regime would no doubt banish the irretrievably corrupt Guomindang party, I expected that the Communists would otherwise allow a pluralistic political atmosphere. I would earn my degree and do what I could to help the new China find its way.

Equally important in my decision was Mother's health. She was making good progress in Dr. Dunlap's care, and he expected her to make a complete recovery and live many more years. I would remain by her side to make those years as happy as possible. Ma Li-chun had told me that she intended to return to her parents' home once we were back in Shaanxi. With the obligation of looking after my sisters-in-law and nieces lifted from my shoulders, I no longer thought Mother and I would return to Zhou-bian village. I would marry Du Chun-fang and together we would make a home for Mother in Xi'an or Xing-ping City. We would visit Wen-shuan and his family in Zhou-bian village often.

I believed Wen-shuan, as honest a man as ever lived, would do well under a Communist government: farming his land, providing for the good of his family, and contributing in his way to the good of all China. The Communists might believe in many radical things, but at least one Confucian principle endured: the respect for the peasant farmer as the most honorable of all China's folk.

Xing-min would also find his way. He had not been at home when the young officer came to evacuate Li Lin-fen and her daughters. But he would not have accepted evacuation since he shared my reasons for remaining with Mother and making a life in the new China.

On May 25, 1949, Shanghai fell to the revolution without the great battle we had all feared. The Nationalist troops had withdrawn from the city. The local pro-Communist underground surfaced to patrol the streets in cooperation with the municipal police. The population waited in a state of fearful curiosity. Xing-min and I went to the street to watch as the Communist troops marched into the city, their gaunt faces alight with triumph. It was hard not to be moved at the sight of the victory bought with so much blood and heroism.

Fighting continued in the eastern suburbs for another two days, eventually dying away. I believed my brother Wen-po was either safely on his way to Taiwan or in the hands of eternity. I could not imagine him surrendering. Friends visited our apartment, revealing themselves as underground Communists. They promised us that we had nothing to fear from the Communists though Wen-po had fought courageously for the Nationalist cause. I had been careful to maintain my political neutrality, and neighbors would observe that I had Communist friends as well as a Nationalist brother.

Mother's reaction to the Communist victory was typical of her fatalistic outlook. The mandate of Heaven had been withdrawn from the Nationalists and given into other hands, another example of the predestination that ultimately ruled the lives of human beings. She grieved for her lost sons, leaned even more on me, and accepted the latest turn of fate. I reassured her of my intention to continue at her side. Then I gathered my neglected books and began studying in anticipation of my return to the university; it was time for me to look to the future as a brave and independent adult.

But two days later a friend burst into our apartment, his face pale with terror. He leaned close to my ear and whispered fiercely. "Your brother Wen-po is hiding in my apartment. You must get him out. He puts my whole family in danger. The Communists will kill us all if they find him there!"

CHAPTER 8

The Tiger at Bay

IN GREAT AGITATION, I FOLLOWED my friend through the streets to his apartment. I'd come to know Du Ru-min when we were law students at Chao-yang University in Beijing in 1947. We had become reacquainted in Shanghai where, despite his youth, he'd become a judge of the district court. When he'd visited our apartment one day, I'd introduced him to Wen-po. Du Ru-min had expressed appreciation for my brother's service in the Nationalist cause and had spoken eloquently over supper about the need to preserve Dr. Sun's vision in this time of great difficulty. But there was none of the confidence of that day remaining in him now. He was terrified and so was I.

Communist soldiers strolled the streets and stood post on every corner. Most were young men from rural China who still looked a bit dazed by the immensity of the great city and the sudden absence of fighting to do. All but a few of them were unarmed, an intelligent policy imposed by the Communist commanders. Nationalist soldiers had looted during their withdrawal to the ships, but these young soldiers of the People's Liberation Army seemed almost passive, more bemused than triumphant at having Shanghai helpless at their feet. We were much more afraid of civilian spies and informers. Everyone we passed on the street from children to aged grandmothers might report a suspicion to the authorities. Our danger extended far beyond our personal safety. Since the days of the ancient emperors, the authorities in China had maintained order by punishing not only offenders but entire families. There was no reason to expect the Communists to behave differently.

At his apartment door, Du Ru-min knocked lightly. His young wife opened it, her eyes wide with fear, a sleeping baby in her arms. Du Ru-min patted her arm. "Make tea. Everything will be all right." She scuttled away to the tiny kitchen.

Wen-po stood up slowly from a dim corner, his shoulders relaxing as he saw me. He wore filthy peasant's clothing, the lower left leg spattered with dried blood. His bloodshot eyes stared from sockets deeply sunken with fatigue. But he managed a rueful smile. "Hello, little brother. The ship left without me and now the Communists will want to kill me."

I hesitated momentarily and then went to him. I bowed as custom demanded and we embraced. "They cannot kill you," I said. "You are Tiger Chang."

He chuckled softly. "Even tigers die. I have killed many Communists, and they will want me badly. But I don't intend to make it easy for them. Come, we must talk. Du Ru-min has risked a great deal hiding me, and I should leave as soon as I can."

The three of us sat. I asked about the blood on his leg. He shrugged. "The former owner had worse luck than I did and had no more need of his pants. Another unfortunate man had no use for his shirt." He said this casually with the practiced demeanor of one who has seen much violent death. But I knew my brother well enough to detect the exhaustion in his voice. To the best of my recollection this is the story he told us:

"For two days after the Communists took the city, our corps fought to hold Wu-song. The shelling was terrible, the Communists throwing everything they had at the port. Ships burned and sank, and the harbor was strewn with floating corpses. On the second night [May 26], our corps finally started going aboard transports. By daylight yesterday, only our division and part of another were still ashore. All day the shelling kept the transports away. By then the men were so tired that we had to scream and shake them. At dusk, several divisions of Communist infantry attacked. We got some fire support from warships but still we had to beat back two human wave attacks.

"Finally, General Liu received orders to take the division off. I stayed back in charge of the rear guard, the last of the last. We fought off attacks until after midnight when I saw we couldn't hold much longer. I left the front line then to see if a ship was alongside the pier to take us off. One was, and I hurried back, meeting the first of my companies withdrawing. The men were still all right, exhausted but not panicky. I left my officers to get them on board and went on to the front to make sure every last man had gotten the order to retreat. The lines were deserted, and I saw that it wouldn't take the Communists long to realize we'd retreated. At best we had half an hour. I hurried back to the ship and went on board to speak to General Liu. Then I returned to the pier to get the last of my men embarked. A few sailors were still on the pier directing the boarding. I suggested to their officer that he should take them on board since there didn't seem much more anyone could do. Just then shells hit the ship two or three times in quick succession. The sailors cast off the lines, and I ran for the gangway, but the concussion of another shell lifted me off my feet. I landed in the water between the ship and the pier, and I thought for a moment I would be crushed. I swam under the pier and then down to the end through bodies, oil, garbage, and shit. A couple of civilian stevedores pulled me out. After no sleep in three days, even that short swim exhausted me. They pushed me under the cover of a truck where I lay barely conscious. By the time I dragged myself out, the ship was just a silhouette against the fires on the far shore. I could do nothing but watch it steam down the channel, and it seemed to me for a moment like that ship was the Nationalist cause and I was all China abandoned to the darkness."

My brother was not a poet but a warrior. Yet his last words touched our hearts. For a few minutes, the three of us wept for the loss of Dr. Sun's dream, a destruction engineered by so many events, causes, and personalities that nowhere could you find an entirely satisfactory explanation. But lost it was.

Wen-po went on in a tired voice. "I knew I couldn't go to our apartment. Too many of the neighbors had seen me in uniform with my jeep and bodyguards. I thought of Du Ru-min and decided to risk coming here since I knew he was a true Nationalist and a brave man." He glanced at Du Ru-min to catch his expression.

Du Ru-min stared at his fine judge's hands, so unused to the hard work of farming or war. "I am a patriot and care not so much for my own life. But I must protect my family."

"Of course," Wen-po said. "I am eternally in your debt. Now that Wen-wei is here, we will find another place for me to hide until I can rejoin the army."

I asked Du Ru-min for a few minutes alone with Wen-po. He understood that I was trying to save him from knowing too much. By the time Du Ru-min came back with tea, we had discussed the only plan I could think of. It would take some hours to make arrangements, and Du Ru-min agreed to hide Wen-po until night. At the door, Wen-po stopped me. I think he was nearly overwhelmed by emotion but embarrassed to show it. Whatever he had to say, he decided against it, saying only, "I'm sure General Liu didn't mean to leave me behind. Never think that of him. He must have thought I'd gotten aboard."

My education had taught me to organize my thoughts in a logical manner, but my fear almost overwhelmed my reason as I made my way through the streets to our apartment. First, I must tell Mother of Wen-po's danger. I worried that in her naiveté she might think that he could simply quit being a soldier and settle down with us until her treatments were over and we could all go home. A small part of me wondered if that were indeed a possibility. Wen-po was a true patriot who put China before any ideology. Perhaps the Communists would pardon him, accepting his services as a soldier or a humble farmer. But that was a foolish idea. The Fifty-second Corps had killed so many Communists in Manchuria that the enemy general Lin Biao had circulated pictures of the ranking officers with special instructions to kill or capture them at all costs. At the very least, the Communists would imprison Wen-po for many years.

To my surprise, Mother took the news of Wen-po's danger extremely well. In the months she had been so desperately ill, I'd come to think of her as completely dependent on me. She was a countrywoman, neither educated nor much interested in the ways of big cities and the wider world. She did not speak Mandarin, English, or any of the Shanghai dialects, so it fell to me to interpret her answers to the doctors' questions and to explain their orders to her. The treatments had made her very weak, and she required an arm to lean on with every step on her poor feet. But I had forgotten that a warrior's mother must herself be a warrior at heart. Though greatly worn by her illness, Mother summoned her strength to face this crisis as she had all the crises in the years we were entirely dependent on her. She brushed away my concerns for her, insisting I must not worry about her until Wen-po was safe from those who would do him harm. She fixed me with a fierce look that might indeed have come from a mother tiger sensing danger to a cub. I would, she informed me, find a way to arrange his escape because I was the smartest of her children just as Wen-po was the bravest. The time had come for me to turn all I'd learned at school to a practical task.

I suppose I could have told her that little I'd learned in school applied in this matter and that Wen-hui's street smarts would have been far more appropriate to the situation. But Mother's command allowed for no excuses. I explained without great enthusiasm the only plan I'd been able to concoct. She agreed to it instantly, and I called the Shanghai Radium Hospital to see if she could be readmitted now that the fighting seemed to be over. Though all the city's hospitals were swamped with wounded, Dr. Wu, president of the hospital, granted permission.

I decided not to tell Ma Li-chun of Wen-po's danger for the time being. She was a good-hearted girl but unsophisticated and not good at hiding her emotions. In this crisis, the less she knew the better. Nor would I tell Mr. Chao Yi, who had already taken far too many risks for our family. When Xing-min came home a short while later, I drew him aside and told him that his father was hiding in the city. He turned pale and had to sit down. I waited apprehensively for him to recover, not sure if I'd done the right thing in telling him. He looked up with tears in his eyes. "We have to save him. What can we do?"

"I told Dr. Wu that Mother wants to go back to the hospital now that the fighting's over. Once she's checked in, Wen-po can hide in her room. We'll tell Dr. Wu and the nurses that he's Wen-shuan come to visit from the country."

We discussed the plan for half an hour, unable to improve on it though we agreed that it was very dangerous. That evening we hired a pair of pedicabs.

Xing-min took Mother to the hospital in the first while I detoured by Du Ru-min's apartment to pick up Wen-po. The streets were crowded for the first time since the fall of the city, the weather warm and the people beginning to emerge from their homes to enjoy the fresh air after the danger of recent weeks. To me everything about Wen-po's short hair, appearance, and manner spoke of a soldier's identity, but we passed through the streets without incident. At the hospital, a nurse settled Mother in bed. Wen-po eased quietly into a corner, the dutiful son watching at the bedside of a gravely ill parent.

When Dr. Wu came into the room the next morning he was startled to find Wen-po with us. "What are you doing here?" he blurted. "I thought you'd gone to Taiwan with the rest of the army."

I spoke up hastily. "This isn't Wen-po, Doctor. This is our brother from home, Wen-shuan. They do look very much alike, don't they?"

The good doctor hesitated a long moment. "Yes, very much. . . . So how is your mother feeling this morning?" He started asking questions while I interpreted and Wen-po did his best to fade from attention.

For a week Wen-po stayed in Mother's room. Dr. Wu didn't question him again though I'm sure he knew the truth. The doctor was an overseas Chinese who had returned to China at the beginning of the war against the Japanese. He could have left many times, but he was a dedicated patriot, a kind man, and—fortunately for us—a sympathizer with the Nationalist cause.

Outside, in the streets of Shanghai, the Communists were pursuing their enemies with greater vindictiveness each passing day. They rousted many Nationalist officers and officials from hiding and arrested hundreds of members of the underworld Green Gang. The *Liberation Daily* published long lists of the enemies of the revolution executed by firing squad. Articles warned against collaboration and gave directions on how to spot fugitives.

Finally, Dr. Wu came to me, a copy of the latest *Liberation Daily* conspicuously under his arm. "The Communists will soon search the hospital. I think it would be better if your brother from home found a new place to stay. He does look very much like your army brother, and we wouldn't want to see any unfortunate mistake." His lips twitched into a wry smile.

I was quick to agree. "The trains will be running soon. He needs to get home to tend our land."

"Yes. . . . Well, better sooner than later, I think."

I had no very good plan on where to hide Wen-po next. I went to Dr. Dunlap, hoping that Wen-po could hide in the doctor's spacious home. The doctor led me outside into the garden and smoked his pipe quietly as I told him our predicament. When I was done, he sighed. "Chang, I wish I could help, but the Communists are watching all foreigners. I employ a cook, a gardener, and a chauffeur, and any one of them might be in their pay. I have all my patients to think about. I can't let one healthy man imperil them no matter what his danger."

I'm afraid that I didn't believe Dr. Dunlap's excuse that the Communists were watching him. Westerners had lived for generations in Shanghai, nearly oblivious to China's laws and police. The Western allies had abandoned the hated policy of extraterritoriality during World War II as a concession to the Chinese war effort. But most of us still harbored a belief that Westerners were somehow above the law. Not long after, I learned that the Communists were indeed keeping the residences of all foreigners under constant surveillance. Wen-po probably owed his life to Dr. Dunlap's gentle refusal that night.

I turned next to the secret societies. Every city in China—and Shanghai in more proliferation than any other—had secret societies called *tongs*. Some *tongs*—like the famous Green Gang—were underworld organizations similar to the Mafia. Others were benevolent associations based on dialect and more akin to the Masons than the Mafia. Emigrants and travelers to the big city sought out *tong*-owned inns for social companionship and business contacts. In these inns, a man's affairs were usually his own.

I ventured into central Shanghai to find such an inn. I was eventually directed to one where the owner and patrons spoke the dialect of my native Shaanxi province. When I first walked in, suspicious faces turned my way. But the moment I started speaking the Shaanxi dialect, everyone relaxed and I was cordially greeted. Though I considered myself quite a cosmopolitan young man by then, I welcomed the sound of the dialect spoken in my distant corner of China.

I arranged a room for my brother and that night brought him from the hospital. For the next six weeks he lived at the inn under the guise of being a business traveler stranded by the interruption in train service. I'm not sure how much his assumed identity was believed. My brother knew nothing of commerce and might have unwittingly revealed his true profession any number of times, but no one went out of his way to question him. All this changed when a Communist officer from Shaanxi took a room. Sensing an agreeable companion, he took a seat opposite my brother at mealtime and tried to engage him in conversation. My brother gave short, simple answers, but the Communist officer continued to seek his company in the succeeding days. Wen-po was not a natural conspirator but a forthright military man. Try though he might, the Communist officer intrigued him, and he probably talked too much and asked too many questions. Several days later I shared a meal with Wen-po and the officer. Though Wen-po seemed oblivious to such things, I thought I spotted an untoward curiosity in the officer, as if he had begun to suspect that Wen-po was not what he seemed. I left the inn deeply shaken. Somehow I must get my brother out of the city before his own natural honesty became his downfall.

We had long since rejected any idea of Wen-po trying to reach Nationalist territory in the south by a direct route. He spoke none of the dialects spoken in the coastal provinces between Shanghai and the Nationalist stronghold at Xiamen (Amoy) and would almost certainly be apprehended. Fortunately, the rail connection most of the way to Xi'an reopened about this time. With Wen-po's permission I'd told Mr. Chao Yi of his presence in Shanghai. He smiled. "I thought you and young Xing-min were sneaking about quite a lot. How can I help?"

I was greatly relieved when Mr. Chao Yi joined our plans. He had traveled much on the roads and railroads of China and could help Wen-po maintain his businessman's disguise along a route where it would be natural to speak the Shaanxi dialect. I bought tickets for them to Xi'an and another for myself as far as Nanjing. I went next to a luggage shop where I bought Wen-po a light suitcase and a small sample case. I'd already, at considerable cost, purchased several boxes of penicillin through a nurse at the Shanghai Radium Hospital. Penicillin was both light and precious, a commodity that Wen-po, for all his inexperience in commerce, might trade for cash or use as a bribe. I now faced the problem of forging a set of travel documents for him. I went in search of someone able to make a copy of the seal of the Shaanxi ministry of commerce.

Even before the Communist occupation of the city, I'd assiduously courted the friendship of our neighbors and the craftsmen plying their trades along our street. It was impossible for us to hide our connection with Wen-po and the Nationalists, but we could appear friendly and nonpolitical. Among the people I greeted daily was a wood carver. He was a cheerful young man who, despite his evident poverty, seemed to have a kind word for everyone. Now I engaged him in deeper conversation, finally mentioning that I knew a rich salesman who had lost his travel documents and was afraid to go to the Communist authorities for new ones.

The carver nodded sympathetically. "They'd suspect he's up to something."

"Yes, but all he really wants to do is get back to his wife and family in Xi'an."

"It's a pity he lost his documents. It may take him a very long time."

"In these times, you could hardly blame him for trying to have a new set made privately."

"No, but it would be very dangerous."

"He's a rich man. He'd offer a great deal of money."

The carver hesitated. "Still, I doubt if anyone would take the risk for even half a tael of gold."

"Oh, but he's willing to pay a full tael."

I could see the light of greed flicker in his expression. "What would a man have to do for such a great sum?"

"Duplicate the seal."

"One would need a copy."

"I have a copy."

For a long moment he meditated. "And after all, since he is honest as well as rich, what harm is there? Let me see the copy."

I slipped Mr. Chao Yi's documents from my pocket to show him the imprint of the seal. "Could you perhaps carve a seal?"

"Yes," he said, quickly pocketing the document. "I'll bring it to you in the morning."

He was as good as his word, delivering a perfect carving of the seal the next morning. He accepted the tael of gold from me with expressions of gratitude and left the apartment. I hid the seal and went to check Mother out of the hospital. She was very weak from a recent treatment but frantic to see Wen-po a final time. I'd briefly thought of taking him to her room late at night, but the risk was too great now that several Communist nurses and aides had begun to work on Mother's floor.

That evening Xing-min and I carefully printed a set of travel documents for Wen-po. He arrived at our apartment at 1:00 a.m. to say good-bye to Mother, Xing-min, and Ma Li-chun, whom we had told of his presence in Shanghai just that day. There is really not much to recount of the farewell since it was filled with tears and heartache rather than words. After embracing Mother, Wen-po stepped to Ma Li-chun, bowed formally, and thanked her for her faithfulness to Wen-hui and the family. "Wen-hui is gone, sister-in-law; you must remarry if the chance comes."

She nodded somberly and wished him well.

He turned to Xing-min, accepted his bow of respect, and took the travel papers. He examined them. "Thank you," he said. "I am very grateful."

"You're welcome, Father," Xing-min mumbled.

For a long moment they stood awkwardly. "Come sit with me," Wen-po said. He went to the bed where Mother lay, took her hand, and after a moment, took his son's hand as well. I joined them and, for the next three hours, we sat together, all dozing at one time or another. At dawn, Wen-po rose, embraced Mother and Xing-min, and walked from the apartment. Mr. Chao Yi and I made quick farewells and followed.

In the street, we set off for the train station. "Walk like a salesman, not a soldier," I hissed. "Behave like you spent your last night in the big city drinking and whoring." He snorted, but adjusted his shoulders and gait.

The train trip to Nanjing was surprisingly pleasant. Good spirits abounded among the passengers, many of whom were returning home after long separation from their families. The guards and officials were relaxed and gave our papers only a cursory look. We feared, of course, that the pictures of the Fifty-second Corps's ranking officers might still be in circulation, but we saw no evidence of this.

For all my coaching, Wen-po still carried himself like a soldier, but at least his hair was longer now and worn in the style of a businessman. Fortunately, he'd had a facial disfigurement corrected during his early months in Shanghai. From birth, the right side of his chin had been distorted by a noticeable indentation, a mar on his otherwise handsome features and the cause of a good deal of rough teasing and the nickname "Mr. Twisted Chin." Taking advantage of the slack period following the transfer of his division to Shanghai, he had visited Dr. Dunlap, who had sent him to Dr. Ni, the dean of the medical school of St. John's University in the city. Dr. Ni removed a small piece of one of Wen-po's ribs and fitted it to the indentation. The surgery left a barely noticeable scar and changed Wen-po's appearance quite dramatically. Over and over on the train trip to Nanjing, I told myself that he was no longer recognizable as the Tiger Chang of old who had killed so many Communists in Manchuria.

We arrived in Nanjing in late morning. I bought two tickets for the ferry across the Yangtze. We kept our farewells formal, aware that anything emotional might draw unwanted notice. I watched until the ferry carrying Wen-po and Mr. Chao Yi reached midstream, waved, and turned back for the walk to the train station. Dangers aplenty lay before Wen-po, but I was immensely relieved to see him out of Shanghai and on his way. The journey would in all likelihood take my beloved brother forever from my life, a realization that brought tears to my eyes for all my efforts at self-control. I wept for a few minutes in the shadow of an alley. Then, telling myself that a brother of Tiger Chang and a son of Chang Wei-sze must comport himself with dignity and a warrior's heart, I set off again for the train station and my return to Shanghai.

Over the years I pieced together the story of Wen-po's journey. Before the Communist invasion of central China, the trip from Shanghai to Xi'an took two days and two nights by train. But it took Wen-po and Mr. Chao Yi two weeks by train, horseback, and foot to reach Xi'an. Several times they were stopped and questioned closely, but their travel documents and explanations held up under scrutiny.

The local Communist underground had emerged to take command of Xi'an. Mr. Lee Shiao-feng, an old friend of Wen-po's, hid him for several days. Mr. Chao Yi continued to his home in Xing-ping City, rested for a day, and then went to Zhou-bian village to inform Wen-shuan that his brother was a fugitive. The brothers met outside Xi'an at a landmark they both knew. The meeting was very emotional after their many years apart. Wen-shuan was under the impression that he was welcoming Wen-po home for good. But Wen-po told him that he dared not enter the village where many would recognize him despite his years away. Wen-shuan tried to persuade him that the villagers would welcome and hide him, but Wen-po refused.

Wen-shuan had always been an innocent, an unsophisticated farmer who remained convinced of the intrinsic goodness of village people and the eternal wisdom of China's traditional rural way of life. Wen-po could come home, could take up the life of farming he had left so long ago. Wen-shuan claimed no preeminent title to the family land in exchange for all his hard work. Our ancestral land belonged to the entire family with him but the latest custodian of that precious inheritance. The wheel of fortune had hit some bumps, had slued from rut to rut as Heaven determined who would next hold the mandate to rule the Middle Kingdom. But none of this altered the eternal verity of the wheel itself. Wen-po need only take up the good life again and all would be well. I can liken Wen-shuan's attitude to nothing except a profound religious faith, so deeply held that he was never plagued by question or doubt. It was an attitude held through scores of generations in China and remained the basis of existence for Wen-shuan and hundreds of millions of rural Chinese. Wen-po was not immune to its temptations, but he knew the Communists and his own danger far too well to agree to Wen-shuan's plan.

They camped near the road that night, sitting close in the dark, the early summer redolent and singing with the life around them. Wen-shuan renewed his passionate entreaties: "I beg you, eldest brother. Don't leave us."

"I must go, younger brother," Wen-po said. "I am a soldier."

"You have fought your battles."

"Yes, and too well. They will kill me if they find me."

"The village will protect you. All this madness will pass."

"No, I don't think so. I must go."

The next evening they arrived unannounced at the home of Mr. Chang Feng-li, Wen-po's friend who had been our family's savior in the great famine. Chang Feng-li was, of course, shocked when Wen-po stepped from the dark, but he recovered with the grace of an old-fashioned host. "Are you hungry, my friend?" he asked.

"Yes, very hungry," Wen-po said, "though I do not want to trouble you."

"Then you are not a ghost; otherwise, you would not care about food and would want to cause me trouble. Come in, old friends."

Again Mr. Chang Feng-li had come to our family's aid. He fed the two travelers and gave Wen-po a bed. Wen-shuan returned to the village to gather food for the journey and to tell Chang Sun-sze of his dangerous errand. She was more sophisticated than her husband, assuring him that Wen-po was correct in continuing his flight. Chang Sun-sze went to see Wen-po's daughter Sher-chen and our sisters Chu-yeh and Ling-yeh, arranging for them to meet Wen-po and Wen-shuan at a roadside temple on the route to Nationalist territory.

But the next afternoon, just as Wen-po and Wen-shuan were about to leave Chang Feng-li's, a young Communist from a nearby village happened by the house. Liu Kuan-ying had gone to elementary school in Xing-ping City with me, and he recognized Wen-shuan. He guessed that Wen-po was another brother from their close resemblance. He knew Wen-po's reputation and was immediately suspicious, surmising that this hard man might be one and the same. He waited for Wen-shuan to introduce his traveling companion, but poor Wen-shuan was an even worse actor than Wen-po. Liu Kuan-ying demanded to know if this was not the famous Chang brother who had risen high in the Nationalist army. Wen-shuan denied it, introducing Wen-po as a cousin who bore a pronounced family resemblance. Chang Feng-li confirmed this explanation, but Liu Kuan-ying did not believe them. Still, he was facing three strong and perhaps desperate men, and he chose not to press his doubts. Leaving them, he hurried to tell his local party cadre of the strangely familiar man traveling with the farmer Chang Wen-shuan. Alarmed by the encounter, Wen-po and Wen-shuan hurriedly departed Chang Feng-li's house, taking a different road than the easier track past the temple where Sher-chen, Chu-yeh, and Ling-yeh waited only to be disappointed.

Fortunately, the local cadre did not put enough credit in Liu Kuan-ying's report to order a pursuit. After five more days of travel, Wen-po and Wen-shuan reached the treacherous borderland where neither Communists nor Nationalists held sway but only bandits and wolves. Several times in their journey, Wen-shuan had become so overcome with emotion that he'd sat by the road weeping until Wen-po managed to urge him onward with gentle words. At the time of parting, Wen-shuan again begged Wen-po to return home to Zhou-bian village, to trust in the traditional loyalty and decency of the village folk. But Wen-po had to tell him no. They embraced then, the soldier and the farmer seeking to clutch the other in remembrance for all time. Wen-po broke the grasp at last and hurried off down the narrow track into no-man's-land, leaving Wen-shuan weeping on the hill.

For several more days, Wen-po made his way toward Nationalist territory in far southwestern Shaanxi. Nearing his goal late one evening, he was wading a stream when a guerrilla rose up from the bushes on the far side and leveled a rifle at his chest. Wen-po raised his face to stare back and suddenly the man started to laugh. "Uncle Wen-po! What are you doing here?"

By the most incredible good fortune, the guerrilla was from our village and clan. Chang Jian-yuan led Wen-po to camp where the commander, too, recognized Zhou-bian village's famous soldier. Mr. Wang Tse-yee and Wen-po had served in the regional defense force before the war with the Japanese.

He welcomed Wen-po heartily, fed him, and gave him fresh clothes. Within hours, word was passed by runner and radio to General Hu Zong-nan's headquarters and relayed to the Nationalist high command in Taiwan that Tiger Chang had emerged from the wilderness to fight again. Two days later he was on a plane bound for Taiwan.

In Shanghai, Mother worried about all her widely dispersed family. She had been relieved to hear that Wen-po had made it successfully to Nanjing and the Yangtze ferry. But when weeks passed with no news from Xi'an or Zhou-bian village, she began to worry anew. I tried to distract her with a discussion of my relationship with Du Chun-fang, which had been too long on an informal basis. She agreed with me, and I wrote to Wen-shuan, requesting that he make a formal engagement for me to marry Du Chun-fang. Wen-shuan was happy to accomplish this in Mother's name, counting himself greatly honored to assume such a responsibility in the absence of parents or older brothers.

With Mother's health improving, I traveled to Shaanxi in August 1949. The railroad was still in pieces, requiring the traveler to walk or ride horseback for long stretches. The countryside was quiet, the cities calm, but everyone still seemed on edge, not quite trusting peace after so many years of war. It took me ten days to reach Xi'an. I visited Mr. Lee Shiao-feng, who related to me what he'd learned from Wen-po during the days my brother had hidden with him. I thanked him effusively for his kindness and the risks he'd taken helping Wen-po.

I rode with a former schoolmate, Li Wei-chong, on the train to Xing-ping City. We arrived in the evening, and I asked him to walk with me to the home of Du Chun-fang's parents. At their gate, I waited while Wei-chong went inside. He found Chun-fang at her loom and told her I was outside. She refused to believe him, told him he was a tease and a flirt who only wanted to get her outside so that they might stroll in the pleasant evening. From the street I could hear their conversation and, unable to restrain myself, I entered. Chun-fang let out a cry, almost as if she'd seen a ghost. The cry was followed by tears of happiness. I stayed that night in her home. Her parents treated me royally, and Chun-fang and I talked late into the night about our marriage and future together.

The next morning I visited Mr. Chao Yi to thank him for all his kindnesses toward our family. I then set out on foot for Zhou-bian village, my heart joyful and my step light. I hadn't been home in nearly three years, and I had to stop several times to speak with friends and neighbors I met on the road. As a result, news of my coming reached the village a good hour before I arrived. Wen-shuan, Chang Sun-sze, Sher-chen, and several cousins greeted me. All my family members were affected, Wen-shuan the most deeply of all. Though a man of few words, his emotions ran deep.

Throughout the afternoon and evening, my sister-in-law Chang Sun-sze acted as hostess to the neighbors and friends calling at our family compound. She kept the mood light, several times whispering to Wen-shuan that this should be a time of joyous celebration, not weeping. Wen-shuan tried to comply, but his tears continued to fall. It was obvious to me that he had been under much greater strain than I'd suspected. He was a simple man, caring nothing about politics or matters of the intellect, but only about the land and his family. Haunted by worries about Mother and the rest of us, confused by the great changes threatening the traditional way of life in China, poor Wen-shuan had been taxed almost to the breaking point. My arrival overwhelmed his self-control.

The next morning we set out to visit our sisters Chu-yeh and Ling-yeh and their families. Wen-shuan had recovered his self-possession and was able to tell me the details of his journey with Wen-po. I was disturbed to hear that a representative of the authorities had visited the village to investigate Liu Kuan-ying's report of seeing Wen-po. But Wen-shuan assured me that he'd held firmly to the story that Liu Kuan-ying had mistaken a look-alike cousin for Wen-po.

For the next several days I reveled in reunions with friends and relatives. After Xi'an, Beijing, and Shanghai, Zhou-bian village seemed a very small place. Yet my joy was undiminished by the absence of cosmopolitan attractions. I was delighted to receive a message that I should stop and see my old schoolteacher Gao Chong-sze in Xing-ping City on my way home. But Chang Sun-sze frowned at the news. "He is a Communist magistrate now. It was he who sent the man to question Wen-shuan about Wen-po."

"But certainly Gao Chong-sze must know that I am no more likely to reveal any secrets than Wen-shuan."

"Everyone knows that Wen-shuan is a man of few words and not likely to say more than he has to. You, however, have a reputation as a talker."

I was offended. "Not on a subject such as this!"

She smiled. "I'm teasing. But be careful your old teacher doesn't trip you up."

I liked Chang Sun-sze immensely, especially for the way she looked after and protected Wen-shuan. I also trusted her judgment and agreed to be on my guard when I met my old teacher.

The night before I left, I found Wen-shuan sitting in the family graveyard, tears streaming down his face. He gestured at the family graves. "I have worked hard all my life so that we never need part from our land and our ancestors. But now we will be buried at all the points of the wind. Wen-hui is gone. Wen-po is gone. Father never came home. Will you come home again? Will Mother come home? Am I to be the only one of us buried here?"

I sat with him a long time, trying to console him. For all Chang Sun-sze's reassurances, Wen-shuan still believed that he might have convinced Wen-po to stay if he'd only had the proper gift with words. He also blamed himself for Wen-hui's disappearance, feeling that if he'd managed to get along better with his restless brother, Wen-hui might have stayed home rather than going off to Manchuria. Poor Wen-shuan. The least worldly of the four of us had through his stewardship of the ancestral land and graves come to see himself as responsible for us all. It was a burden beyond him—would have been beyond any of us—yet true to his stubborn nature he refused to lay it down.

The next day, I visited my old teacher in Xing-ping City. Gao Chong-sze seemed unchanged by his responsibilities as a Communist magistrate. We talked easily and at length. He had been my favorite teacher, and his pride in my academic achievements made me feel very good. But at length he paused, fixing me with a searching gaze. "We had a report from your former classmate Liu Kuan-ying that he saw Wen-shuan in the company of a man who looked much like you but older. Would that have been your brother Wen-po?"

"Oh, no," I said. "Wen-po fought for the Nationalists. He was evacuated to Taiwan."

"Why aren't you with him?"

"You know I am not a political person. And I have my mother to look after."

He inquired politely after Mother's health and then returned to the subject of Wen-po. "We heard he missed the ship."

I was fairly certain that this was a chance guess at the truth. "No, I'm sure he left."

"Perhaps he came back to make trouble."

"Oh, I can't believe that's true, *Lao-sze*. Liu Kuan-ying must have mistaken one of my cousins for my brother. All of us Changs look alike."

For another long moment he gazed at me. I tried to look innocent, trusting that he didn't really want to trip up a favorite former student. Then he muttered a proverb about honor to brothers, teachers, and sovereigns, and changed the subject.

I worried that suspicion would continue to cling to Wen-shuan and me. But there was nothing I could do, and I tried to banish my fears as I rode the train to Xi'an where Du Chun-fang was waiting at an aunt's. For the next three days, I visited friends and went for long, wonderful walks with her. I was supposed to meet her a final time at the station when she boarded the train for the return trip to Xing-ping City. But I was delayed and, to my chagrin and guilt, missed a tender parting with her.

Back in Shanghai, I continued to live quietly with Mother, Xing-min, and Ma Li-chun. I was extremely careful in my dealings with people, keeping my political views entirely to myself. Although Dr. Sun Yat-sen remained a hero to both Communists and Nationalists, I had no way of knowing if the Communists might one day decide to purge his memory and contributions to the revolution. So I avoided even acknowledging my loyalty to his principles. I was hardly alone in my reticence. Many students at Soochow University adopted similar wait-and-see attitudes.

I counted among my friends several dedicated Communists. Wang Tian-lu, one of my former schoolmates, had been appointed a police court judge. He visited us often, always enjoying a home-cooked meal in place of his usual bachelor fare. The university's student council president invited me to apply for membership in the Communist Youth League. It would have been foolish for me to refuse, and I completed the membership forms. However, others involved with recruitment must have retained some doubts about my loyalty, and I was granted only candidate status. I considered this the best of all possible outcomes since it allowed me to continue to maintain my low profile.

Even the most stubborn Nationalists no longer believed that victory could be achieved on the mainland. Peng Dehuai's Communist army pushed west from Xi'an to occupy China's wilderness northwest. In late September distant Xinjiang province submitted to Communist rule. Lin Biao's army struck into southern China, occupying Changsa in August and Guangzhou in October. A third army advanced into the southwest, occupying Guizhou and Sichuan provinces. Anticipating final victory, Mao declared the formation of the People's Republic of China (PRC) on October 1, 1949. Chongqing, Chiang's wartime capital, fell in November. Xiamen, the last Nationalist foothold on the coast, surrendered after a bitter struggle late in the month. Across the strait from Xiamen lay Taiwan, invisible to the soldiers on the mainland shore but looming large in the history of the rest of the twentieth century.

Late in 1949 we received the sad news that my eldest sister, Chu-yeh, had died of pneumonia at age forty-six. I had seen my gentle, easygoing sister during my visit home in August, and she'd seemed in good health. Now she was gone, and we grieved deeply. The loss was particularly hard on Mother. Chinese tradition puts a great emphasis on male children, and the birth of Wen-po had been the greatest moment in her life. But Chu-yeh had been her first child, the daughter who had helped her raise a bevy of younger children through the long years of my parents' stormy marriage. Chu-yeh had been married eight years before my birth to the shopkeeper who was later very insulting to Mother during the famine. But Chu-yeh remained loyal, helping us when she could despite her difficult husband. Her death shook Mother to her innermost core. She looked at me one day, her eyes swimming with tears: "My little ducks are growing few. Promise that you will outlive me and do honor at my grave." I promised and constantly reassured her of my devotion, but she remained disconsolate for weeks, counting and recounting the losses in her life.

Mother was nearly seventy. She had mourned the loss of parents, mother-in-law, husband, two brothers, and a much loved daughter-in-law. Her stepdaughter, Bei-yeh, and her daughters Chu-yeh, Koo-yeh, and Reou-yeh had died, leaving only Ling-yeh. Her son Wen-hui had disappeared, probably forever. Her son Wen-po had departed on a spring morning, vanishing beyond her summons. That I, too, would one day abandon her became her greatest fear.

For Mother, Wen-po had lost the reality of a living man. I tried to explain the geography of China to her and how, given good luck, Wen-po would long since have reached the safety of Taiwan. But she did not have the capacity to grasp the wideness of the world. Until well into her fifties, her life had been entirely lived within an area of a few square miles in a remote corner of rural China. Before 1938, when we visited the provincial capital of Xi'an, she had never been farther from the neighboring villages of her birth and marriage than Xing-ping City. Recent years had added Beijing and Shanghai to her travels, but the world's true size and complexity were utterly beyond her comprehension.

Xing-min and I studied. Ma Li-chun marketed and cooked. Mother had her treatments and, when she felt well enough, visited with another elderly lady from Shaanxi. As she began to rally emotionally, we were not unhappy as a family. We still had enough savings for adequate shelter and food. We had never displayed wealth or reactionary politics and felt fairly safe from Communist persecution. We carried on with our lives, enjoying simple pleasures when they came our way.

One evening in early February 1950, I answered a knock on our door to find two men waiting outside. They didn't reply to my greeting. The first held up a letter to show me the distinctive brush strokes of Wen-po's calligraphy. The other placed a simple gold bracelet in my palm. I recognized the bracelet as the one my mother had pressed on Wen-po's wife, Li Lin-fen, on the night she'd left for evacuation to Taiwan. With shaking fingers I accepted the proffered letter. The two strangers disappeared into the night, never having spoken a word.

The letter was brief. Wen-po had survived the dangerous crossing of no-man's-land to Nationalist territory. By August he was in Taiwan, where he was reunited with Li Lin-fen and their two small daughters. He was assigned to command the Fortieth Division of the Fifty-second Army Corps on the island of Chusan, eighty miles south of Shanghai. With the usual parting words of respect and fidelity, he signed the letter, "Your dutiful son and brother."

We were all overjoyed to hear of Wen-po's safe escape, but the manner of the letter's delivery troubled me. Had the two men been members of the

Nationalist underground? Or had Communist intelligence intercepted the letter and sent agents to test our loyalty? I discussed the matter at length with Xing-min. There was a definite argument in favor of turning the letter over to the authorities. Wen-po had revealed nothing of military importance, and our demonstration of loyalty would do much to secure our safety in the future. But showing the letter would also draw attention to us and, for all its expediency, seemed a disloyal act. We resolved to take our chances keeping it secret. Mother had no doubts of the wisdom of our decision; for her family loyalty could never be compromised even in the smallest way.

For weeks we lived in fear of arrest. Yet nothing seemed to change in our lives. My friend Wang Tian-lu, the Communist judge, still came to eat with us every week or so. The neighbors were friendly. Xing-min and the nephew of our next-door neighbor became particularly close. Xing-min and Xiao Kuai chummed together and often played basketball until dusk. Our period of peace ended in the middle of an April morning when the president of the student council at my university intercepted me. He handed me a note: "The law student Chang Wen-wei is summoned to garrison command by Mr. Zhang Jian-xin."

Garrison command was the headquarters of Shanghai's martial law government. I felt bile sear my throat. "Is it about my candidacy for the Communist Youth League?"

He lifted his shoulders. "I wouldn't know. I'm to pick you up after your last class and take you there. That's all I was told."

For the rest of the day I couldn't concentrate on my classes. What I feared most was that my role in Wen-po's escape had been discovered. Perhaps the man who'd carved the seal had been arrested and interrogated. Perhaps someone at the hospital or the inn had voiced suspicions. Perhaps my old teacher in Xing-ping City had decided to contact the authorities in Shanghai about the possible sighting of Wen-po in the company of Wen-shuan.

The president of the student council was no more communicative on our trip to garrison command. Whatever he knew he was unwilling to tell. He left me in a waiting room with a cool nod and hurried off, obviously wanting to be rid of any association with me as quickly as possible. I waited on a hard bench amid the hurried comings and goings of officers and messengers in uniform. There were also many people in street clothes. In my fear, they seemed particularly sinister—either informers or agents—though I suppose many of them held entirely innocent employment. A clerk at a desk called me brusquely, pointed down the hall. "Mr. Zhang's office is the third door on the left. Hurry. Don't make him wait."

I entered Mr. Zhang Jian-xin's office with trepidation, expecting an interview with a harsh, unfriendly interrogator. To my surprise, I was greeted by a smiling, handsome man in his late twenties. Mr. Zhang shook my hand warmly, gestured me to a chair, and offered me a cigarette, which I declined, fearing that it would make me ill. "So how are you finding life in our glorious People's Republic?" he asked in Mandarin with a Shandong accent, his tone slightly ironic.

I assured him that I was very happy with the restoration of peace and civil order and my opportunity to continue my education so that I might be of service to China.

"You have candidate status in the Youth League?"

"Yes."

"And your mother is receiving treatment at Dr. Dunlap's clinic and the Shanghai Radium Hospital. How is her health?"

"Better." I explained at some length, feeling his cool, sardonic gaze on me.

"So, then . . ." He glanced at a sheet on his desk. "You live with your mother, nephew, and sister-in-law."

He went on asking questions, most of which I could answer with a simple affirmative. Gradually it dawned on me that, for all his pleasant manner, he was delivering a message: he knew a great deal about us, including things that could only come from someone intimately acquainted with our family.

Finally, he leaned back. "As you can see, your family has been of considerable interest to us."

The statement required reply and I chose my words with care. "We have nothing to hide. We are loyal Chinese: two students, a sick old lady, and a young wife whose husband disappeared during the battle for Anshan in Manchuria."

"Your brother Chang Wen-hui?"

"Yes."

"Perhaps I could find out something about him."

"We would be very grateful."

Mr. Zhang made a note. "Can you guess the reason why we have been interested in you?"

I could, of course, and to deny it would be a lie. Yet I didn't want to talk of Wen-po unless Mr. Zhang mentioned him first. I remained quiet.

Mr. Zhang smiled slightly. "We are interested because of who your eldest brother is: Wen-po, the Guomindang general."

"I see."

"A very effective commander I'm told. And a good son. He came to visit your home often?"

"Yes."

"His wife and daughters lived with you?"

"For a time, yes."

"Before he evacuated them. Why didn't he arrange for the rest of you to go?"

"None of us had any desire to leave. We are not political people, and Mother is very ill."

"In the People's Republic, all people will need to be political so that we may be united in building a new China."

I let this pass without comment, though it was obvious that I would have to find another excuse to avoid political discussion.

He stubbed out one cigarette and lit another. "Would you like to know who gathered information for us?"

"I'm sure he meant only to assist the authorities. We have nothing to hide."

"He's a young man well acquainted with your nephew. A neighbor lad, Xiao Kuai."

"Yes, I know him."

"He saw your brother come to the apartment. Before the Nationalist flight to Taiwan, he worked as a stevedore on the docks loading an American warship. He saw your brother about the port."

I felt a rush of panic. Had Xiao Kuai possibly seen my brother stranded on the pier?

Mr. Zhang exhaled, watching me through the smoke. "But then the American ship left and he didn't have a job. After that he didn't see your brother. I assume the general made it safely to Taiwan?"

This was the first time I'd been forced into a corner where the wrong answer might betray me. I opened my hands in a gesture that I hoped carried no direct answer. Surprisingly, he did not press me, but continued: "Xiao Kuai did the job he was assigned, fairly and without prejudice," he said. "Don't be too resentful."

"I'm sure he simply did his patriotic duty. We have nothing to hide."

"And you are not political people." He smiled slightly.

"No, we are not."

He watched me, his eyes amused. "Have you seen *The White-haired Girl*?"

For a moment I thought he was referring to a real person, but then I realized he was speaking of the popular revolutionary play. "No, I haven't."

"You should. It's very good. How about *Thought Reform*?"

"No."

"I'm surprised. Well, I'm going to *The White-haired Girl* tomorrow night. Shall I pick you up at the university?"

I agreed, though much confused why this smooth, educated man should be interested in taking a callow student to a play. We again shook hands. "Let me know if there is anything I can do for your mother," he said. "I would be happy to help if it's in my power."

I barely slept that night, turning the interview over and over in my head. Mr. Zhang had been dressed in civilian clothes that gave no indication if he was an army officer, a civilian detective, or what. I suspected from his questions that he was an army intelligence or political officer. From some details he'd known about us, I suspected that my friend Wang Tian-lu, the Communist judge, had also made a report on us. But no one seemed to suspect our complicity in Wen-po's escape or to think our relationship to him unduly dangerous to the revolution. Indeed, Mr. Zhang's interest in me seemed more in the nature of a job interview than a hostile interrogation.

The next evening he picked me up at the university in his jeep. During the ride and again when we drank tea after the play, we chatted in a relaxed fashion. Not once did he mention politics, the civil war, or Wen-po. I still didn't know if he was a military officer in mufti or a civilian official, but I asked no questions, only listened politely as he reminisced about his student days.

The following evening he again picked me up and we went to see *Thought Reform*. By then I'd convinced myself that he was mainly interested in furthering my political education as a candidate for the Communist Youth League. Perhaps I had been identified as a potential civil servant in the new Communist government. Perhaps a judge like Wang Tian-lu. I was used to winning acclaim for my academic talents, and this explanation seemed entirely plausible. I was flattered. If the laws were reasonable and applied fairly to all, I could serve a Communist government in good conscience.

Several days later Mr. Zhang again summoned me to his office. After the usual polite inquiry after Mother's health, he said, "We have information that your brother Wen-po is commanding the garrison at the port of Shenjiamen on Chusan Island."

I made my best show of gratitude for the news. "Thank you for telling me. Mother will be happy to hear that he is safe."

"He's safe for the moment. However, our military commanders are readying a force to capture the island. I expect that there will be many casualties on both sides." He smoked reflectively. "Would you like to help your brother?"

I hesitated because to say "yes" might be interpreted as meaning that I would willingly spy for Wen-po. "He is my brother," I said cautiously. "I would like to see him survive all battles."

Mr. Zhang seemed to take no notice of my response. "There is a way. You could go to Chusan Island and tell him that he shouldn't resist our landing. He is an able man, a patriot; he could join us rather than fighting history. We are not monsters. There is room for all in the People's Republic except those who exploit the people. He would go through a period of political reeducation and then take up a responsible position. Certainly not as high as under the Guomindang, but his ability would guarantee his advancement."

He paused, waiting for me to reply. I couldn't think of anything to say.

"So will you take on this honorable mission for us?"

"I'm sorry, Mr. Zhang. I am grateful for your cordiality to me and my family, but Wen-po would never agree to what you propose. He is not the sort of man who changes his mind, no matter how mistaken his loyalties may be. And I can't leave Mother. She is completely dependent on me."

He sighed, lit yet another cigarette. "My young friend, you need to do this because it is your patriotic duty and also greatly to your personal advantage. I will personally see that your mother is well looked after in your absence. When you return, I will guarantee that she continues to receive the best possible care."

I heard the warning beneath his solicitude about Mother's care. If I didn't cooperate, the Communists might deny us everything. The hospital might no longer admit her for radiation therapy, our apartment might be confiscated, and we might find ourselves on a train heading home. Or, in my case, perhaps bound for a reeducation camp. "You don't know my brother," I said weakly.

"No, but I know you. You have an astute mind for one so young. We will expect you to convince your brother of the proper action. I'll send for you in a few days when I have some arrangements made."

He spoke as if I had already agreed, but I returned home knowing that I had a painful decision to make. On parting, he had warned me against upsetting Mother, and I knew his advice was correct in this regard. I confided in Xing-min after she was asleep. We both wept. We had lived on the edge of a razor for two years and found it very unfair that we should be confronted by this new danger. Certainly many families had suffered far worse, but Xing-min and I were very young, our nerves terribly jangled by decisions beyond our maturity.

The next day I sought out the son of one of Mother's friends at the hospital. Mr. Ma was a former newspaper editor who had brought his mother from Xi'an for treatment at the Shanghai Radium Hospital. Overhearing the other's dialect, the old ladies had become friends, introducing their sons to each other with the usual motherly pride. Through several conversations, I'd been impressed with Mr. Ma's learning, worldliness, and hardheaded good sense. Perhaps he could suggest a way out of my predicament.

But Mr. Ma's analysis provided no easy answers. If I didn't cooperate with Mr. Zhang's request, the Communists would punish me and the entire family. At the least, we would be shipped back to Shaanxi, all hope of eventual escape from China cut off if we found life under the Communists intolerable. There were also risks acceding to Mr. Zhang's request: the crossing itself would be dangerous. I might be shot by a sentry on the shore of Chusan Island or jailed as a spy. Even if I managed to get to my brother, would he still trust me?

I was rocked by this question. Of course Wen-po would trust me. How could he possibly expect treachery from me?

Mr. Ma smiled bleakly. "These are strange times. No one, not even a brother, can be entirely trusted. Wen-po has great responsibilities. You cannot expect him to lay them aside even for love of you. I think you only know the brother, not the general."

He let me brood on these things for several moments before going on. "There is no good choice here, only one that is not quite as bad as the other. I think you have to go to Chusan Island and hope that somehow you can return here to care for your mother. There is great risk in that choice, but if you don't go, the Communists will destroy you and everyone in your family. Don't underestimate how ruthless and vengeful they can be, even the smooth, sophisticated ones like your Mr. Zhang. "

Xiao Kuai and Wang Tian-lu came to visit me that night. They readily admitted that they had made reports on us but assured me that they had done so only out of patriotic duty and had spoken highly of us. They were aware of the terrible choice being asked of me, and I believe they visited out of genuine sympathy. They pledged to help Mother in any way they could in my absence. I accepted their assurances of goodwill.

Two days later I was again called to Mr. Zhang's office. This time his manner was stern. "So have you reconciled yourself to your duty?"

"I would need your promise to do all in your power to arrange my return." Though I had practiced beforehand, I now realized that this sounded a little like a demand. I hurried on. "Mother depends on me, and I owe her all the devotion expected of the youngest and only unmarried son. If I'm shot by a sentry or arrested as a spy, she will suffer terribly."

He waved a hand. "You overestimate the dangers. People go back and forth between here and Chusan Island all the time. You'll sail there on a junk, show your student papers, and go on about your business. Very simple."

"But suppose I'm not allowed to return, Mr. Zhang? It is true my brother Wen-po fought for the Guomindang, but my beliefs are my own. I have no desire to leave China. I am a patriotic student who wants to complete his education in order to be of service to China."

"You will serve China on this errand. You should feel privileged and not attempt to bargain with me."

"Please excuse me. I only wish to stress how I must return for my mother's sake."

"And for the sake of your future service to China," he said dryly.

"Insofar as my modest talents allow."

"If I promise that we will take every possible precaution to ensure your safe return, will you go willingly and uncoerced?"

If I'd dared, I would have laughed at his suggestion that I was not being coerced even as he spoke. But I had no time for dangerous ripostes. "I would beg you also, Mr. Zhang, to find out what you can about my brother Wen-hui."

"I have already given you that promise."

"I simply wish to emphasize the great importance the question has for my family."

"Of course."

Though I knew I had obtained about all I could hope for in the way of guarantees, I continued to avoid making a commitment. Mr. Zhang was patient, explaining that sailing junks regularly made the crossing between Shanghai and Chusan Island. They were licensed by both Communist and Nationalist authorities and carried about twenty passengers, mostly traders who had family on the island. This was a surprise to me since I'd thought all communication entirely shut off. "I will not ask you to take note of the island's defenses or to meet with any agents," Mr. Zhang assured me. "You will not be a spy but only the bearer of a message."

My mind was eased by his words. Still, I delayed. "But certainly I will be questioned by the guards on the docks."

"Yes, and here is how you will answer." He coached me how to respond to any question that might be asked. At the end of half an hour, he leaned back and lit another of his cigarettes. "Now I think it is time for you to stop stalling. You need to tell me if you will go to Chusan Island or not. It may well save your brother's life and the lives of many of his soldiers. And consider this, Wen-wei. If you do not go and he is killed, it is you who will be to blame for his death and for the sorrow it brings your mother. Not us, but you. But if he responds in a reasonable and patriotic way, your mission will not only save his life but enable him to return to your mother as a welcome participant in our revolution."

I thought of saying: once he's been reeducated in one of your camps for a few years. But again this was no time for ripostes. I knew Wen-po would never agree to surrender to the Communists: my mission was doomed and, hence, entirely unnecessary. But there was no way to convince Mr. Zhang of this. "I have not spoken to my mother yet," I said. "If I receive her permission, I will go."

He sighed. "Very well. I will have to hope that she is as wise as I expect she is. Let me call the comrade in charge of licensing the boats."

He spoke into a phone and a couple of minutes later I was stunned when Wang Tian-lu joined us. He smiled sympathetically at my obvious shock. We lived in a time of unexpected surprises, never knowing in what capacity a friend might suddenly appear. At Mr. Zhang's request, he laid out all the details of my trip to Chusan Island. Though I was somewhat unnerved that so much planning had already been done, I was glad that it was being done by someone I knew well.

That evening I spoke again with Xing-min. We agreed that I had little choice but to undertake the journey to Chusan Island. We braced ourselves for a difficult evening and went to explain the situation to Mother. We propped her up in bed to listen. "Mother," I said, "I have an opportunity to go see Wen-po on Chusan Island. I should be back in about ten days. Wang Tian-lu and his superior Mr. Zhang at garrison command have everything arranged. I hope to get some money from Wen-po so that we can stay comfortably in Shanghai until you are well. Wang Tian-lu and Mr. Zhang want nothing from me except to ask Wen-po not to resist when the Communists land on the island. They say that they will land in great numbers and that Wen-po and his men will probably all die if they try to resist."

Mother did not fully comprehend at first. She was ailing and never comfortable visualizing what was outside of her immediate experience. "We don't need more money," she said. "We are all right."

I explained carefully that we did need more money.

"If living here is too expensive, let us go back to Zhou-bian village. I feel fine now."

I explained that Dr. Dunlap needed more time to ensure her cure.

"I don't want you risking your life between two armies."

I assured her that I would be back in Shanghai before any battle.

She returned to the issue of money and her health, forcing me to fight through her objections several more times. Finally, she said, "There are storms on the sea. Can your all-powerful Mr. Zhang protect you against those?"

"No," I said, "but it is before the stormy season and Wang Tian-lu will put me on a good ship."

The argument lasted for hours. When she was too tired to go on and fell to weeping continuously, I lay beside her until she fell into a troubled sleep. I could not sleep, nor could Xing-min, and we sat up for hours drinking tea and mulling over the straits life had brought us to.

The next two days were very difficult for all of us. Mother had exhausted her arguments and could only weep disconsolately for being once again the victim of forces beyond her power to comprehend or alter. Wang Tian-lu and two kind colleagues from the garrison command visited to assure her that they would do all in their power to bring me back safe. During my absence they would personally see that she had transportation to her medical appointments and whatever help she needed.

At one point Wang Tian-lu spoke of patriotism. Mother responded with a stinging and tearful speech: "Don't talk to me of patriotism, young man. Since he could walk, my Wen-wei has lived a patriotic life. Every step has been taken so that one day he could be a magistrate and govern our district fairly, keeping the stupid warlords and the bandits away from us, making sure we have food in time of famine, keeping the tax collector from stealing, making sure the holes in the roads are filled in. But you, you privileged city boy, wouldn't understand what country folk need. Instead you want to get my Wen-wei killed for your stupid revolution, leaving his mother and his village to suffer! So don't speak to me of patriotism. While you were living in luxury, this poor village woman was reduced to begging for food so that her son might live to become a magistrate and be the worth of any ten of you."

It was an extraordinary speech and took Wang Tian-lu and his fellow officials utterly by surprise. Wang Tian-lu spluttered about having come from a poor background himself. One of the other officials tried to explain that the revolution was intended to cure the woes that beset the rural peasantry. Mother paid them no attention, turning on her side and presenting her back to them.

I guided Wang Tian-lu and his friends from the room. Outside he lit a cigarette with fingers that shook slightly. "I hadn't realized what you were up against. She could flay a shark with her tongue. Still, you must go. There is no alternative. No pleasant one, anyway."

Mother stopped arguing after that evening. In the next few days I would catch her watching me, her eyes brimming, but she accepted that I must go to Chusan Island. She was an extraordinarily brave person. Once she'd done all that she could in a situation, she accepted the outcome and carried on.

The day before I departed from Shanghai, Dr. Wu readmitted Mother to the hospital. On May 5, 1950, Wang Tian-lu took me to the harbor and put me aboard a junk captained by a wizened old man who might have served as the main character in a Chinese version of *The Old Man and the Sea*. We made the two-day crossing to Chusan Island under sail, arriving at the port of Shenjiamen in midafternoon. Half the passengers passed through customs and security inspections with no problems and disappeared in the company of happy families. After an hour of additional questioning, another three were released. The remaining seven of us resigned ourselves to answering the same questions again. Meanwhile, our interrogators, like people at the lowest level of bureaucracies everywhere, sought to shift responsibility onto others. After a time, a slightly higher official arrived to ask the same questions. He, in turn, departed to consult with his supervisor. Despite the delay, I was not unduly worried. I had no contraband and carried only a suitcase of cigarettes for my brother. My papers were in order and my explanation for my trip true if incomplete. My brother was a powerful man whom no one at a low level would want to offend. I simply had to wait until an official of sufficient intelligence arrived to order my release—no doubt with apologies for the delay.

I was wrong. After a third and more intense round of questioning, much of it concerning what I'd observed of the Communist defenses of Shanghai, I was again left to wait. Several times I had asked my captors to call my brother, who would certainly send someone or come himself to obtain my release. But my requests no longer received even a polite reply. An even more senior official arrived to tell us that since the hour was late we would be housed in a building down the street until questioning could resume in the morning. I was quite agitated as we walked down the street under a loose guard. These people didn't seem to quake at my brother's name as I'd expected. Perhaps he had been transferred or fallen from grace. In either case, I would be in for a very difficult time.

Desperate, I grabbed the arm of a young man lounging on the street. I asked him for a match (I rarely smoked) and then slipped him two packages of cigarettes and my brother's address. "Please go to my brother. Tell him that I am being held by the port police." I had no time to say more before I was pushed rudely from behind by one of the guards. At the end of the block, we entered a grim concrete building and were ushered into a bare room where we were told we would stay until morning.

The young man I'd slipped the cigarettes to might have been a thief, a student, or an agent of Chiang's feared secret police. I was never to know, but he delivered my message and a half hour later I was called to the guardroom at the front of the building. A middle-aged lieutenant shook my hand warmly, explaining that he'd known my brother since Yunnan when he'd cared for Wen-po's horse. He had risen to higher responsibility in the years since and now had charge of the communications center in my brother's headquarters at the address I'd given the young man. My brother was in a meeting with his regimental commanders, but I wasn't to worry. He would personally tell Wen-po of my whereabouts as soon as possible.

I wish I could remember the good lieutenant's name. He gave me some cold rice cakes and two army blankets, again told me not to worry, and returned to his duties. I waited for two more hours. Finally, I heard a jeep pull up outside and a commanding voice telling the guard on duty that he'd come for the student Chang Wen-wei. My rescuer wore the uniform of a colonel. He shook my hand, introducing himself as Colonel Ku, an old friend of my brother, who was waiting for me at the colonel's house.

We rode through the spring night, driving by the dim illumination of the tiny blackout lights of the jeep. The colonel was not talkative, concentrating on his driving, but I sensed sympathy. At his home, he ushered me into a comfortable parlor. My brother rose from a chair, his face wearing not joy but a dark scowl. "Why are you here, youngest brother?" he snapped.

So great was my shock at this greeting that I stammered. "I thought you would give me money to help care for Mother."

"So you want money so you can return to Shanghai and live under the Communists? Get him out of here, Colonel. Turn him over to the police. I do not acknowledge him as my brother!"

The colonel appeared almost as shocked as I was. "General, please. My wife is cooking a light meal for us. Let's eat and talk things over calmly."

"Tell her to stop cooking! I will not sit down with a man who accepts living under the Communists, even if he calls himself my brother. Get him out of here!"

"They made me come," I blurted.

"I don't give a damn if you were snatched off the street and dropped here by an eagle! You say you want to go back and that is not permissible for a brother of mine. You will stay here or cease to be my brother."

"But Mother needs me," I begged, tears welling in my eyes.

"Our mother is not the concern here; your decision is! Do you choose to obey me or do you choose to deny me as your brother? In this war, I have lost a son and a daughter. I have lost two brothers and their wives, all my remaining sisters and their husbands, all my nieces and nephews. I must lose my mother, but I will not lose you. You shall stay here!"

"I cannot. I must—"

"All you must do is obey your eldest brother. That is the rule taught us from birth. Or have you become a Communist, one of the scum who would tear down all China's traditions? Tell me what it will be, youngest brother? Will you obey me? Or shall I disown you for all time?"

At this point, Colonel Ku intervened, pulling me from the room into a narrow passageway. "Listen to me," he said. "This can go very badly for you. I command the Nationalist agents in Shanghai. I was the one who sent your brother's letter. We know of Zhang and his plots. Your brother left you in police custody because he wanted to scare you. And you might have remained there two or three days if his former groom hadn't intervened out of ignorance and a good heart. Your brother lost patience and had you brought here. If you refuse to stay on your own, he will turn you over to the secret police. And once you're in their hands, no one but the Generalissimo himself can have you released. Do you understand?"

I closed my ears against all the colonel said, turned rudely away, and reentered the room where Wen-po stood, his fists clenched. Before he could again demand the answer I could not make, I asked a question of my own. "Who is to care for Mother if I do not return?"

"That is no longer your concern."

"The Communists want you to surrender when they land."

"Surrender?" He thumped his chest. "I am a Guomindang general! I kill Communists. I have killed thousands in this war, and I will kill thousands more if they land here."

"I told them you would never agree. But they sent me anyway, not as a spy but as a messenger. I don't fear them."

"Then you are a fool! No one who fails them goes unpunished."

"Then let them punish me. I must care for Mother. I am her true son even if you are not!"

For a moment his eyes flashed with a rage like no fury I had ever seen. "I am a truer son to her than you can ever understand. But she is an old, sick woman. Let her die!"

I stared at him in horror. "You cannot mean—"

"Yes, I can! You are young. I will not permit you to live any longer under the Communists."

"But Xing-min—"

"Xing-min is my concern, not yours. I will get him out of Shanghai in the future. But enough. Do you obey me, youngest brother? Or shall I have Colonel Ku turn you over to the secret police as a traitor who only calls himself my brother? Choose now! Once and for all time!"

I collapsed on a chair, my body racked with sobs as my will gave way entirely before this monster people called "the Tiger." Whether I agreed or not, he would never let me return to Shanghai, never let me return to Mother's bedside.

He resumed his seat and picked up a report from a low table beside his chair. After ten minutes of my sobbing, he snapped: "That's enough! Get command of your emotions. You were taught to be stalwart."

When I'd managed to quiet my sobbing, he asked sternly, "So will you stay as I command you?"

I nodded, my eyes squeezed shut, tears running down my cheeks. In a somewhat kinder voice, he said, "All right then. Now act with courage or you will embarrass me and make me ashamed of you. Courage now in all that you do."

He summoned Colonel Ku and thanked him for his services to us. On the way to his quarters, Wen-po rode beside his driver while I perched in the back of the jeep. Our tires hummed on the hard-packed road, the jeep's engine a base counterpoint to the singing of cicadas joyous with the coming of summer. Above the harbor, searchlights probed the night sky for warplanes. Along the shore, more searchlights swept the dark waves for raiders by boat. Beyond the breakers, eighty miles of the East China Sea separated me from the room where my mother lay in the Shanghai Radium Hospital. I had broken my promise to her. I would not sit at her deathbed, would not hear her call my name, would not hold her hand in the last moments of her life. I would not accompany her funeral procession nor do her honor beside the quiet grave she deserved.

For years after her death, her spirit would roam unquiet, weeping for her lost sons. Wen-shuan would labor in the sun, hearing her spirit begging to know what had become of his brothers. He would have no answers for her. And I . . . I would live in the Occident, marry someone she had never met, become a father, an American, and a modestly respected scholar. But never in all the remaining years of my life would I be able to cross that dark immensity to her.

CHAPTER 9

Exile

I WOULD NEVER COMPLETELY UNDERSTAND my brother's harshness that night. After my capitulation, he seemed embarrassed by the intensity of his emotional display. That night and the next day he treated me kindly but without intimacy. I was physically and mentally exhausted, and he let me sleep most of the day in a corner of his office while field phones rang and messengers and staff officers hurried in and out. Everybody expected the Communists to land any day, and my brother had his men digging trenches and constructing fortifications along the stretch of coastline assigned to his division.

Late in the day, he roused me for a supper of army rations. He told me that he had phoned to see if his superior, General Liu Yu-chang, wanted to interrogate me. But General Liu had left everything to Wen-po's discretion.

My mouth had gone dry at the word *interrogation*, and now I mumbled, "Thank you, eldest brother."

He studied me critically. "I am going to send you to the officers training camp. You look run-down and weak. They will feed you up and get you in better condition. I don't ask you to enlist, but don't embarrass me either."

I nodded. I felt that I should make one final appeal to return to Mother, but when I looked up, his eyes warned me. I had made my decision and it was irrevocable.

I departed the next morning for the officers training camp. I spent a miserable week there, trying to master drill, the manual of arms, and military regulations. I think only my brother's high position kept the instructors from publicly berating and humiliating me.

In the middle of my second week on Chusan Island, Wen-po came to address the officer candidates. Before he could start, however, he was summoned from the podium by General Liu. They talked earnestly for a few minutes and then my brother gave rapid orders to the camp's commandant. All was chaos for the next hour as we rushed to get ready for the field. We were issued rifles and rations for three days. Then we marched off, not knowing where or for what purpose.

It seemed that every soldier of the 100,000 on the island had been mobilized. We bounced off one shoal of marching men after another. For three days we marched back and forth, no sooner establishing one position before marching off to another. As I dragged along behind the fitter young men, I excoriated my brother for this ordeal. Every time we came on an island man or boy of remotely military age, he was hustled into ranks and forced to carry part of our equipment. Any stumble or plea was answered with a kick or a rifle butt. I was appalled by this brutality and averted my gaze from their beseeching faces. I could never be a soldier, could never exhibit the contempt for human suffering of my fellow cadets.

About fifty of these terrified islanders were with us at dawn on the fourth day when we marched to the harbor and boarded a large military transport. Instead of repelling an invasion, perhaps we were going to make one on the mainland. If so, what had been the purpose of exhausting ourselves with three days of pointless marching beforehand?

We were still on deck, waiting to file below to the berthing spaces, when the ship cast off and started for the harbor mouth. A sudden commotion broke out as three of the civilians bolted for the rail and leaped over the side. Cursing, an instructor pushed his way to the rail, took aim, and emptied his rifle at the swimming men. The light was bad, the men's heads and backs barely visible as they swam for the shore. But the instructor was a good shot and one of the figures jerked, rolled over, and lay still, a dark stain of blood trailing as the corpse bobbed in the wake of the ship.

Beyond the harbor mouth we entered the open sea, the transport's vast bulk beginning to roll beneath us. We filed below. Many of my fellow cadets climbed into hammocks and were insensible in moments. Exhausted as I was, I couldn't stand not knowing what was happening above. Others were likewise anxious, and several of us crept on deck. We were greeted with a spectacular sight. All around us ships steamed on a wide expanse of flat, blue sea. I counted close to a hundred ranging in size from tugboats to transports even bigger than ours. Warships ranged along the edges of the formation. Overhead fighters patrolled, their wings reflecting the sun.

For hours we steamed north at a few knots while the fleet formed up. In the middle of the afternoon we turned east for Taiwan. That night a holiday mood prevailed on the berthing decks as men laughed, sang, and told stories. We were sailing east toward at least temporary safety, not west for a bloody landing on the mainland. I should have been elated, too, but my mind kept coming back to the unfortunate islander left floating in the harbor with a bullet in his back. I watched the merciless instructor laughing in the company of several other corporals and sergeants. Had they already forgotten the killing? Or was the recollection what these hard men laughed about?

For hours after the lights went out, I thought about the incident. Had the islander been trying to get back to an ill mother, to a sweetheart, or simply to a beloved patch of ground? What did he care about wars, politics, or the great currents of history on which nations and ideologies contested for brief supremacy? For that matter, what did I? I wished only to be of service to my mother, repaying a small part of her love for me. I wished to marry a girl in far-off Shaanxi, making with her a home for Mother and our children. If fortune favored us, perhaps we would settle in old age in the village where I had been born. If I could in a small way be of service to China in the years between marriage and death, so much the better. But I was no warrior, lacked utterly the ferocity of my brother and the tough young men sleeping near me. I lay in the dark, feeling the throb of the great ship through the deck beneath me, sensing beyond its steel skin the depth of a measureless sea and the workings of machineries I could never understand, as all the while my eyes leaked tears for my mother and my distant home.

We landed at the port of Keelung two days later. At the foot of the gangplank, a short, smiling woman in a fur coat handed us each a package of cigarettes as photographers filmed and bodyguards hung nearby. "It's Madam," soldiers behind me whispered to each other as we moved slowly forward. When it came my turn, I accepted my pack of Lucky Strikes with an abashed bow. Close up, Madam Chiang Kai-shek, until recently the most powerful woman in China, looked unspeakably weary. "Thank you, soldier," she said. "Welcome to free China."

To my great relief, my brother came for me the next day. I turned in my rifle and uniform and became a civilian again. We drove to the apartment he'd rented in Hsinchu for Li Lin-fen and their two daughters. For the next several months I lived there, a displaced person with no work and little hope of returning where I was needed. I tried to help Li Lin-fen with the children, but I fear I was more of a hindrance. I had no room of my own but slept on a folding cot in the dining room. The weather was hot, the small apartment almost unbearably stuffy. The streets outside offered little relief. Though I had registered with the police, I was hesitant to wander lest I be picked up as a deserter. I could not understand the local dialect, nor could I make myself understood. Wen-po was immensely busy, rarely returning home and then only for a meal and a short reunion with his wife and daughters. He had no time to help me, and I drifted.

The mood in Taiwan under martial law was extremely tense. Chiang Kai-shek had reassumed the presidency, forcing Li Zongren to flee to Hong Kong. With him went any small hope of a negotiated peace with the Communists.

The Nationalist troops worked from dawn to dusk building fortifications to repel a Communist landing. It seemed that the Americans and the British had entirely abandoned the Nationalist cause. Many of the wealthy families fled to Hong Kong. Everyone else lived expecting catastrophe any day.

On June 25, 1950, Communist North Korea invaded South Korea. The invasion immediately restored the Chinese Nationalists to the status of honored American allies. Within days, the American Seventh Fleet patrolled the Taiwan Strait. General Douglas MacArthur flew to Taipei to consult with Chiang Kai-shek on mutual defense arrangements. Arrogant as always, Chiang held out for the best possible terms, dangling the possibility but never committing Nationalist troops to the conflict in Korea.

It seemed likely that the battle-hardened Fifty-second Corps under General Liu would become one of the first Nationalist units deployed in Korea. Wen-po went from preparing to hold against a Communist invasion across the strait to preparing his troops for battle in Korea. He was even less available to help me, and I became deeply despondent worrying about Mother, my other family members on the mainland, and my fiancée, Du Chun-fang. My nights were racked with nightmares and my days with an endless cycle of self-recrimination for the weakness that had landed me on Taiwan.

I had not written to Du Chun-fang before my coerced mission to Chusan Island. I had not wanted to worry her, especially when I expected to return to Shanghai in a few days. Even as the newspapers howled of the Communist atrocities on the mainland, I held out hope that I might yet return to Shanghai.

In these months, it was still possible to pass in and out of China through Hong Kong. Wen-po and I discussed sending for Du Chun-fang, but she was an only child and would never abandon her parents to join me in Taiwan.

I considered taking a flight to Hong Kong, hoping that I could explain my apparent treachery to Mr. Zhang once I reached Shanghai. But I had little money, and Wen-po had forbidden my return to the mainland: an order demanding absolute obedience under Confucian tradition. Had I been raised in one of the West's more flexible ethical systems, I might have dared to disobey him. But obedience to an older brother was one of the five relationships expressing the central axiom of Confucianism, the *jen*. According to the Confucian philosophers, the *jen*, or man's natural sympathy for other people, dictated his need to live within a social order. Disobeying Wen-po would not only break our fraternal bond forever but put me in opposition to one of the central beliefs of Chinese society. Would Du Chun-fang want to marry such a man? Would Mother truly want such a son at her bedside?

I cannot describe my torment in that summer as I wandered without purpose, bedeviled night and day with worries and guilt. I took the risk of writing to Xing-min through Hong Kong. News reports indicated that the Korean War and the presence of the American Seventh Fleet in the Taiwan Strait had caused the Communists to crack down on all dissension and disloyalty at home. Mr. Zhang would have lost considerable face when I failed to return from my mission to Chusan Island. Had he revenged himself on Mother and Xing-min? I hesitated a long time before mailing the letter, afraid that it might represent an additional danger to them. But I had to know if Mother was all right, and eventually I sent my letter.

At the same time that I worried about what the Communist authorities might be doing to Mother and Xing-min, I worried that the Nationalist secret police might be watching me. Many Communist agents or supposed agents had been arrested, brutally interrogated, and executed on Taiwan. In my first hours on Chusan Island, I had been interrogated three times on the assumption that I was a Communist agent. In the atmosphere of paranoia on Taiwan, might I still be under suspicion? To this day I'm not sure if I was being watched. Whatever the case, I was never questioned. Indeed, my entire mission to Chusan Island seemed entirely forgotten by everyone except me. Wen-po never brought it up. General Liu never questioned me. No army intelligence or secret police ever came to call. The event that had upset all my plans, separated me from my mother, and denied me the companionship of the girl I loved seemed entirely unimportant to everyone else.

In this desperate time in my life, M. T. Yang, an old friend from junior high school in Xing-ping City, came to my aid. (Like many progressive young Chinese, he had adopted the practice of putting the surname after the given name. Many young people also dropped the hyphen between the halves of their given names and began using only the initials in their professional lives, a practice popularized by the powerful finance minister T. V. Soong.) In 1944, my friend had responded to Chiang's call for a hundred thousand educated young people to form a youth corps in the war against the Japanese. After Japan's surrender, he had joined the Fifty-second Corps, serving as division accountant under my brother. He was still serving in this capacity when we renewed our friendship. No doubt to Li Lin-fen's great relief, I moved out of the crowded apartment and into his quarters. He often took me with him when his duties sent him to Taipei. He paid for my train ticket and meals and took me to the theater for plays and movies. With his encouragement, I tried to gain admission to Taiwan University Law School in the fall of 1950. But this proved impossible without transcripts or any influential friends among the professors and administrators.

I was at the point of despair when I learned that Mr. Chu Cheng was living in Taipei. A retired statesman, he had been chairman of the board of directors at Chao-yang Law University in Beijing during my time there. I went to his residence to beg him to intercede for me. He greeted me with great kindness and listened patiently to my story. When I'd finished, he explained that he was out of favor with the government and had no influence at Taiwan University. He could, however, recommend me to his son-in-law, Mr. Chang Ming, who was president of Tamkang English College, a new private college in Tamsui township outside of Taipei. The next day I enrolled as a sophomore at Tamkang English College. I found that my rudimentary English courses in high school had given me only the shallowest foundation in the language. I worked like a madman to catch up, an English-Chinese dictionary constantly at my elbow. But at least I was studying again after my months of aimless drifting.

About this time I received a return letter from Xing-min. He wrote that he was doing well in the new People's Republic and that Mother continued to make progress in her treatments. They were glad that I was safe, but if I couldn't return to Shanghai, I shouldn't write them again. Xing-min's injunction not to write was a broad hint that they were under surveillance.

Though brief and circumspect, his letter brought me great relief and new hope. I undertook to make the best of what Tamkang English College had to offer. The college had no campus or buildings of its own but rented classroom and dormitory space from a private missionary high school. I lived in the dormitory with a number of other young men from the mainland. Many had stories similar to mine. Samuel S. Wang had been a freshman at a university in South Korea when the Communist invasion had forced him to flee to Taiwan. We were both from the Yellow River region of northern China, spoke similar dialects, and had been distantly acquainted at school in Beijing. We became lifelong friends during the winter of 1950–1951. Samuel had a scholarship for the fall of 1951 to George Fox College in Newberg, Oregon. He suggested that once my English skills improved, I too might want to study in the United States. I still hoped to return to Shanghai and resisted the idea. Nevertheless, it began to take root in my imagination.

I was largely ignorant of world affairs and hadn't yet realized that the deepening Cold War would make my return to China impossible for many years. Through the summer of 1950, South Korean and United Nations forces retreated under a furious assault by the North Korean Communists until they fought with their backs to the sea in the Pusan area at the southeastern tip of the peninsula. On September 15, the situation changed dramatically when General MacArthur executed a daring amphibious landing at Inchon far behind the Communist front. Under assault front and rear, the North Koreans retreated and kept retreating nearly to the Yalu River separating Korea from China. General MacArthur alarmed China's Communist leaders with inflammatory statements advocating a second front on the coast of China by Chiang Kai-shek's Nationalist army. The People's Republic warned the United

Nations against pushing to the Yalu, but MacArthur and President Truman ignored the warning. Throughout November frontline United Nations troops reported brushes with Chinese soldiers. Still, United Nations command was unprepared when the People's Liberation Army attacked in overwhelming force on November 26, routing United Nations forces.

That winter it became impossible for me to ignore the effect the Cold War was having and would have on my life. Radio reports, newsreels, and newspapers carried reports of hot spots on nearly every continent, all threatening to erupt into World War III. Gloomy with my prospects, I kept at my studies in the hope that one day the world might regain a little sanity.

I like to think that it was not entirely by chance that Miss Lillian C. Wells entered my life when I most needed spiritual comfort. Miss Wells had come to China as a Presbyterian missionary in the 1920s. She taught in northern Jiangsu province until forced to leave after Pearl Harbor. At the end of the war, she and many of her fellow missionaries returned to their mission stations, only to be forced to flee again by the civil war. Settling in Taiwan, she taught English at Tamkang College and conducted Bible classes at her residence in the Canadian mission compound.

When I first met her, Miss Wells was in her late sixties, a slender woman of rather schoolmarmish appearance. But her smile was quick, her manner open and friendly, totally lacking the condescension and arrogance of many Westerners. She liked Chinese people, saw them not as ignorant and backward heathens, but as fellow seekers of the Light. She invited Samuel S. Wang, me, and our friend Alfred Huang to her Bible classes. At first I went for the companionship and out of intellectual interest in the strange religion that my mother had found so appealing during her stay in the hospital in Xi'an. But Miss Wells spotted a spiritual yearning in my sad demeanor that I, myself, had not recognized. We stayed late after every class, questioning her and learning from her explanations. She did not push the message of Christ but opened it for our hearts to accept. Samuel and I became converts. Alfred declined because his parents were Buddhists and would be greatly disappointed if he accepted a religion alien—in their view—to China. She gave everyone in her class a Christian name, and I became David Chang to my fellow students.

When school let out for the summer, Samuel and I stayed on in the dormitory, eating our meals with a neighborhood family. Sitting outside on warm summer evenings, we watched the moon rise to twine itself in a million stars as dusk blue faded to black. We were as happy as we had a right to expect in such a difficult time for our land and our families. We had heard and accepted the message of Christ and would soon be baptized. Samuel looked forward to studying in the United States, saying that he would try to arrange a scholarship for me to follow him. I no longer resisted quite so loudly. A week before

Samuel's departure for the United States, we were baptized. Miss Wells stood as our sponsor, positively glowing with pride in us, as if we had been the first converts she had helped to find Christ rather than only the latest of many.

In my second winter in Taiwan, I became Miss Wells's assistant in her Sunday school classes. She had a tremendous influence on me, becoming in many ways my surrogate mother. During the frequent air raids, Miss Wells would remain in her classroom while her students took shelter. I stayed with her, not because I had become oblivious to fear but because I accepted the will of God over my life. Together we prayed for the end of war and the deliverance of China from its long suffering. We prayed for my mother and my family, asking God to keep them in his care. That they had not come to know the Christian message—or in my mother's case only in its barest outline—only increased their importance to us as fellow children of God.

I became well acquainted with Miss Wells's circle of missionary friends in Taiwan. Without my knowledge, she began working with them to arrange for my education in America. One day she asked me to stay for a moment after class. She produced an official envelope and handed it to me, obviously relishing the small drama of the moment. Inside was a letter from the World Mission of the Southern Presbyterian Church informing me that I had been awarded a full scholarship to Southwestern College (now Rhodes College) in Memphis, Tennessee. I was, of course, greatly surprised and thanked her profusely. She explained that the scholarship would pay for my tuition, room, board, and books. If on graduation I felt the call to the ministry, I might continue my studies on a scholarship to the Presbyterian seminary in Richmond, Virginia. "God will let you know when the time is right," she said. "But you can be certain that he has special work for you to do."

Going to visit Wen-po that night, my elation began to fade. The scholarship was very generous, but how could I afford the trip to America? I didn't have suitable clothes or even a suitcase. Though his responsibilities were large, his pay was not, and he had his growing family to support. Was it fair to impose on him for so much? By the time I reached his home, I had thoroughly discouraged myself. But Wen-po was greatly excited by my news. I saw in his relief how much he had worried about my future. He was not himself a Christian, but he respected Miss Wells and her circle as dedicated workers for the welfare of the Chinese people. He congratulated me warmly and gave his permission for me to accept the scholarship. "But how can I afford the trip?" I asked.

"We will find a way. I will take up a collection among my friends, perhaps ask General Liu for a loan." He would hear no defeatism on my part and we were soon deep in talk of the future.

The good General Liu made a gift of five hundred dollars toward my trip to America. Through the generosity of Wen-po, Miss Wells, and their many friends, I was able to make travel reservations. I would fly to Hong Kong and there board a liner, the S.S. *President Wilson*, for the voyage across the Pacific.

Before my departure, Miss Wells spoke frankly about the dangers and temptations I would face in America. I should avoid alcohol, which never did people, American or Chinese, any good. I should learn that Americans were an informal people without a rigid system of etiquette. I shouldn't be too quick to take offense at facial or verbal expressions that seemed impolite. Nor should I be unnerved by the emotional openness of Americans, who were a good-hearted people if rather boisterous by Chinese standards. Finally, I should be aware of the racism of far too many Americans. The Negroes got the worst of it, but I should expect to have some unpleasant incidents. But if I conducted myself as a Christian in a spirit of charity I would have nothing to fear. Finally, when I decided to marry, I should marry a Chinese woman for my own comfort and for the sake of our children. This was wise and motherly advice, and I resolved to follow it.

Going to study in America forced me to confront a task too long delayed. I loved Du Chun-fang, but our marriage was no longer a realistic possibility. The time had come for me to release her from her promise to me. I wrote her a loving letter, hoping that whatever censors intercepted it would let it pass on through the mails to the virtuous and kind girl I had left behind.

The night before I left, I was racked by doubts. Would I ever again see Wen-po and his family on Taiwan or Mother and my loved ones on the mainland? Was going to America a betrayal, a final surrendering of hope? I prayed for hours. Though my mind cautioned me to beware of the sin of pride, my faith told me that God had opened this way for me, that he had led me to Miss Wells and the knowledge of Christ, and that this scholarship was another expression of his will in my life.

I left for Hong Kong on March 4, 1953. Wen-po and his family, Miss Wells, and several of her friends came to see me off. In Hong Kong, I met with Dr. Dunlap, who had held on in Shanghai until the Communists made it impossible for him to continue in practice. His household and clinic staffs demanded pay raises he could not afford; the Communists seized his property investments; government bureaucrats threw obstacles in his way at every opportunity. Finally, with great sadness, he closed his office in November 1952 and left Shanghai.

As always, he greeted me cordially. He told me that he had continued to treat Mother successfully, eventually removing the entire tumor on her vocal cords. He had seen her after that for checkups and found no reoccurrence. When he attempted to contact her shortly before his departure for Hong Kong, he found that Ma Li-chun had taken her back to Zhou-bian village. I was greatly relieved when he assured me that the tumor was gone for good after seventeen surgeries. We strolled along the boulevards of Hong Kong in the spring evening. "And what of your young lady at home?" he asked. "I recall you were engaged."

"I posted a letter to her today, telling her that she must find another."

He nodded. "The world is a sad place for lovers. Have you read Shakespeare?"

"Only a little."

"Well, he will be someone for you to study. There is great solace in his plays." He laid a hand briefly on my shoulder as we walked. "You did the honorable thing."

I arrived at Southwestern College in April 1953. From the first, I found myself welcomed with warmth beyond anything I could have imagined. Teachers and administrators extended every kindness. My fellow students were universally well mannered, kind, gentle, soft-spoken, and religious. At meals, they sought places by me. I appreciated being included in their community, but they spoke so rapidly and used so many colloquial expressions that I had great difficulty participating in the conversations. An even larger problem was that I couldn't tell them apart! I could tell girl from boy, but otherwise they all looked much alike. Sometimes out of sheer exhaustion I sought a place where I could sit in privacy, but these kind American young people rarely allowed me to isolate myself. The girls in particular sought me out, refusing with many giggles to let me sit alone.

I studied English very hard through that spring and summer to prepare myself for a full load of courses in the fall. I bought an ancient radio for a dollar and slept with it under my pillow to avoid disturbing my roommate. I sat through the same movies over and over, often confused by the story but getting every penny's worth of instruction from my ten-cent admission. On Sundays I attended several services and Sunday school sessions. At nights I studied books and newspapers until my eyes stung.

I was one of four Chinese students to enroll for the fall semester of 1953. My course work required many hours of study every night, but I was accustomed to the long hours demanded of a student in Chinese schools. Thanks to many kind people, particularly my roommates and professors, I thrived. Unfortunately, my fellow Chinese students had more difficulty, and I was the only one to return for the spring semester of 1954.

As I gained a good command of English, I found that I could excel in the American university system. Deeply as I believed in the message of Christ, I did not feel a call to the ministry. I would study political science instead in the hope that I might one day return to China to become a public official, working for the good of the rural folk and fulfilling my mother's ambition.

I remained in touch with many friends, especially Samuel S. Wang, who had embarked on a distinguished career in organic chemistry; Dr. Dunlap, who had retired to the Washington, D.C., area; and "my friend in Christ," Miss Lillian C. Wells. In every case their friendship supported me, but I ached for some contact with my beloved family in China. Many nights I lay sleepless, watching the moon through my dormitory window and remembering how Mother and I had watched it rise over the fields at home.

The Communists had shut the mainland tight, barring the citizens of the People's Republic from any correspondence with relatives on Taiwan or overseas. Taiwan's laws were even stricter, carrying fines, imprisonment, and even death for attempts to make contact with people on the mainland. Wen-po was an honored member of the Nationalist military and had assignments of increasing responsibility, including for a time the defense of Little Quemoy Island in Amoy Bay, but even he was forbidden the right to travel abroad. In the United States it was the era of McCarthyism and Communist witch hunts. For fear of FBI investigation and deportation, Chinese immigrants and students gave up their attempts to contact family members in mainland China. It was impossible for me to reconcile myself to my continued separation from my family, but I had to accept it.

After graduation from Southwestern College in 1955, I enrolled at the University of Minnesota, earning my master's degree in March 1957. With the encouragement of Dr. Dunlap, I next enrolled at the University of Illinois in Urbana, not far from his family home. In 1960, I was awarded my Ph.D. in political science. By that time it was obvious that I could never return to China to become a public official. Mao was thoroughly in control, his brand of Communism more erratic than ever. The Great Leap Forward had failed, and shortly the even more disastrous Great Cultural Revolution would begin. Nor was there a place for me in Taiwan, where the Nationalist government repressed civil rights and dealt severely with liberals like me. I lamented for China and the sad events that made it impossible for me to go home. I must plan for a career in America.

In the fall of 1960, I began teaching at the University of Wisconsin, Oshkosh, where I would remain on the faculty for the next thirty-five years. Married friends in Chicago introduced me to a sprightly, intelligent young woman, Alice Tan. She had been born into an educated family in Sichuan province. Her parents had emigrated with their seven children to Singapore in 1930. Her father became a senior civil servant and was able to send his children, boys and girls, to Catholic school. Alice became a high school teacher and a temporary school principal. Wanting to further her education, she came to the United States to attend Mundelein College in Chicago. We were a perfect fit—or at least I thought so. Once she'd gotten to know me and met my friends, she agreed. We were married in 1962 in Oshkosh.

My dear friend and mentor, Miss Lillian C. Wells, retired to Morristown, Tennessee, where she died in 1963. Her legacy was almost entirely spiritual, and she left behind only a few possessions. I was deeply honored to receive her most precious: a worn Chinese Bible.

In those years I knew many times of fulfillment and joy. Alice and I were blessed with two wonderful sons, Christopher and Victor. We enjoyed a comfortable American life. By 1967, I was a full professor and chairman of my department. I authored books and published numerous articles. My expertise was recognized with accolades and awards. I was active in the Presbyterian Church, Alice in the Roman Catholic Church. As our children grew older, I became concerned that this division of affiliation might complicate their religious education. Alice was a third-generation Catholic, and I did not feel that I could ask her to abandon her treasured family tradition. So I left the Presbyterian Church to become a Roman Catholic—a decision that I'm sure Miss Wells would have understood. In 1968, Alice and I stood before a judge to swear our allegiance to our adopted land and became U.S. citizens.

For all my happiness and achievement in America, never a day passed when I did not mourn for my lost family in China. Was Mother still alive? Had Death carried away others among my dear ones? Were the Communists persecuting my family because of Wen-po and me? I could get no answers to these or a thousand other questions. I could turn on my television to hear American astronauts beaming back messages from the moon, but I could not send a simple letter to China to find out if my mother still drew breath among the living, still looked for the return of her prodigal son.

CHAPTER 10

America and the Prodigal's Return

IN MY CHILDHOOD AND YOUTH in northern China, I received a considerable education in coping with freezing weather, but I earned my advanced degree in cold at the University of Wisconsin, Oshkosh. Overlooking frozen Lake Winnebago, the university is a dreadfully frigid place in January and February. Students in the winter term assume a lumpiness of outline not entirely dissimilar to that assumed by Chinese students half the world away. American winter wear is certainly more colorful and stylish than the bulky padded coats of the Chinese, but whether in Oshkosh or Beijing the observer can only guess the true shape of the muffled figures making their way over the frozen landscape.

A similar cold dominated relations between the United States and the People's Republic in the 1960s and early 1970s. As a professor of political science and international relations, I watched the thermometer for the slightest hint of a gradual warming. For years diplomatic contact between these two immensely important countries was conducted in meetings between their representatives to Poland. When Soviet advisors quit China in 1960, many Chinese intellectuals in America hoped that the deterioration of the Sino-Soviet alliance would open the way for a rapprochement between the United States and China. But the slight movement toward better relations during the Kennedy administration came to nothing with the young president's assassination, the intensification of the conflict in Vietnam, and the opening of the Great Cultural Revolution in China. Meanwhile, the U.S.S.R. started preparing for possible war with its one-time Communist ally and China worked feverishly to build a defensive nuclear arsenal.

Among Chinese scholars in America there was a deep sense of frustration. We published papers and met at academic conferences. We tried in our classes and lectures to persuade Americans not to judge all Chinese by the actions of Mao and his Red Guard fanatics. The vast majority of Chinese people were sane and decent, wanting peace every bit as much as Americans. China was not historically an aggressive, expansionist power but quite the contrary.

Hence, much of American foreign policy, particularly in Southeast Asia, was based on an utterly false premise. But I'm afraid little of what we said or wrote penetrated the public consciousness or moderated the government's attitude toward China in the years of the Johnson administration.

In January 1968, Richard M. Nixon took office as president. Although a lifelong anticommunist, Nixon was a political realist. He appointed as the principal architect of his foreign policy the likewise pragmatic Dr. Henry Kissinger. Their careful probes of the mood of the government of the PRC revealed a willingness to improve relations. Kissinger and Premier Zhou Enlai, another sophisticated pragmatist, began careful negotiations through third parties.

From 1969 to 1971 I taught as a visiting professor of international politics at the graduate school of National Cheng-chi University in Taiwan. In the summers I traveled as a field lecturer for the United States Information Agency, speaking in Taiwan, the Philippines, and Malaysia. In every country I interviewed high officials and found them all intensely interested in the diplomatic minuet between the United States and the PRC. By the spring of 1971, these contacts had reached the level of sufficient cordiality that the Chinese felt confident in making a public gesture of goodwill by inviting the American table tennis team, then visiting Japan, to extend its tour of the Far East with a visit to the PRC.

When news of China's invitation and the American acceptance reached Taiwan, my colleagues at the university were immediately suspicious of American motives. Was this the first step in a betrayal of Taiwan and the Nationalist cause? My own reaction was more optimistic, though I had to be restrained in my comments. I thought I detected the subtle maneuvering of Zhou and Kissinger at work. I knew Kissinger slightly and was thoroughly familiar with his scholarly work. I did not entirely agree with his analysis of global balance-of-power politics, which seemed to me drawn almost entirely from European history, but I had confidence in his intellect and finesse—vital components in any diplomatic negotiations with the Chinese. Zhou was an equally brilliant and subtle diplomat, a pragmatist who had moderated some of the grosser excesses of Mao's policies. I hoped fervently that these two men might negotiate a safer, more stable alignment of the world's competing powers and ideologies.

Several months of "ping-pong diplomacy" followed. In July 1971, Kissinger slipped secretly into China for face-to-face negotiations with Zhou, a trip that was kept secret until the public announcement that the PRC had invited President Nixon to visit China in the early months of 1972. Like most people, I was greatly surprised by Kissinger's journey and the announcement that Nixon, that dedicated cold warrior, might actually visit a nation he had so long and so virulently denounced.

Though bitterly opposed in the United States by conservative pundits and the "China Lobby" funded by the Nationalist government on Taiwan, Kissinger's negotiations proved extremely popular with the American public and the international community. The Nixon administration abandoned as "futile" American opposition to the PRC's membership in the United Nations. In October 1971, the PRC assumed seats in the General Assembly and on the Security Council. Probably only a Republican president of Nixon's anticommunist credentials could have engineered such a profound reversal of American policy. In February 1972, Nixon made his journey to the PRC where he met with Mao and Zhou. Like tens of millions around the globe, I watched in amazement and hope as the dramatic scenes played out before the television cameras.

Wen-po and I discussed developments often. For a decade after the fall of the mainland to the Communists, he had held important field commands in the defense of Taiwan and the smaller islands held by the Nationalists. He met with Chiang Kai-shek and become personal friends with Chiang Ching-kuo, the Generalissimo's son and political heir. Transferred from field command, Wen-po attended the Joint War College and then took a position on the army general staff. After his retirement in 1966, high government officials frequently sought his advice.

Wen-po and I were initially very skeptical of the Communist government's sincerity in seeking warmer relations with the United States. We knew the Communists' duplicity and ruthlessness from hard personal experience. Nor did we entirely trust the good faith of the United States. After the heavy cost of the Vietnam War, would the Nixon administration maintain American defense commitments to Taiwan? Or would Nixon and Kissinger sacrifice Taiwan to achieve better relations with the PRC and a more stable global balance of power?

But on a personal level, we were tremendously excited by a possible "opening" of China. We ached for news of our family on the mainland. Mother would be an extremely old lady by now, approaching ninety, but I held out hope that she was yet alive. More than anything in life, I wanted to kneel before her to explain why I had never returned, to apologize with my words and tears for all the days of my absence from her side.

Wen-po cautioned me against making plans to visit the mainland until formal relations were established between the United States and the PRC. The Communists had long memories and might yet take revenge on me for my failure to return from Chusan Island in 1950. As a teacher, scholar, and social scientist, I had openly criticized the Communist government for its social and economic mismanagement. The Great Cultural Revolution seemed an experiment gone wild, beyond even Mao's power to control. While negotiations for Nixon's visit went on, Red Guards continued dragging intellectuals and pragmatic government officials through the streets, beating them, and forcing them into confessions of crimes against the people. Might I not suffer the same fate even if I were only returning to visit relatives?

For a while I held off writing to Xing-min and Wen-shuan. I did not know under what sort of pressure they might be living because of their relationship to Wen-po and me. Whatever our eagerness for news, we did not want to make life worse for them. We watched the coverage of Nixon's visit and waited for further indications of China's political direction. It seemed that the Cultural Revolution was ebbing, the pragmatists regaining some influence. Friends told us that they had exchanged letters with relatives in China with no untoward consequences. Finally, I sat down to write to Wen-shuan.

Six months passed before a return letter arrived, dictated by Wen-shuan to his eldest son, Ping-fan. The letter was brief, obviously the cautious words of people unsure how much and how honestly they should speak. My brother and sister-in-law were happy to hear from me. They were in good health. They had three sons and three daughters, all enjoying a good life in "Liberated China." Finally, came the news I had long feared: "Mother lived for three years after she returned to the village. She had a stroke in 1954. She lived another year and died on July 8, 1955. She missed you always and called out for you on her deathbed."

Much as I had long suspected that Mother was no longer among the living, the news triggered a terrible grief in me. For weeks I mourned intensely, weeping often. My wife and my sons tried to comfort me, but I was inconsolable. Finally, we arranged for a mass in her honor, a memorial to her that helped me accept the finality of my loss.

Gradually, I established correspondence with others in my family. Xing-min wrote from Shanghai. He had become a physical education teacher and was married to another teacher, Fan Jin-nan. Together they had two sons and a daughter. Pu-chao wrote to tell me that he and Sher-chen lived near Zhou-bian village and had a son and four daughters. Ping-fan wrote often for his father, Wen-shuan. All these early letters were brief and restrained, assuring me that all was well in their lives in "Liberated China." Several former school-mates wrote, telling me of their families and of the improvements in China. Their comments were general, avoiding politics and the intimate details of life under the commune system.

Wen-po and I were cautious in our responses, avoiding any subject that might put our loved ones at risk. He established a postal box address in Hong Kong to avoid the restrictions on correspondence still maintained by the Nationalist government on Taiwan. We enclosed small amounts of cash in our letters. We couldn't risk too much since the authorities would confiscate any unseemly amount, but we were proud to make the lives of our relatives a little easier.

Wen-po and I had long wanted to have the bones of our father returned to Zhou-bian village. In 1974, we sent money to Xing-min and Wen-shuan for the trip to Gansu province. But the village party cadre denied Wen-shuan's travel request since the time and expense would violate the commune's "thriftiness" policy. My cousin Chang Wen-de stepped forward. He was the son of my uncle Chang Weng and the concubine he'd purchased following his son Pao-wa's death. Uncle Chang Weng had never prospered following the division of the family property in the late 1920s. By the time of his death about 1940, he was nearly penniless, leaving the concubine and Wen-de to live in abysmal poverty in a small Buddhist temple.

Wen-hui and Wen-po had helped Uncle Chang Weng in so far as they were able and, after his death, had sent what they could to the concubine and her son. Still, Wen-de had grown up an angry and bitter man with a grudge against all who had better fortune. After Liberation, the Communists chose him as a production team leader, more for his sense of aggrievement than his talent. He had given Wen-shuan a very hard time over the years, but on this day he remembered family honor and protested the village cadre's decision. When the cadre refused to change his position, Wen-de stepped close. "My uncle Chang Ying had a terrible temper. My father always said I inherited it. I have fought for control in the face of your unreasonableness, but it would be wise for you to reconsider now." The cadre looked at the hard-muscled farmers watching the exchange, most connected in one way or another to our clan, and decided that he would rather violate the "thriftiness" policy than absorb an extravagant beating.

My nephew Xing-min later told me how heavily the responsibility for burying the family's elders weighed on Wen-shuan. Their trip to Gansu province allowed him to pay a long-overdue obligation, alleviating some of his sadness. His uncanny memory led him to the exact spot where he and Wen-hui had buried our father thirty-four years before. In a short time, Wen-shuan and Xing-min managed to disinter the bones, wrapping them carefully and placing them in a bag for the trip home. Back in Zhou-bian village, the family held a simple traditional ceremony in our house. Many older villagers came to show their respect, recalling our father's services to the education of the children; his willingness to help illiterate neighbors with their accounts, letters, and contracts; and especially his extraordinary generosity in opening the family granary in the time of the great famine. Enclosed in a small casket and clothed in the best material available, our father's bones were buried next to Mother's. Though our parents' married life had been stormy, in death they would now lie peacefully side by side.

In 1976 I was invited to attend the National Development Conference in Taipei. In my next letter to Xing-min, I casually mentioned my planned trip to Taiwan. He wrote back in great excitement that if I could arrange to bring his father to Hong Kong, he had permission to meet us there. Wen-po, who had always regretted allowing his son to remain behind in Shanghai in 1949, greeted the possibility of a reunion with equal excitement.

Wen-po was still forbidden to travel outside Taiwan because of his high military rank. For years the government of Chiang Kai-shek had feared the political impact if one of its senior generals or officials defected to the PRC or sought political asylum in another country in order to voice criticisms of Chiang's rule. In addition to these paranoid fears was the genuine danger of trouble with Communist agents abroad. By the mid-1970s, however, the political mood in Taiwan had begun to shift toward a more liberal outlook. Chiang Kai-shek died in 1975 and was succeeded by his son Chiang Ching-kuo, who had been premier since 1972. Wen-po and Chiang Ching-kuo had been friends for years. My brother did not want to impose on that friendship, but he felt somewhat protected by it as long as he traveled quietly and incognito. I couldn't resist kidding him when he again assumed the disguise of a businessman as he had in his escape from China in 1949.

We met Xing-min and several members of his wife's family at the airport in Hong Kong. It was a very emotional scene, Xing-min and I weeping, Wen-po so overwhelmed that he could not even shed tears but only hold our hands during the taxi ride. We stayed the next five days at the home of Fan Jin-nan's maternal uncle, Mr. Chu Kuo-pao. This gracious gentleman gave us a bedroom and the privacy to recall all the long years since our dangerous days together in Shanghai. Xing-min related many things that he hadn't been free to include in his letters.

After my failure to return from Chusan Island in May 1950, Mr. Zhang Jian-xin had several times called Xing-min to his office for questioning. It seemed to Xing-min that Mr. Zhang had never put much hope in the success of my mission but that he was very upset that I had broken my promise to return. For a time, Xing-min feared that the Communists would deny Mother further medical care. But Mr. Zhang proved to be a man of decency and, once he was satisfied that Xing-min had no complicity in my disappearance, great generosity. He visited Mother to assure her that she would continue to receive the best medical care. He obtained a teaching job for Xing-min and protected him from further interrogation. Xing-min continued under surveillance by Communist police. When my letter arrived later that year, explaining that I had been forbidden to return, Xing-min felt that for his and Mother's protection he had to send me a cool answer along with the request not to write again.

In 1951, Mr. Zhang was transferred to a post in Beijing. In 1952, Wen-shuan traveled to Shanghai to take Mother and the ever-loyal Ma Li-chun home. The Communist authorities would not give Xing-min leave to accompany them, probably because they wanted him close at hand in case Wen-po or I tried to contact him. The surveillance and periodic interrogations continued for many years.

Xing-min found teaching agreeable. He maintained a low profile, avoiding any hint of disloyalty to the government and the party. In 1960, he married Fan Jin-nan. They were both practicing Catholics and suffered for it during the Cultural Revolution, Jin-nan serving six months in jail for refusing to denounce her religion. Before and after President Nixon's visit, the authorities questioned Xing-min about his contacts with Wen-po and me. To his surprise, he was encouraged to write us.

At this point he paused in his narrative. "I think our old friend Mr. Zhang Jian-xin was behind that. The guide the tourist board sent to keep an eye on me has a letter for you. Apparently, Mr. Zhang hasn't forgotten any of us."

This news startled me very much. What possible interest could Zhang Jian-xin still have in my life? Later that evening, I sought out Mr. Deng Hui-siong, the good-natured representative of the tourist board. The letter he gave me from Mr. Zhang was an invitation on behalf of the government to visit the PRC, assuring me of a friendly reception and the opportunity to interview many scholars and officials. I read the letter several times. From the day I'd received Xing-min's letter saying that he could meet us in Hong Kong, I had wondered why the authorities would so readily grant him permission for such a trip. Was this letter the reason? And why would they be so interested in me? I pondered this for a long hour. I was not an influential person, no maker of foreign policy, but I did have extensive connections in the community of China scholars in America and Taiwan. Mr. Zhang, or whoever was behind the letter, probably thought that my relationship to Wen-po gave me access to people of importance in the government of Taiwan. To some degree this was correct.

Mr. Zhang would be in his late fifties by now, apparently still holding a responsible position despite the dislocations of the Cultural Revolution. That would be like him: a cagey survivor like Premier Zhou Enlai. He mentioned in his letter that he'd served in the Chinese embassy in Jakarta, Indonesia. Was his specialty still intelligence? And if so, was he looking for the opportunity to once again make me one of his agents?

This thought brought me up short. On my second and third readings of the letter, I had flattered myself that my modest academic reputation might have attracted the invitation. Now I began to suspect a darker purpose than an exchange of ideas with a visiting scholar. How could I know the truth? I couldn't. I folded the letter carefully, slipped it deep in a pocket of my briefcase. For a few moments I had dreamed of going home to Zhou-bian village, of seeing Wen-shuan, Sher-chen, Ling-yeh, and all those I loved. But I would not risk becoming a tool of the Communists, the Nationalists, or the Americans. I was a scholar, and my academic integrity must always be my most precious possession. I would go to China only when I could be sure of my personal safety and the safety of my reputation.

Mr. Chu Kuo-pao continued to be the most gracious host through the rest of our visit. He took us to see the offices and warehouse of his trading company, guided us to the Hong Kong sights, and took us to wonderful restaurants. Xing-min, Wen-po, and I continued to sit up late every night talking. Xing-min told us what he could of Wen-shuan's life. They had been together on the journey two years before to retrieve our father's bones from Gansu province. Wen-shuan was still a reticent man, hardworking and uncomplaining. He had been questioned on a number of occasions in the 1950s and 1960s about communication with Wen-po and me. After Nixon's visit to China, some Red Guards had interrogated him harshly. All political factions did not agree with the invitation to the American president, and the radicals—represented at the lowest level by the Red Guards—resented it intensely.

Wen-po and I wept when we heard how Wen-shuan had suffered for our sake. Xing-min let us weep. "I have thought about Uncle Wen-shuan a long time," he said quietly. "He is like a stone. He has even come to look like he is made of stone. He has been weathered by sun, rain, wind, and suffering. But none of that can break him. He endures, remains fixed in the earth. Do not weep too much for his life. He would not want that."

We cried into our hands, nodding, knowing that Xing-min was right: our quiet, gentle brother would not want us to weep for his sake. After a meditative moment, Xing-min smiled. "And do not forget that he has Chang Sun-sze by his side. You may be 'the Tiger,' Father, but she is also one. She will stand up for him against anybody. Uncle Wen-shuan may not have words to spare, but she has plenty and they come quick and hot. Back in the early years after Liberation when other villagers denounced him as a rich farmer, she told them off, reminded them how he had worked like a beast of burden all the years since the great famine to buy back the family land. If they were going to take his land because he worked harder than others, so be it. But don't say that Chang Wen-shuan had exploited anyone, because they all knew it was false, that there was never a more honest, a more generous man in the village."

"Did Wen-shuan tell you this?" I asked.

"A little of it. Most of it Sher-chen told me. Wen-shuan doesn't care to talk much, but he lights up whenever Sun-sze is mentioned. After all these years and six children, he's more proud of her than ever. She's day, night, sun, moon, everything to him. In the short time we were away in search of Grandfather Chang Ying's bones, Wen-shuan longed for her constantly. Some of the villagers are frightened of her and don't like her, but the others treat her with the respect they used to have for Grandmother Wei-sze. I think she is a very great person."

He went on to tell us what he knew of the circumstances surrounding the confiscation of the family land. The story of land redistribution, collectivization, and communization lies at the heart of the sad epic of China under Mao. For my brother Wen-shuan and literally hundreds of millions of rural farmers, no amount of improvement in other aspects of their lives could ever compensate for the loss of their land. Since time immemorial, land ownership had represented economic, social, and spiritual fulfillment to the Chinese peasants. Following Liberation, the Communist authorities instituted land reform throughout China. Since Wen-shuan had managed by great thrift to acquire a few extra acres, he was denounced as a "rich farmer" and much of his land taken away.

In the mid-1950s, the Communists collectivized agriculture, taking all the land out of private ownership. I was far away in the United States, but reading of this policy, I could imagine how the loss of the remaining family land tore at Wen-shuan's soul. Collectivization destroyed a farming economy based on millennia of trial and error. The Chinese peasants had neither the flexibility nor the motivation to adapt to a new system in which they could see little solid personal reward. When collectivization failed to produce an agricultural miracle, Mao blamed the conservative Confucian beliefs that, despite half a century of revolution, still dominated rural life. In 1957, he instituted the commune system, bringing all aspects of rural life under control of the government.

The commune system deprived the rural folk of most of their remaining personal liberties and all property but minor personal possessions. It became an economic and social disaster of unparalleled proportions. As a scholar in America, I puzzled over how Mao—himself of rural origins—could blunder so utterly in the reform of agriculture and rural society. Some form of land redistribution was long overdue to correct the injustices of the past, but forced collectivization was an immense mistake, the succeeding commune system a catastrophe. Together they struck at the heart of Chinese culture, character, and initiative.

Mao's agricultural policies were based, at least in part, on a faulty analysis of history. Though rich landlords shamelessly exploited the peasants in some areas, Mao accorded them too prominent a role in the rural economy. Throughout much of China, particularly in the wheat-growing north, the traditional agrarian economy depended upon cooperation among small independent farmers. The peasant farming village was a communal endeavor millennia before Marx, Lenin, and Mao formulated their theories of communism. The overwhelming historical evidence is that life was not only tolerable but good in the traditional land-based social system. Yes, it was hard. The rural Chinese suffered greatly in times of natural disaster, famine, war, and revolution. They desperately needed improved health care, education, and social services. But the rural traditions as they existed were not irretrievably flawed. Instead of destroying them, Mao and the Communists could have used them as the basis for an enlightened socialism as embodied in the concept of "the People's Livelihood" in Dr. Sun Yat-sen's philosophy. Instead, they attempted to bring about a change in the very nature of Chinese life through force and edict. Hundreds of millions of rural folk suffered the undeserved consequences in one of the great tragedies of history. My brother Wen-shuan was one of them.

The United States and the PRC established formal diplomatic relations on January 1, 1979. I was at last confident that I could travel in China without undue risk. Alice and I immediately began planning a family trip with our sons Christopher, then sixteen, and Victor, eleven. We arrived in Guangzhou on June 5, 1979, twenty-nine years after my forced departure from China. The Communist travel service in Hong Kong had arranged our tour with great consideration for our comfort. This attention came as a welcome surprise, but I was conscious of my brother Wen-po's warning that the Communists never did favors without expecting a return on their investment: "They cannot do anything from the heart, youngest brother, because they have no hearts."

I wasn't as suspicious as Wen-po and was prepared to be gracious in response to their generosity. At the same time, I would accept nothing that might compromise my scholarly objectivity. After thanking the government travel agent warmly for the hospitality and cooperation, I made it clear that we would pay all expenses for the trip. With a bit of reluctance, he agreed.

We were assigned to the keeping of Mr. Kao Wei-chun. With his unfailing good humor, energy, and efficiency, Mr. Kao guided us through the maze of Communist bureaucracy. He bought our tickets, booked tours and hotel reservations, and made arrangements for my scholarly researches. Though we knew he was the eyes of the government, we enjoyed him immensely. He got along very well with the boys as they adjusted to the reality of a China they'd only seen in pictures. Christopher was fascinated by everything he saw and took delight in his role as the trip's photographer. Victor, only eleven, had a more difficult time. He disliked the food, was uncomfortable at the curiosity of Chinese youngsters, and found the cultural sights of little interest. Mr. Kao's sympathy helped Victor a great deal.

I was anxious to visit Zhou-bian village as soon as possible to see my relatives and do honor at my mother's grave. Mr. Kao, however, told us that we must visit Shanghai first. He had made arrangements for me to interview several important officials, he said, and he did not want to put them off. Only later would I learn all the reasons behind this change in our itinerary.

Shanghai was larger and more bustling than ever. We had a wonderful time with Xing-min and his family. I interviewed local officials and received tours of schools, factories, communes, and community centers. Mr. Kao arranged a boat trip to Wu-song harbor, where Wen-po's division had held back fierce Communist attacks in the final stages of the Nationalist evacuation. Without explaining my exact purpose to Mr. Kao, I visited my friend Du Ru-min to thank him for hiding Wen-po in the dangerous early hours of his escape.

After a week in Shanghai, we made the long train ride across central China to Xi'an. The towns and the landscape reflected both the progress and the failures of thirty years of Communist rule. The railroad now had two lines of well-maintained tracks, many new schools stood in the villages, and all was peaceful and orderly. But the poverty of rural life had, if anything, worsened. Men, women, and children labored with their beasts in the hot sun, only the occasional tractor indicating any change in age-old methods. Housing was crowded and poor, electricity and running water still a rarity. How, I wondered, could so many have worked so hard under Communism and made so little progress?

The longer I rode the train, the less able I was to absorb what I saw. Each mile brought me closer to my childhood home and a confrontation with my past. I had longed to stand by my mother's grave, to call on her spirit to forgive me for my inconstancy. But now the prospect terrified me. I had visions of collapsing utterly, of being reduced to a howling child pursued by all the wolves of my nightmares through the dark streets and alleys of an unredeemable past. With every hour I became more agitated. I could not eat for fear of vomiting. Alice insisted that I try to rest, but sleep brought terrible nightmares. I paced the train's corridors, mumbling to myself like a man possessed by spirits. Alice again made me sit, smoothed my forehead, hummed to me as if I were a child disturbed from sleep by ghosts. I slept at last, my dreams so deep and turbulent that when I awoke I had no memory of specifics, only the sense of being tumbled amid forces of such immensity that they were entirely beyond naming or definition.

The train pulled into Xi'an in midmorning. As our coach slowed, I leaned out the window, craning to see if I recognized anyone on the approaching platform. Suddenly, a man broke from a knot of people and came dashing alongside the train. "Wen-wei! Wen-wei," he cried. I gaped at my brother Wen-shuan. I reached out my hand for his, our fingers just brushing across the gap, and then clasping as the train ground to a halt. We were sobbing, unable even to speak each other's name. My legs shook, and I felt Alice and my sons holding on to me, keeping me from falling. A pair of young men, nephews I had never met, boarded the train to help me off.

On the platform, relatives surrounded us, their hands reaching out for me, touching, patting, welcoming. But I had eyes only for my beloved brother.

We stood weeping, our hands again clasped. A short, officious man pushed through to us. "Come, uncles," he growled, "you're making a spectacle of yourselves." He guided us to the station, his voice sharp as he cleared a path through the crowd. Entering a small waiting room, he ordered everyone out, barring the door even to our families. "I am Cheng Jing-ting, your sister Koo-yeh's son," he told me, his handshake brusque. "I work for the party. I am to welcome you here and guide you through your visit."

He hesitated, his voice becoming almost pleading. "I will do everything I can for the honor of our family and to justify my superiors' trust. But, uncles, we must maintain some dignity. It is unseemly for mature men to display such emotion in front of strangers. There might be . . . misinterpretations. Please remember that. Now I will leave you alone until you regain your composure."

I could understand my nephew's mortification. Some of his superiors were no doubt in the crowd of strangers watching our family group. That all should go smoothly was for Cheng Jing-ting a test of his ability, our incapacitation in grief and joy an unseemly breach of the bureaucratic need for order. But Wen-shuan and I cared nothing for such considerations as we sat in the waiting room, arms around each other, tears flowing, as we tried to voice all the regrets, longing, fears, and love that had bound us together over three decades.

After ten minutes, Cheng Jing-ting opened the door, his face still clouded as he ushered in two women. They approached, smiling shyly, both much older, much more careworn than I'd expected. They started to introduce themselves but there was no need. I rose, my tears again flowing, to embrace my sister Ling-yeh and my dear niece Sher-chen, the playmate of my childhood.

With the circle expanded to four, our mood lightened. The women brushed at my thinning hair, poked my belly and arms to see if I had become a fat capitalist. We giggled, wept, laughed. By the door Cheng Jing-ting relaxed. He let others join us, admitting them in twos and threes until they ignored him and all pushed in. My sister-in-law Chang Sun-sze took charge, ignoring Cheng Jing-ting and Mr. Kao, who seemed entirely satisfied for the moment to carry our bags. Leading us out of the terminal, she herded us into a shining new bus, probably the pride of the Xi'an municipal fleet. Seated by Wen-shuan, I had an opportunity to reach across the aisle to take Alice's hand for a moment. She patted it, smiled at me. Victor was trying to look small beside her, quite overwhelmed by the tumult, but Christopher was in his glory, the family camera snapping away in his hands.

The way northwest from Xi'an to Zhou-bian village lay straight and smooth, the rutted, twisted dirt roads of my youth replaced by an asphalt highway. I had difficulty identifying the villages we passed, so different did they appear from what I remembered. Our village no longer had a gate or a defensive wall, both demolished to make room for new construction. As we slowed, I saw a large crowd gathered in our street. Had so many people lived in our village before? No, of course not; an entire generation had grown up and had children of their own since my departure. Only the middle-aged and the old would remember me; to the rest I would be an alien, a curiosity from a far distant land.

Emerging from the bus, Alice, the boys, and I were engulfed in a sea of friendly people, many of them wishing to touch our colorful Western clothing. Cheng Jing-ting and Mr. Kao had anticipated this moment and gave us cigarettes and candy to distribute: small gifts of appreciation for the welcome. We could not endure the press for long, and after a few minutes, they managed to maneuver us through the crowd to the door of the family home.

I had made my homecoming in stages, stepping first into the world that is China when we arrived in Guangzhou, next into the arms of my brother, then into the village, and now into the family home with its cool shade on this warm day, its multitude of memories, its heartbreaking familiarity to Chang Wen-wei, who had been baby, boy, and youth within its shelter. I took the seat pushed at me by Chang Sun-sze, accepted the restorative cup of tea, and tried to let the house speak to me. But I could not listen yet, not until I had taken the remaining step: the last, the most longed-for and feared.

Wen-shuan hung at my shoulder, unwilling to get more than a foot from me. I reached for one of his strong, callused farmer's hands, as used to the hoe handle and the feel of earth as my soft professor's hands were to the pen and the shuffling of paper. "I must go to her now," I said. "She is waiting, and I have been gone a very long time."

He squeezed my hand, all the love, understanding, and patience of this good, quiet man in that gesture. "Wen-wei," he said, "I must tell you that it is not like the cemetery you remember. The Communists made us plow it flat." He started to weep.

Sun-sze continued the explanation. "The local cadre said that the new China could not afford to waste good farmland on the dead and a bunch of old superstitions. So Wen-shuan and our neighbors had to plow the graves under. When word came of your visit, the cadre told us that we must identify your parents' resting place and raise a new grave. He was worried, almost frightened, urged us to raise a grave even if we didn't know the exact location. Wen-shuan knew exactly where it was, of course, but the grave is just fresh earth, raw and filled with clods."

She glanced to see if Cheng Jing-ting and Mr. Kao were within hearing. "The Communists made a big effort for your visit. We thought you were coming before, but they wanted to raise the grave higher and arrange for a big turnout. That's why they had you arrive on a Sunday when people weren't working."

I nodded, understanding now Mr. Kao's insistence that we visit Shanghai before going to Shaanxi province. Sun-sze patted our shoulders. "Now you brothers need to go speak to your mother. Be happy that you have lived to see this day."

While Sun-sze gathered the family to follow us, Wen-shuan and I, our arms linked, left the house, crossing the rough ground toward the family cemetery and our mother's grave. That the family might have gone alone was, of course, too much to expect. This was China, where the right to bear witness is so ingrained as to be almost a civic obligation. A large crowd followed behind us. Scores could claim kinship or past friendship, but the vast majority were unknown to me. The most intense moment of my physical and spiritual life would play out at the center of a wide circle of strangers, interested and sympathetic but for the most part simply curious, like the audience to some immemorial drama, expecting in the witnessed suffering some liberating catharsis, a fleeting connection with the truth at the heart of the tragedy bequeathed us by the gods, Man's fall, or simply the fact that we are all merely, though I believe redeemably, human.

The grave stood alone, a low mound of raw earth unsoftened by rain, wind, and time. Mother might have been buried yesterday, departing this life only hours rather than a quarter century before my return. I stopped short of the grave while Ling-yeh, Sher-chen, and my cousin Mian-wa knelt to keen in ritual and true grief. I had feared dissolving in my sorrow, but I found myself rendered numb by the realization that I had come at last to this instant and this small spot in a distant, troubled land. I was overcome by a sense of utter desolation. My accomplishments, my family, my struggles seemed entirely without significance. I had abandoned my mother, left her to suffer and die without my comfort, her heart broken and crying out for her lost sons, of whom I had been the youngest, dearest, and most culpable for the final tragedy of her life.

"I am home, Mother," I whispered and could say no more.

In an ancient Chinese lament, a mockingbird or a dove might have given voice at this moment in derision or sympathy for a wanderer's sorrow. But all the birds in Zhou-bian village had been snared and caged or eaten long ago, and I stood by my mother's grave without welcome from this world or the next.

That afternoon we feasted, the gathering a giddy rejoicing after the pain of our visit to the grave. Toward evening, Mr. Kao took Alice and the boys back to Xi'an, where they could rest in a modern hotel. I stayed on for two days. Many friends and relatives from the old times came to see me. They would ask if I recognized them, but I could put a name to only a few, so old had hard work and hard times made them. I gave small gifts of money, asked after their families and their lives.

On the morning of the third day, as I was about to leave by bicycle with one of my nephews for Xing-ping City, I became extremely fearful. I had left Zhou-bian village those many years before never imagining that I wouldn't return for three decades. Would I ever return again? Hard-liners might retake control of the government, reinstating the ban on foreign visitors so long in place under Mao. I might not live long enough to see another change in the political climate. After this day, I might never see my village, my ancestral home, or my relatives again.

I had written a long memorial to my parents before leaving America, but at the graveside I had entirely forgotten to read it. I begged Wen-shuan to accompany me to the cemetery where I might do them the honor I had neglected. But I was nearly hysterical, and he was afraid what might happen if we visited the grave a second time. Counseled by Sun-sze and two of my adult nephews, he refused, made me lie down instead with a damp cloth over my eyes. In an hour, my agitation eased, and we were able to talk sensibly.

In the street I embraced Wen-shuan a last time. "Go," he said through tears. "I know you will be back."

In Xing-ping City I visited several old schoolmates, though I was prevented from visiting the school itself by a bureaucratic foul-up that I could not resolve in the absence of my national guide. I visited the grave of my old teacher Gao Chong-sze to thank him for not probing too deeply into what I knew of Wen-po's escape during our meeting in August 1949.

In Xi'an, the authorities had arranged for the use of the People's Hall so that I could greet all the people who might come to see me. For two days I met with scores of people. Many were distant relatives and old acquaintances come to pay their respects. Others were strangers with messages for me to carry to relatives in America. Toward the end of the first day, an elderly but robust woman approached the couch where I was sitting deep in conversation with an old schoolmate. She waited politely until I looked up to see the mischievous grin and merry eyes of my sister-in-law Ma Li-chun, Wen-hui's widow. I jumped up and, laughing and weeping, we embraced. "You go on a simple errand," she said, "and—poof—you're gone for thirty years. What are we to do with you?"

I had a wonderful conversation with her over supper. After returning to Zhou-bian village with Mother in 1952, she had been courted by a widower from another village. They married and adopted two children. After her second husband died in the early 1960s, Ma Li-chun became like the good aunt in Mother's story: always available to help in times of birth, death, or illness. At the end of our evening, I made her a small gift of money and promised to seek her out on my next visit. She grinned and tapped my forehead with a knuckle. "Now that you have found the way again, I will expect it." Long ago, when she had first come into our family, many of us had wondered why Wen-hui would choose a wife so much his opposite. But like the good trader he was, he knew the resonance of true gold ringing deeply to the heart.

On the second day I received a message from Wen-po's old division commander, General Ping Er-ming, who had not been lucky enough to escape China in 1949. Would I agree to meet with him? I was surprised by the question until I reflected that even in old age General Ping would be a political untouchable. But I was an American now and would meet with whom I chose. That night we had supper together. His clothes were threadbare and his body bent by his many years of prison and abuse by the Communists. Yet he maintained a quiet, irreducible dignity. When I ordered him a bottle of Chinese beer, his eyes misted. He explained that in all the years since the revolution he had never been able to afford a drop of beer. Despite his poverty, he protested against accepting money from me when we parted. But I insisted. Later Wen-po and other old friends would manage to send General Ping enough money for him to enjoy a little comfort at the end of his life.

By the morning of the third day I had entirely lost my voice and was tottering on the edge of emotional and physical exhaustion. Mr. Kao took charge, insisting that I end my interviews. He spoke to Alice, suggesting that I take a few days of complete rest. She agreed, and the next day we flew to Yan'an, Mao's wartime headquarters in northern Shaanxi. We returned briefly to Xi'an five days later and then took the train to Beijing, where I had the honor of lecturing at the Social Science Academy. I was taken aback by the lack of response to my talk, only to find later that the scholars had appreciated it very much but were leery about asking questions in the presence of senior party officials. I soon found that they were not the only ones who feared speaking openly. The interviews I had with several high-ranking officials were all strikingly similar, each official informed of the answers I'd received in earlier meetings and sticking firmly to the party line.

On our second night in Beijing we drove to Mr. Zhang Jian-xin's home for supper. Though he no longer had the trim, soldierly bearing of the man who had blackmailed me into my fateful trip to Chusan Island, the elderly Mr. Zhang was still a handsome man. Over dinner in his comfortable home he charmed Alice and the boys with his ready wit and faintly ironic smile. But his eyes were quiet and watchful. He said he was retired from the diplomatic service, but I don't think intelligence agents ever really retire, and I guessed that he would make a report on our visit. He never spoke of Chusan Island, Wen-po, or politics. He asked after Xing-min, and I assured him that my nephew still enjoyed the job Mr. Zhang had obtained for him those many years ago. He nodded with satisfaction.

"I inquired into the fate of your brother Wen-hui," he said. "I'm sorry, but I could discover nothing."

"Thank you," I said. "And thank you for looking after Mother."

"You are welcome. Now tell me of your visit to Zhou-bian village."

When I finished, he sat toying with his glass for a moment. "Going home," he mused. "I should do that, too, though sometimes I forget where it is exactly."

At the door we again shook hands. "It appears that life has worked out for you," he said.

"And for you."

"Yes, we have been among the lucky ones."

I spent fifty-five days in China in 1979. Since that trip, I have returned to China and Taiwan a dozen times to do research, lecture, and visit my relatives. At times I have been entrusted with messages between the governments as the "two Chinas" seek reconciliation. I always traveled trying to observe not only for myself but also for Wen-po, who because of his high rank could never return to the mainland. Usually I stopped off in Taiwan on my way back to America to report to him. He would listen avidly, savoring every bit of news about our relatives.

In 1984, I was invited to lecture in Manchuria. I received permission to visit Anshan, where I made every possible effort to determine the fate of my brother Wen-hui. I found no evidence of use and had to accept at last his complete disappearance. Yet I needed to make an act of remembrance before I could say good-bye. I made inquiries and was directed to a small Taoist temple where I paid for a ceremony for the repose of my brother's soul. I cried helplessly as the monks performed the simple ceremony.

Later that summer I told Wen-po of my failed search. He nodded. "Yes, I had evidence of his death even before I left Manchuria. Many times I tried to lead you to the realization, but you always resisted. It is good that you have accepted his death at last."

"I will love and remember him always," I said.

"Yes. As will I." He sighed. "We have seen so many pass away from us. I am afraid to recite their names lest I forget one. But none is truly forgotten. They are with us always. . . . But, come, let us call for tea and talk of the living."

When I saw Ma Li-chun a year later, I described my search and my final acceptance. "In my heart I always knew," she said quietly. "When I went back to find him after we were separated, I thought I caught a glimpse of his body through the smoke. It was all torn by an explosion and half buried in rubble. There was no hope that he was alive, and I could not get closer because of the firing."

"Why didn't you ever tell me?"

"Oh, Wen-wei," she said. "There was no point telling you that I *might* have seen his body. You loved him too much to abandon hope. You are a stubborn man, brother-in-law; you will love when all others have lost hope. It is your greatest failing and your greatest virtue." She smiled at me through her tears.

In the end, Wen-po and Ma Li-chun—the general and the simple country widow—brought me to the same realization. For much of my life I had let regret constrain my love. My hope of finding Wen-hui alive when he was almost certainly dead, the guilt I felt at leaving my mother in Shanghai, though I'd had no real choice, had deprived me of the joy I might have taken in remembering them in all their striking vitality. In the years since, I have tried to put aside my old habit of mourning in favor of a love unrestricted by regret or remorse. So it is that around me now I feel all my family, living and dead, their love warming me, lighting my way.

Books must end though stories do not. Wen-po died in 1986, a wise and honored patriot who lived his life according to the ancient Confucian principles learned from our father, Chang Ying. Ling-yeh died in 1989 of stomach cancer, a courageous woman to her final day. In 1997, my gentle brother Wen-shuan died. As he feared, he was the only one of us four to lie in the family graveyard. But I am sure Mother's spirit comforted him. Sher-chen's husband and my dear friend Nan Pu-chao died in 1998. In 2001, my redoubtable sister-in-law Chang Sun-sze was laid to rest next to Wen-shuan.

Sher-chen, Xing-min, Ma Li-chun, Li Lin-fen, and I live on. Each time we meet or speak by telephone, we talk of Mother and home. A scene often recalled is of Mother weaving in the courtyard as she often did on days of sunshine and soft breezes. It is a peaceful memory: Mother's hands passing the shuttle as she hums a tune suited to the task and the day. Perhaps she dreams of colored silk thread in place of the coarse gray cotton beneath her fingers, of a chance to weave something not just of utility but of beauty. The shuttle blurs from one of her quick, capable hands to the other, laying down another row, weaving her life into the tapestry of time, as the breeze plays gently at the strings of the loom as if it were a harp.

Postscript

I AM PROFOUNDLY GRATEFUL THAT I spent my early years in a traditional Chinese village. Many writers and social scientists in the twentieth century, particularly in the revolutionary decades, derided the traditional village system, denouncing it as "feudal." In reality, the village traditions of mutual cooperation, Confucian social harmony, and conformity to standards all understood produced an economic and social system that worked very well for a very long time.

Perhaps the greatest wisdom of the Confucian social order was the positioning of the peasant farmer at the top of the hierarchy of public virtue. The Confucian intellectual seeking admission to the mandarin civil service did so not to gain an ascendancy over the common folk but to become their servant. It has been one of the bemusements of my life that the word *intellectual* is so frequently a pejorative term in America. I suppose it is an attitude born of the militant and often touchy democratic impulse that resents any assertion of superiority; hence, the broadness of the American middle class in which virtually everyone claims membership.

Rural Chinese society had a different solution to the problem of equality. On the village level, everyday life was probably more democratic than in virtually any society on earth. Yet certain class distinctions and rituals were recognized and preserved as part of the natural and benevolent order of things first elucidated by Confucius. From early in my schooling, I was viewed as an intellectual in training. With this came both respect and obligation: school was my preparation to serve the greater good of China. When my uncle Wei San or one of the village men patted me on the shoulder and told me to study hard, it was an injunction to study not only for my own good but also for the good of the larger society in which our village was a small but integral part. In practical terms, I might become a magistrate whose judgments would have a direct effect on the prosperity of our village. But even if my service to China took me far from home, those who remained behind could take comfort that somewhere I was working in the interests of the rural folk.

In America it has seemed to me that some intellectuals feel obliged to behave contrary to social or political norms as an assertion of scholarly independence. Many, indeed, seem defensive about their intellectuality, adopting either a prickly eccentricity or a self-conscious folksiness. In the China of my youth, the former behavior would have been considered insulting, the latter preposterous if not insane. For me and for the other serious students of my youth, becoming an intellectual was an honorable and patriotic goal.

Like many Chinese intellectuals, I feel a sense of guilt that we as a class were not able to steer China on a better course through the middle of the twentieth century. Tragically, Mao Zedong would make *intellectual* a loathsome word during the Cultural Revolution, though his colleague—and for me a great patriot—Zhou Enlai was one of the preeminent intellectuals of his time.

When I first began to study Western social theories while a young student in Taiwan, I was struck by how similar the traditional Chinese village was to John Locke's idealized "State of Nature." Locke premised his theory on the basic goodness of human beings and the natural tendency of human society toward cooperation. No organized government was necessary so long as people lived in the State of Nature, becoming necessary only when society reached a mass where forces opposing cooperation began to interfere. Then people should enter voluntarily into a "social contract," wherein all agreed to a limited government to enforce laws for the common good.

As a graduate student in political science in America, I became familiar with the rival theory of social organization proposed by Thomas Hobbes. In Hobbes's view, man in the natural state was a selfish individualist constantly at war with his fellows. Hence, life in the natural state was "nasty, brutish, and short." Only the need for protection against violence persuaded human beings to form governments and to cede some of their independence to authority.

My experience growing up in a Chinese village argued against the misanthropy of Hobbes and in favor of Locke's humanism. For the 80 percent of Chinese people then living in rural communities, cooperation, peace, and tranquility were the norms, not the exceptions. The central government did little for people living in the countryside. Most people resented and feared the government as an instrument of oppression. They blamed government for wars, warlords, and the unrest that spawned bandits and all manner of unnecessary hardships for the rural folk.

Further study brought me to Thomas Jefferson's vision of an American society based on agriculture and small towns, and Alexander Hamilton's opposing vision of an America based on industrial development and cities. It may be that the tranquil and peaceful life I knew as a boy cannot coexist with the advancing forces of industrial development and modernization in China. However, I refuse to abandon the peace and contentment of Confucian humanist philosophy in favor of materialism's insatiable greed. Perhaps in the new China emerging today, the common people will find a way of marrying tradition and modernity in a system that preserves the best of the old and the new. For all the tragedy of my mother's life and all the terrible suffering China experienced in the twentieth century, I remain convinced of the basic goodness of human beings. Given time, the old principles of cooperation for the common good may yet triumph.

About the Authors

Dr. David Wen-wei Chang is emeritus professor of political science at the University of Wisconsin, Oshkosh. In a distinguished career of forty years, he has been a field lecturer for the United States Information Agency; Visiting Professor of International Politics at National Cheng-chi University, Taiwan; a visiting scholar at the Institute of East Asian Studies, University of California, Berkeley; and Fulbright professor at People's University, Beijing. He is the author of six scholarly books in the field of China studies, including *China under Deng Xiaoping* (1988) and *Politics of Hong Kong's Reversion to China* (1998), as well as numerous journal articles. Born in Zhou-bian village, Shaanxi province, China, he has lived in the United States since 1953. He resides in Silver Spring, Maryland, with his wife, Alice. They have two adult children, Christopher and Victor.

Alden R. Carter is the author of thirteen novels and thirty nonfiction books for children, young adults, and adults. The author of three histories of China for various ages, his latest is *China: From the First Chinese to the Olympics* (2008). He resides in Marshfield, Wisconsin, with his wife, the photographer and fabric artist Carol Shadis Carter. They have two adult children, Brian and Siri.